W9-AQW-832

I AM ANASTASIA

TSAR NICHOLAS II OF RUSSIA WITH HIS FAMILY: *l. to r.*, Grand-Duchesses Olga and Maria, the Tsar, the Tsarina, the Grand-Duchess Anastasia, the Tsarevich Alexis, the Grand-Duchess Tatiana

# I Am Anastasia

*The Autobiography of the*
*Grand-Duchess*
*of Russia*
*With Notes by*
*Roland Krug von Nidda*
*Translated from the German by*
*Oliver Coburn*

HB

HARCOURT, BRACE AND COMPANY
*New York*

C.3.59

*Published in Germany under the title* Ich, Anastasia, Erzähle
*Published in England under the title* I, Anastasia

*Thanks are due to Gleb Botkin for permission to quote material from his book* The Woman Who Rose Again.

*Library of Congress Catalog Card Number: 58–10907*
*Printed in the United States of America*

*Genealogical tables are on pages 276 and 277*

Dates in Anastasia's life from her arrival in Germany
to her visit to America

*February 20, 1920* Attempted suicide.

*March 30, 1920* Admitted to Dalldorf asylum.

*Autumn 1921* Confesses her identity to Nurse Thea Malinovsky, later Mrs Chemnitz (who afterwards makes declaration on oath concerning this).

*March 1922* Klara Peuthert, who has been in Dalldorf under observation, informs Russian emigrés she has seen Anastasia.

*May—August 1922* At the Kleists'.

*August 1922 to end of 1923* Stays with various people, mostly Klara Peuthert.

*January to September 1924* With Inspector Grünberg.

*August 1924* Visited by Princess Irene of Prussia (Tsarina's sister).

*August—November 1924* West-End Hospital, Berlin.

*November 1924—January 1925* With Klara Peuthert and Bachmanns (coal-heavers).

*January—June 1925* With Grünberg. Reappearance of Serge Tchaikovski. Visited by Princess Cecilie. Meets Harriet Rathlef.

*June 1925—April 1926* Mommsen Nursing Home, Berlin (operations by Dr Rudnev).

*July 1925* Confronted by Volkov, Gilliard and Shura.

*July—October 1925* Grand-Duchess Olga (Tsar's sister) in Berlin.

*April 1926* Lugano with Harriet Rathlef.

*June 1926—March 1927* Stillachhaus Nursing Home, Oberstdorf. Beginning of Shanzkovski story.

*March 1927—January 1928* With Duke George of Leuchtenberg at Seeon Castle, Upper Bavaria. Confronted by Felix Shanzkovski.

*February 1928* Sails for America.

I FIND it more difficult than other people to write down the story of my life. If external happenings alone were important, my experiences have been so manifold that I could easily fill a book with them; only the reader would learn little about me as a person. But the task is far harder if I am to reveal my opinions and emotions, for I should first have to know myself, and how much self-knowledge do I possess after living almost forty years in semi-darkness and a long while in a sort of twilight? All I can be sure of, is that I have already died several times and been made to go on living; that in my misery I have even despaired of God.

I have become thicker-skinned than nature made me, and these days I prefer to retire into myself. Anyone who reads these pages will understand why, despite their lack of order and method. That lack is due to the severe injuries I have received and to my illness, which together have left inexplicable gaps in my memory, so that I can scarcely fit together all the fragments making up my life. I have to grope forward step by step through the maze of my thoughts, even though I may sometimes lose my bearings. But any fair-minded person will realise my determination to be honest, since my sole object is to re-establish my identity, to have a name, like any ordinary person, that is recognised by the world.

Without a name, a human being is deformed, as if by a distorting mirror. No one else trusts him or believes in him, he is rejected even by those who were once close to him. Everything about him is remote, distant as a dream that escapes before you can catch it. Life itself turns into a dream.

Why has God punished me so hard? I often think of this, wondering what ill I can have done. Of course I was often naughty as a child, but surely not vicious; and childish pranks would never earn the punishment I have suffered. It has been my lot to stay behind alone in a world utterly strange to me; I was not permitted to die with my family. All I want now is to forget, to live quietly in the shadows, in the calm of my little cottage, the no-man's-land I have been forced to make my home. But for my own self-respect I still need my name.

When I look back, I feel that few people can have had lives that split off so clearly into two parts, separated like a landscape at dusk by the dark line of a river. Or perhaps the dividing line is more an ocean than a river, for the two parts are two different worlds which have nothing in common. On one side of the ocean is my short, happy, untroubled childhood, when I looked on the bright day without any idea that another and a cruel world existed. The second part is enveloped in a darkness which seems never-ending: it began with the outbreak of the First World War, when I was only thirteen. Gradually the thunder-clouds gathered, in March 1917 the storm burst, and my life disintegrated on the terrible night of 17th July, 1918, when we all stared death in the eyes and death took my dear parents, sisters and brother.

The youngest daughter of Nicholas II, last emperor of Russia, I was born on 5th June, 1901 at Peterhof Castle not far from St Petersburg. This wonderful castle on the Gulf of Finland, famous for its extensive fountains, was built by Peter the Great. My mother was Princess Alix of Hesse, but on being converted to our Russian Orthodox Church she took the name of Alexandra Feodorovna. She was the daughter of the Grand-Duke Louis IV. As everyone knows, my parents' marriage was not prompted by any political considerations.

I was called Anastasia first after my godmother, Anastasia Nikolaievna, wife of my uncle the Grand-Duke Nikolai, and secondly after the Grand-Duchess Anastasia of Mecklenburg, daughter of the Grand-Duke Michael of Russia and mother of the German Crown Princess Cecilie. My godmother was one of two daughters of King Nikita of Montenegro who married into Russian families and were commonly known as 'the Montenegrins' (the other being Milica, wife of the Grand-Duke Peter). Aunt 'Stana' (as we used to call her) was a high-spirited woman; and unlike another sister, the Queen of Italy, whose eyes I remember as always looking sad, 'Stana' had particularly merry and vivacious eyes. She was first married to an uncle of my father's, Duke George of Leuchtenberg, but did not get on with him, so their marriage was dissolved. My parents thought her an intriguer, and no doubt much amusement was caused by the telegram Duke George sent to the bridegroom on her remarriage: 'Cannot congratulate you, she's a quarrelsome wench.' Seeing how slight was my connection with Aunt 'Stana' apart from our name, it seems an irony of fate that many years afterwards as a refugee I was given hospitality by the nephew of her first husband, at his castle in Upper Bavaria.

My parents had four children besides me: my sisters Olga, Tatiana and Maria, all older than me, and my brother Alexi, who was younger. My parents had to wait a long time before they got the son they so much wanted.

My two eldest sisters were always referred to as 'the big girls,' Maria and I as 'the little girls.' Tatiana was the tallest of us. She was very gay like me, and a good sport; the two of us had a lot of fun together. She had the best voice of us four, and I well remember our singing hymns in Siberia with Mama and the nuns who came to visit us; Tatiana's voice could always be heard above the rest. We all loved her dearly.

Olga was the quietest. She drew and painted very well, and once, as a present for Papa, she painted a scene in the park he was specially fond of—it was where the five trees grew that had been planted at our births. The picture turned out extremely well, and Papa was very proud of his present.

Maria was a really good-hearted girl, always thinking of others, never of herself. I feel she had a better nature than any of us.

We deeply revered our parents, who made no favourites. But we very soon realised their anxiety about Alexi, who suffered from hæmophilia. Indeed, worry over her son made Mama more and more retiring as the years passed. It was natural that he should be treated as something special, for apart from his illness he was heir apparent, and also the baby of the family, spoiled and adored by everyone. When in health he was the merriest boy, and he was also very clever, making good progress in lessons despite his continual illnesses. Mama was far more with him than with us girls, and never left him alone for long. When he was ill, she sat day and night at his bedside, though this always exhausted her, so that in the end she had to retire to bed herself.

I have many other memories of Alexi. Once he gave our parents a terrible fright, by hiding somewhere for hours—I think it was in the banqueting hall—and letting us search for him. Mama was so upset she got quite ill, and Monsieur Gilliard, our French tutor, was also extremely worried, because he was responsible for Alexi. My brother had no idea how we were all fearing the worst, he was merely delighted at having managed to hide so cleverly and not being found. He did the same thing on another occasion, but that time he hid under a large plant in the park. We all hunted for him desperately, and again Mama was sick with worry.

Like us girls, Alexi loved anything to do with soldiers. When he was still very small, he liked standing to attention with his arms held stiffly at his side, as Nagorny the Marine had taught him. Alexi was very fond of Nagorny, who behaved almost like a nanny and had a good influence on him. I don't think Nagorny can have been married, though the other Marine with Alexi certainly was, for he had two sons.

Despite his illness, my brother had a very cheerful disposition. He recovered quickly from the severest attacks, and was again serene and happy once the pain had gone. But he minded a great deal being unable to romp and play as he would have liked to, and always had to be very careful not to hurt himself. He was never allowed to climb trees, ride a horse, or a bicycle, because they were all too dangerous; also he had to wear a sort of splint on his leg. But he had a tricycle specially made for him.

There's another thing I must say about Alexi's illness. When he was laid up, he was in such pain one could hardly bear to see it. None of the doctors could help him, and the only person who could was Rasputin, whom we called Father Gregory. He only needed to come and pray, and Alexi was better at once. Because of this Mama trusted him completely, and we all thought of him as a saint. Had he stayed alive, the great misfortune would never have come upon us. It is appalling that he should have been murdered by a cousin of ours, we could none of us grasp that a member of our family could commit such a crime against him of all people. We sisters also saw quite a lot of him. He was in Siberia during the first part of the war, and was Papa's best counsellor, the only one who told him the truth and warned him against the war, the only one who knew that it could bring nothing but misfortune on us all.

Although Mama was German, she had become a true Russian

in her faith and in her love for her people. But we did not often speak Russian with her; it was mostly English, because her mother, the second daughter of Queen Victoria, had died very young and the Queen often had her grandchildren with her for long periods, so they got used to speaking English. When we were alone with Papa, we often talked Russian, but when we were all together, it was always English. Mama never liked speaking Russian with us, and she hadn't a very good accent—she was still a foreigner in that. Yet she loved only Russia, it was her true country. During the war she was particularly bitter about Germany. I can still remember how shocked my parents were at the news that the Emperor William had proclaimed Poland a monarchy, which was the most terrible blow for them. They spoke of the Emperor in extreme bitterness and disgust. By trying to hurt us, he had hurt himself just as badly.

I can remember plenty of other things about our life at home. When we were small, Papa was very fond of playing with us. I can still remember his taking us on the chute. For we had a room in Tsarskoe Selo where there was a chute; actually it had been built for my brother. In the winter we romped with Papa in the snow. Sometimes we threw him into it, so that he was quite white. We laughed loudly, but he got his own back by throwing *us* in afterwards. Papa would have been a happier man if he hadn't always been burdened by the cares of state.

In the summer we played tennis with our parents. Papa was very good at the game, he could move about the court quickly and was very supple. I once had a snapshot at home, of Mama and Tatiana being coached at tennis. I think it must have been taken in Germany, when we were there with relatives.

I played mostly with my brother and my sister Maria. I got on very well with Alexi, we were always thinking out some new game together; he was such a jolly little boy when he was well. I myself was a very hoydenish girl, I liked racing about, and climbing trees in the park. I often tore my clothes doing that, which vexed Mama. Still, I could be very funny, and the family were always laughing about me because I did such amusing things, like hanging round my neck a wreath of *sushki*, our Russian cracknel, so that I could always eat some when I wanted.

As a child I also played with dolls, of course. I had very

beautiful dolls. One I had was a present given me in a convent we visited. I can also remember some funny dolls which could dance; and when I was quite small we had a toy I was particularly fond of—a little mouse with a real mouse-skin, which ran across the room when you wound it up with a key. For Papa I was always 'Malenkaia,' the little one, for I was very short: that was a special pet-name of his. Yet Papa was once very cross with me, and I am quite ashamed to tell this story. We were on a ship where there was a sailor on guard. He had to stand very still, of course, so I amused myself by tugging at his uniform, giving him kicks and generally tormenting him. Suddenly Papa came up from behind, took me by the hair, which I always wore down, and dragged me away. He was very angry, and I was dreadfully ashamed.

We all grew up very close to Nature, and specially enjoyed gardening. It was so lovely to see everything budding and growing, and we liked physical work. Papa too used often to join in the digging, and also chopped wood, not only in the hard times when we were prisoners but before as well in the happy days. How long I pined to have a little garden of my own, as I at last have now.

We also had a lot of pets. Animals were always something wonderful in our eyes. My brother had a funny old dog, I had a dog myself, and Tatiana even took hers along to Siberia. Once we had a white Angora cat and a cockatoo, and I remember we kept guinea-pigs as well. In Tsarskoe Selo we even had an elephant, a very good-natured beast—its keeper was a coloured man.

When we were small, we used to go out in a pony-trap. I can still remember a snow-white pony which a Cossack had presented to my father. We also had a small cart, and since Alexi wasn't allowed to ride, there was a horse-drawn carriage for him. But we had a donkey, too, to draw us.

When I was older, I was very fond of riding side-saddle; our horses were dark brown. We also took part in parades, which we thought were the finest thing in our lives. If only I could be in one of those parades just once more! Yes, we were real soldier's children, interested in anything to do with the military.

We always liked best being in Tsarskoe Selo. The castle had a big park with nice ponds, which had black swans swimming in them, and there was a little chalet that was our special joy; but we could romp about anywhere in the grounds to our hearts' content. We children had our rooms on the castle's upper floor. I can't remember properly all the other people who were on that floor. Shura our nurse, who afterwards married Monsieur Gilliard, certainly had her room there, and so did Miss Schneider, my mother's companion, whom we called Aunt Trina and who was later shot by the Bolsheviks. Then M. Gilliard must have had his schoolroom next to Alexi's bedroom. That's all I can think of, and there are a lot of names I have completely forgotten.

In the mornings Mama used to have us girls come to her room. We said good morning to her and then sat in a corner near her dressing-table, and she talked to us while she was having her hair done. Her bedroom had a big, light-coloured bed, made of metal as far as I recall. It stood with the head towards the wall, and at its foot there was a small sofa. Papa's bedroom had darker furniture, and his bed too, I fancy, was darker than Mama's.

Near her bedroom Mama had a room with a lot of icons in it; it was there that she went to pray, though there was also a chapel in the house, where services were held. One of her rooms had wicker furniture and there were flowers from our hot-houses in all the rooms. One of the small rooms between Mama's and Papa's sitting-rooms was full of photographs, with many albums on the tables. They contained all the pictures that had ever been taken of our family. In another of Mama's rooms there was a large picture of the unfortunate Queen of France, which had once been given her, I believe, by the French government.

Usually we breakfasted with our parents, and we only stayed upstairs when Mama was ill or tired from long watches at Alexi's bedside. I liked fruit for my breakfast, and we always got that. On Wednesdays and Fridays a Lenten diet was observed, and this rule was kept to very strictly.

The whole day was mapped out for us, for we had many lessons—which didn't please me at all. Our two foreign tutors were Monsieur Gilliard and Mr Gibbs. One of the Russian tutors was very old, his name was Peter Vassilievich Petrov. My sister Olga was the hardest-working and most conscientious, taking her lessons very seriously. It was quite different with me, I was always wanting to be outside playing in the garden.

Monsieur Gilliard was there chiefly for Alexi, but gave lessons to us girls as well. Coming from the French part of Switzerland, he was very French in his manner, vivacious, imaginative and able to fit in with any situation he might find himself in. Outside lesson-time, for instance, he was very good fun; he and I often teased each other, and laughed a lot. He was the same with the others too, except for my eldest sister, who didn't like this, so he behaved differently with her. Olga wasn't so merry as I, and took everything very seriously. Later on, when all the troubles burst upon us, it was she who bore the brunt of them with Mama and suffered with her.

Mr Gibbs, the English tutor, was quite different from M. Gilliard, but we were extremely fond of him too. He always held his head slightly to one side, I remember. In his whole personality he was a typical English gentleman. When we were at Tobolsk, he came to us there for a time. Both tutors afterwards went back to their own countries.

We did a lot of gymnastics too. I used to have my feet massaged because they were always hurting. I think I got that from Mama, who often complained of her feet, and after big receptions was quite ill from having had to stand so long.

I loved playing the piano, although I didn't like practising; but I was very fond of music. One of my special favourites was a fine cavalry march. I can't remember now what it was called, but I know I enjoyed playing and singing it. We also did needle-work, which I liked very much. I always admired Mama's work greatly, and therefore tried hard to learn quickly everything she showed us. She did a lot of embroidery, and when it was for churches she always used gold thread; those embroideries were specially beautiful. We used to like sitting and working with her. When we were older, we once made ourselves blouses with a many-coloured cross-stitch pattern. I think we were still wearing these blouses at Tobolsk; and on the last day before that terrible night in Ekaterinburg, I had just started on a new piece of colourful embroidery.

* * *

Gilliard, afterwards one of the strongest sceptics on the subject of Anastasia's identity, has this memory of her childhood:

'The schoolroom at Tsarskoe Selo. I have just finished a lesson with

Olga Nikolaievna; by myself again, I am expecting her sister Tatiana. The door opens, and instead I see a very small girl coming towards me. She is carrying under her arm a big picture-book, which she ceremoniously puts down on the table in front of me; then she gives me her hand and says in Russian: "I would like to learn French too." And without waiting for my answer, she climbs on to a chair, kneels on it, opens her book, and asks me, putting her tiny forefinger on a huge elephant: "What's that called in French?" Then I am confronted with a whole succession of lions, tigers, and well, almost all the creatures in the Ark. I join in her game, very pleased with her great seriousness about this first lesson. Then the door opens again, and this time Tatiana comes in. The little girl, whose finger has just lighted on the boa-constrictor, claps the picture-book shut and jumps up. She holds out her hand to me once more, and in a very low voice says: "I'll come again tomorrow." Then she runs out of the room, clasping the book to her chest.

'This was how I first made the acquaintance of Anastasia Nikolaievna, who was then four and a half. I need hardly say that no lesson took place on the next day.

'During the following months I saw more and more of her. She would come running into the schoolroom as soon as she knew I was alone, and would tell me about all the important happenings in her life. She had a child's picturesque turn of phrase, and the melodious Russian gave her voice a soft, almost wheedling note. Sometimes she even got me to let her sit and listen when I was teaching one of the older girls. She would sit on the carpet for preference, and watch everything in devout silence, for she knew that at the first interruption she would be banished from the schoolroom—which at that time she evidently regarded as a sort of forbidden paradise. But these good intentions were seldom strong enough to resist the terrible temptation of making a voyage of discovery under the desk, and such adventures usually ended with a humiliating expulsion from the room, causing a flood of tears.

'The years passed, and in 1910 Anastasia became my pupil. She was then eight and a half, and I have seldom seen such zeal for learning in a girl of that age. She had a remarkable memory and made amazingly good progress. It was like a game to her to learn by heart anything she wanted; and as she had an excellent French accent, she recited it very successfully, whether prose or poetry. Grammar, alas, was never her strong point, even in Russian, and disaster occurred when we came to participles. Facing this difficult part of speech, she developed the instinctive fear of a young colt with which one is trying to jump a fence it thinks too high. Again and again I led her up to the obstacle, but every time at the last moment she shied back.

'In the autumn of 1913 I was appointed house-tutor to the Tsarevich and moved over into the palace. About this time I noticed that Anastasia's zeal for learning was less and less in evidence; in fact she became distinctly lazy. My colleagues and I were in despair, for till then we had always been very satisfied with her. I tried in vain to fight against the pronounced indifference she showed during lessons, but it only turned them into tearful scenes without producing any results: right to the end she remained a lazy pupil. This did not in the least spoil our good relations, however, and since I had got to know her as a very little girl, I was on more familiar terms with her than with her sisters. Because of her age she was much closer to her brother, and was far more interested than her elder sisters in his life and even in mine. She would come running into my study just to get a "yes" or "no" in answer to a question she wanted to ask me. Sometimes she came to me with scarlet cheeks, trembling with emotion, to tell me in her comical French about all the little upsets of her life. Often, too, there was a great joy she wanted to share with somebody at once and couldn't keep to herself a moment longer.

'Ingenuousness and utter simplicity were the most characteristic qualities of Anastasia Nikolaievna. As a small child she was very mischievous, spotting at once the comical traits in people's characters and afterwards imitating them very skilfully, so that it was irresistibly funny. But as she grew older, this rather irreverent habit became less common.

'I never noticed in her the smallest trace of mawkishness or dreamy melancholy, not even at the age when girls easily fall a prey to such tendencies. She was the imp of the whole house, and the glummest faces would always brighten in her presence, for it was impossible to resist her jokes and nonsense. She was very boisterous, and sometimes a good deal too temperamental. Every impulse, every new sensation was something she immediately had to indulge to the full; she was aflame with life and animation. Even at sixteen she still behaved like a headstrong young foal that has run away from its master. In her play, in realising her wishes, in her schemes, in everything she did, there was the same impetuousness and youthful enthusiasm—except, alas, in her lessons. I have mentioned that when she was younger this failing caused many scenes. When I rebuked her then, I felt she positively hated me, and her eyes went quite dark; but her rage vanished as quickly as it had come. A quarter of an hour later all was forgotten, and a happy smile would appear on her cheeks, where the last tears were still drying.

She took calmly any punishment she felt was justified, but was deeply injured by any unfairness, and fought against it with every fibre of her being. For all her weaknesses you were bound to love this child, because you could not escape from her irresistible charm, made up of freshness, enjoyment of life, ingenuousness and simplicity.'

The other tutor, Mr Gibbs, writes:

'I came to the Imperial court in 1908 as successor to the English tutor Mr Epps. The Tsar's daughters were still very young then, the eldest, the Grand-Duchess Olga, being thirteen, and the youngest, the Grand-Duchess Anastasia, only seven. The little Tsarevich was just four. My duties were to teach English to the three eldest. Anastasia was not yet old enough for serious lessons, and I did not start teaching her that year, because I had only just taken up my post and the children did not yet know me. She began, however, in the autumn of the following year, 1909—before that she had only had lessons in scripture, Russian, and also music, I believe. She was a frail little girl then, but her movements were quick and animated, her eyes betrayed intelligence and were full of life. Despite her transparent complexion and delicate appearance she possessed the physical strength so characteristic of the family. She was usually cheerful and contented, and enjoyed finding peculiarities in the speech and behaviour of people around her. She was particularly good at putting on a very solemn expression—I don't think I've ever met another child who could do this so cleverly.

'Nevertheless, the Grand-Duchess as a child was not easy to teach, especially by the traditional methods of teaching. At Cambridge I had taken courses in the sciences and child psychology, and I tried to introduce new methods as far as I was entitled to. Our lessons were usually very peaceful, but sometimes there were storms, too. On one of these occasions, after a lesson that had been more laborious than usual, I refused to give the Grand-Duchess the best mark—five. At that she gripped my shirt, and I at once feared the worst for its cleanliness. (We had to be immaculately dressed when giving our tuition.) Finding she could not get what she wanted by this method, she left the room, to come back soon afterwards with a bunch of flowers. Perhaps flowers would achieve more than violence could.

' "Mr Gibbs, will you change my mark?"

'I looked at her, and she was so upset that I already felt pangs of conscience. Then I contemplated the flowers—really, I couldn't let myself be bribed. I shook my head. At this she drew herself up to her full height, and went off to the next room, where she discovered the dear old Russian professor, Peter Vassilievich, and said: "Peter Vassilievich, allow me to present you with these flowers."

'According to all good tutorial rules, the professor should have refused this present, but he accepted it; even professors are human! Later the whole thing blew over: she again offered me flowers, as she always used to do during the first years, and as for me—well, I was more careful in marking her. We had both learnt our lesson.

'I recall these details to show the intimate terms we were on with the Tsar's children. They grew up under our eyes and were the objects of our lively interest. I gave them up to eighteen lessons a week, not counting walks with the Tsarevich. Later on, when I became his tutor, I was not only required to give him sixteen lessons, but also to make him familiar with the duties of his position, an assignment I shared with my colleague Pierre Gilliard.'

* * *

Time still scarcely seemed to move, and although bad news must sometimes have come, as I could tell from my parents' worried faces, we children still grasped little of what was happening in Russia and the world. In summer we went on many journeys with our parents, including journeys abroad. We visited Germany, England, France and Rumania, and usually stayed with relatives who had already enjoyed our hospitality in Russia; but I had only met a fraction of our extensive family abroad.

In the main we lived very quietly, and as children went about little; I had almost no experience of big society occasions. After all, I was only thirteen at the outbreak of war, so my elder sisters really had more of their life than I did. They were more or less grown up before the war, and could attend parties, whereas I never once went to a real ball. Yet I liked dancing, and we often danced with the officers on my father's yacht, the *Standart*. I was always very happy then.

From the journeys inside Russia I specially remember the ones to Poland, the Crimea and the Finnish Islands. In Poland Papa had a hunting lodge he was particularly fond of called Spala. From the windows there we could watch the game coming out of the forest and stopping quite near the house, a wonderful sight. Altogether the forest was a great joy for me. I could not pass an ant-heap without inspecting it. I specially liked a pool in the forest; more than a pool really, I think, a regular lake. We enjoyed playing there, and it was grand to take off our shoes and stockings and wade into the water, but we weren't allowed to often. All the same, I sometimes did when no one was watching.

We often went to the Crimea. That was the most beautiful district I ever saw in Russia: the flowers and plants were even more luxuriant there than those I saw afterwards at Lugano. The gardens of Livadia were splendidly kept. Our parents always made a good recovery there from the exertions of the winter. An uncle of my father's, Peter Nikolaievich, had a castle here that was completely white.

But perhaps it was even more beautiful in the Islands. We were always quite on our own there. Few people came with us on the yacht, only a few officers, who were very jolly and used to tease me a lot. I wish I could go to the Finnish Islands once more. I can't help thinking of them wistfully, and I believe I should get well again if I could be there for a while as in the old days.

We seldom went to Finland itself, only sailed to and fro between the islands in our *Standart*. We were taken in a small boat to the shore, where we played between the rocks all day and could also paddle in the water. Papa was fond of one very small boat, which had room for only two people, so that he could never take more than one of us children. Sometimes I was allowed to row, which I came to do well, but Papa often went out on his own. Once there was an accident, when the *Standart* ran on a rock; it was a frightful shock for us all. There was something that happened to Alexi, too, and Mama got very upset about it, but I can't recall what it was now.

Another time we sailed to Riga. Papa took a long time deciding to go, for he did not trust the population of the Baltic Provinces. They were always the worst, he said, and he was continually having trouble with the Balts. So the parents were at first very apprehensive when we went there. Afterwards, however, we often recalled with pleasure those days in Riga.

I think I remember our visit there being the occasion for the unveiling of a statue, for which special platforms were built. When the parents were fetched, we four sisters drove into the town in a carriage. We were still children then and all wore our hair down. Alexi hadn't been allowed to land with us. For one thing he was much too small, and besides, Mama was very nervous about him. But I can still remember quite distinctly that while we were in Riga he was allowed to roller-skate on the yacht.

From another visit to Riga I have a memory of our having to plant seven trees somewhere, one for each of us. I shovelled the earth myself for the tree that was being planted for me. My brother wasn't with us this time either, nor was Mama. I think we were accompanied by Princess Obolenski, one of Mama's ladies-in-waiting. It was she also who took us to the banquet in the famous *Schwarzhäupterhaus*. In one of the rooms there we saw pictures of the Russian Emperors, beginning with Peter the Great right down to my father. We were also shown a collection of silver, but I made nothing of this.

The Balts cheered us and welcomed us with a warmth we could never have anticipated, but afterwards, during the war, my father often spoke of them with great bitterness. They fêted us when we visited them, but in the war we knew they were only waiting for the moment when the Germans would move into the Baltic provinces. Papa was wounded and embittered by this, and could never forgive it. Yet the many Balts with us at Court had always been well treated, and indeed some of them were very pleasant. Our marshal, Count Beckendorff, was a Balt.

We went to Germany several times. Mama liked going to the German spas for her health. In one of these spas, but I have forgotten its name, Mama had a Russian church built, and we all attended its dedication. We also visited our uncle, the Grand-Duke Ernest Louis. He had a castle, the *Wolfsgarten*, where it was very beautiful.

Several of our German relatives had previously stayed with us in Russia, so that we knew them already. One of these was Mama's sister, Aunt Irene, wife of Prince Henry of Prussia, whom we called Aunt Nini; and another was our uncle from Hesse, who had brought his sons with him to Russia—they were nice boys. I think the last time I saw Aunt Irene was at Spala in 1912, when she was accompanied by her son, Prince Sigismund of Prussia, whom I saw again many years afterwards. In fact it was this brother and sister of my mother's who were later to cause me such disappointments.

Several of the Prussian princes had stayed with us, and I have clear memories of Prince Adalbert's visit, perhaps because we did not care for him and thought him very conceited. I found the Crown Prince much nicer. He and Princess Cecilie stayed with us at St Petersburg in 1911, but of course I was very small then, and I only know that he was very jolly and everyone liked him.

We visited England, too, though not London. We went to somebody's summer residence at the seaside, and I played with the English children, including the Prince of Wales. There was a young Prince of Leuchtenberg there with his sister, nephew and niece of my later benefactor, Duke George. Once Papa watched us all playing in the park and took a film of us without our knowledge. I can remember our being called into a room and shown the film as a surprise. It was very funny seeing ourselves at play on the screen.

The other person I remember particularly from pre-war days is my grandmother, Maria Feodorovna, widow of Alexander III whom my father succeeded when he died in 1894. She was a princess of Denmark, and as a girl had been called Dagmar. It was her youngest brother, Prince Valdemar, to whom in later years I had reason to be extremely grateful.

Grandmama was always very good to us children. When she invited us, we were always very happy, for we knew this meant a fine time for us. Just as she did at home, Grandmama had Negroes to open the door; they wore large white turbans. Her footmen all wore black livery.

Mama and Grandmama did not get on well together, and they met only on terms of superficial politeness. I was told that since the German-Danish war Grandmama was against everything German, and didn't like Papa marrying a German princess; she would have preferred a French one, I think. Altogether her love went more to her youngest son, Michael, who was next in succession to my father after the death of her second son, the Grand-Duke George. But my grandfather finally gave his blessing to the marriage. Nevertheless, people later talked of the 'great court' of my parents and the 'small court' of the Empress-Dowager Maria Feodorovna. Several grand-dukes soon attached themselves to the 'small court' and took part in violent intrigues against us, which certainly contributed to the collapse of our country. After the Revolution Grandmama succeeded in escaping from the Crimea and getting back to Denmark. She died at Copenhagen in 1928 at the age of eighty. without my having the chance to see her again. It was one of my bitterest disappointments.

A truly sincere friend was my Aunt Olga, Papa's youngest sister. Mama too loved her dearly, she was closest to Mama of all my aunts. She was kind to us all, and had no taste whatever for intrigues. She was very amusing as well, and since I was the same way inclined, we were very fond of each other and enjoyed a lot of silly things together—she used to call me 'Shvipsik.' Aunt Olga also managed to get out of Russia after the Revolution, and lived with my grandmother at Copenhagen. In 1925 she visited me at the nursing home in Berlin, and I shall come later on to the great hopes and disappointments bound up with this meeting.

We were often with the family of the Grand-Duke Constantine, who lived at Pavlovsk near St Petersburg during the summer and at the Marble Palace during the winter. A very cultured man, the Grand-Duke was president of the Academy of Sciences. He was a son of Alexander II's brother and, like his father, had married a Princess of Saxony. His wife, the Grand-Duchess Elizaveta Mavrikievna, was known in our family circle as Aunt Mavra—I had to think a long time before I remembered this abbreviation of her name. She was a very warm-hearted, motherly woman, who never got mixed up with politics, a reason why Mama too specially favoured the relationship with her.

There were a great many children at Pavlovsk, for the Grand-Duke had six sons and two girls, and it was always very jolly there; the children often came to us on visits. One of Constantine's daughters was already married when I was still a child, so I don't remember her. But I have all the more vivid memories of Prince Gabriel, from whom I received a letter in 1928, when I was leaving Europe to go to my cousin Xenia in America. He wrote to me familiarly, and as one writes to a dear relative after long separation. I was naturally very pleased to hear from him, but must admit that at the time I had no strength left to be grateful.

Less happy memories are associated with my great-uncle, the Grand-Duke Nikolai, the husband of my Aunt Anastasia. As a child I had heard something dreadful about him. I was always a great animal-lover, and I was once told that he often behaved very cruelly not only to men but also to animals. On one occasion he was inspecting the litter in the kennels of the Imperial court, and apparently considering that there were too many dogs, he had the puppies brought out and himself smashed their skulls with his whip, leaving his servants to deal in the same way with the older dogs. I was terribly shocked at this.

This uncle gave my father a lot of trouble, for he was an unscrupulous and ambitious man, only interested in getting his own way and paying no more attention to Papa's wishes than he could possibly help. On the other hand he had a good reputation as a soldier, and showed great energy in the war.

Papa also had a lot of trouble with other relatives. The Grand-Duke Cyril had later married Victoria, the divorced wife of my uncle Louis of Hesse, which was naturally not very agreeable for my parents. This led to strained relations between the main and collateral lines of our family which reached their tragic climax in 1917. My father at the time was at his headquarters in Mogilev, while the Grand-Duke was commander of the Marine Guard at Tsarskoe Selo. In this position he owed special loyalty to us, instead of which he was the first to desert, presenting himself with a red cockade in front of the Duma and joining the Provisional Government. Of course we were all disgusted at this betrayal, and it was something my father took particularly hard. Many years later, when I met the Grand-Duke's daughter, I was still made to feel the after-effects of this family conflict. At any rate I don't believe that it was the Russian soldiers and peasants who made the Russian revolution. It had quite a different real cause, and the highest circles in the land were to blame. They lived off the fat of the land, and finally they betrayed us.

* * *

By this time the war was already casting its shadows ahead. Since the murder at Sarajevo every intelligent person in Russia knew that frightful things were in the air. All observers were struck by the Tsar's uneasiness and anxiety. With great apprehension Nicholas II realised that he was facing critical days, and what was worse, that the decision would be up to him too.

The Tsar was a reserved and introspective man, full of ideals and humane principles, but a dreamer. His eyes were melancholy, and their expression was tired, sad, almost distraught. He smiled rarely, spoke little, and when he was talking usually looked at the ground.

He had always considered reforms, but because he was weak-willed, opinionated and stubborn, he returned more and more to the absolutism of his father, Alexander III, although in his youth he had foresworn despotism. He was genuinely convinced that he must carry through the duties enjoined on him as Tsar, but he surrounded himself with people he had not the ability to control and command. He acted on principle, because he considered it his solemn duty to use his strength for the position entrusted to him by God—as the sole Christian monarch combining absolute worldly power with the high office of protector of the Greek Orthodox Church. Like most Russians, he had a superstitious belief in signs, and was always looking out for omens.

His wife Alexandra Feodorovna was perhaps the most pathetic and misunderstood woman in Russia. She was unusually beautiful, but shy, even awkward, mystically inclined; her eyes, too, always looked sad. She loved her husband no less passionately at forty than she had at twenty, with a humble devotion and a deep fervour, although recognising his weakness of will, his susceptibility to outside influences, his indecision and lack of the firmness so necessary in a ruler. But she accepted these failings because she loved her husband.

Having in her youth once made the decision to leave her German home and Protestant faith for Russia and the Greek Orthodox Church, she gave herself to her new country with the same passion as to her husband. She suffered all the more from the cool reserve shown her by the members of her Russian family, starting with the Empress-Dowager, Maria Feodorovna, as well as by a large part of court society. Maria Feodorovna persisted in preceding Alexandra, nodding graciously to right and left with a friendly smile for everyone; she was sure of her rank. After all, she had been wife of the heir to the throne for eight years before becoming Tsarina: she knew her Russia. Alexandra, on the other hand, entering the country only as Empress, received little notice from anyone. She was constantly afraid of speaking bad Russian, so preferred to stay silent; and this reticence was put down to pride. Public receptions would find her blushing with nervousness and embarrassment, searching laboriously for something to say to the guests, and only longing for the reception to end. Then she could return to her household, where instead of the extravagant brilliance of her mother's court a great simplicity reigned, almost suggesting a cosy bourgeois home. She was happiest sitting near her husband's desk, bent over some knitting or embroidery. Her family meant everything to her: Nicki, as she called him, her children, and especially her invalid son.

It was through this son that she came in touch with Rasputin, who was brought into the house originally by the intriguing yet strongly religious Anastasia Nikolaievna. Because she helped Rasputin to a position of great power, the coolness between Alexandra and the Russian court grew to a bitter hatred. Rasputin was a strange person who seemed to embody in himself all the Russian characteristics, good and bad. He had a mysterious charm against which the Tsar stood out for a long time; but Nicholas was so much influenced by his wife that in the end he gave the man his head. And thus, on the day of mobilisation, Rasputin dared to send the Tsar from far Siberia the famous letter with its beacon-fire warning against war:

'Dear friend, I say it once more: a terrible storm is threatening Russia. It is a misfortune, unspeakable suffering. It is dark, and no light shines through. A whole sea of tears. And what a torrent of blood! What am I to say? I can find no words. Indescribable grief. I know they are all demanding war from you, even those who are loyal; they do not see that they are hastening their own fate. Hard is God's punishment. If He takes away your reason, it is the beginning of the end. You are the Tsar, father of the people. Don't let the lunatics triumph, don't plunge yourself and the people into destruction. Germany may be defeated. But what will happen then in Russia? If one thinks of it, there has never been so great a martyrdom. Russia is drowning in blood. Great is the misfortune, boundless the grief.'

Despite pangs of doubt, the Tsar rejected this warning. He had been worked on ceaselessly by the anti-German 'small court' of his mother, the foreign minister, the court camarilla, and above all the military party headed by the war minister and the Grand-Duke Nikolai. They drummed it into him that war was an unavoidable necessity; and so the avalanche began to roll.

Many people saw the war as a way out for other reasons. Long before its outbreak Russian society had begun to sink into the abyss of Bolshevism. All classes, from the court down to the proletariat, were disintegrating in uncontrollable moral decline. Mysticism and spiritualism spread. Even in the highest circles socialist ideas flourished in the most various forms, with prominent writers adopting them enthusiastically: the only parallel is the collapse of French society before that revolution. The downfall of the Russian Empire may well have been largely caused by the intrigues at court, which took on more and more ugly forms, and by suspicions and disunity at the head of the state—since even the Tsar's enemies could not bring themselves to unite in a common cause. Although the court camarilla got rid of Rasputin, their palace rising did not enable them to stop the Socialist Revolution, which (as they signally failed to grasp) was soon to develop into

Bolshevism. There was no stopping the flood-tide of March 1917, to which the tremendous blood-letting at the front contributed its own impetus.

*   *   *

Despite the war, time seemed to stop once more. The sky and the sun, the green in the park, the flowers in their beds—they were still the same in Tsarskoe Selo. We never really grasped anything of what was happening at the front, except perhaps when a hospital train came in and the casualties were unloaded.

Mama worked with Olga and Tatiana in their hospitals. They acted as ordinary nurses, helping at serious operations, and thereby set a fine example of self-sacrifice and Christian charity. But Maria and I also had a hospital under our patronage. It was billeted very near the Palace in the houses belonging to the Cathedral, with fifty beds for private soldiers and fifty for officers in another building, but the beds weren't always occupied.

We were mostly sent officers from our own regiments. Olga was commander of a regiment of Hussars, Tatiana had Lancers, Maria a regiment of Dragoons, while Papa and Alexi were commanders of Cossack regiments. Although I was only fifteen and really still a child, I became commander of a regiment, this exception to the rules being made because it was war-time. I can't remember the regiment's name now, but I believe I even received a delegation on taking it over. When I think of how the people always cheered us whenever we showed ourselves, with what gratification our appearance was hailed everywhere, my thoughts become all confused, and I just cannot grasp that things happened as they did.

I was naturally very proud of our hospital. Maria and I were allowed to go there at least once a week, sometimes even more often, and talk to our wounded, who called us their 'hostesses.' We played halma and draughts with them, sometimes a gramophone record was put on, and one of the officers sang to it; or else they played billiards, but I didn't grasp much about that. Anyhow it helped to pass the time for them, and they liked it when I joked and laughed with them, even though Maria cast disapproving glances. She was always much more serious than I, talking only about the terrible war, the privations and the cold, the Cossacks and the police, who were too hard on the poor people.

Sometimes I brought my Kodak with me, posed a group together, and took a few snaps. As soon as they were developed and printed, they went into our albums. We also brought these with us to show our officers, as we did our poetry albums, in which they had to write something. We might stay to tea with them, and sometimes there was a big block of *halva* on the table. This is a sort of Turkish nougat, and I would pounce on it ignoring protests from Maria, for I was terribly fond of it. *Halva* is really delicious.

Those officers who couldn't go home for Christmas received a silver cigarette case with our monogram as a present, while the privates got silver watches. And everyone being discharged from the hospital received as a souvenir a picture with our signature and a small gold medallion with our initials on it.

By a strange chance I came across such a medallion again in my later life. In the summer of 1927 I was visited at Oberstdorf by Tatiana Melnik, daughter of Dr Botkin, my father's personal physician; she had also worked as a nurse in our hospital, where we saw a lot of her. At Oberstdorf one evening I came into her room while she was changing for dinner. After a while she brought out a handkerchief in which she kept her jewellery, and in it lay a medallion from our war-hospital at Tsarskoe Selo, which belonged to her husband. I recognised it at once. The initials A., M. and N. (Anastasia, Maria Nikolaievna) were unmistakable, so it was not from our elder sisters, but one of our own. I was shattered to take it in my hands. How many people and treasured possessions had perished since then, yet just this little piece had survived!

Mention of Dr Botkin makes me think of something else, although I only heard the details afterwards from Mama and the sisters. It was early March of 1917, the last days we spent, in fact, at our beloved Tsarskoe. For some time there had been in the air an atmosphere of feverishness which had come over both army and population. We heard talk of disturbances breaking out, but Mama allayed our fears, and Papa, as so often, went to his Mogilev headquarters, although Alexi had fallen ill the evening before and had to go to bed. This time, however, it was a different illness, for it soon turned out that he had got measles, and it was not long before we sisters went down with it one after the other. Mama was very worried, because the illness took a serious form, our temperatures sometimes rose to 104, and Maria and I developed pneumonia and neuritis. It was a succession of misfortunes.

I can't remember now how long we were all laid up like this, but I do remember the good Dr Botkin, who was assisted by Derevenko, Alexi's doctor, always coming into our room with noiseless steps and then returning to Mama to report on our condition. It must have been over a week before the crisis was reached. Beside all her other cares Mama now had the worry about our health and the strain of nursing us. Then came the turning point. But that day, when Dr Botkin entered Mama's room with its pale and delicate colours, he found it in semi-darkness. He wanted to give her the news that the greatest danger was past, but Mama was sitting at the table asleep. In her over-tired state she had put her head on her arms and closed her eyes. Sleep had overcome her for the first time in fifty-two hours. I have never forgotten this example of my mother's devotion.

It was in these days that the St Petersburg rising took place, which was to end our freedom. Being ill, we had no idea, of course, what was going on in the capital or at headquarters either. But even some time later, when we were being guarded like prisoners, indeed like criminals, by soldiers with red badges on their sleeves, we still did not grasp the seriousness of the situation, thinking it was a nightmare from which we should soon awaken. We were convinced there were enough regiments in Russia to restore order. We were tragically mistaken: the last act had begun.

* * *

The following days are part of world history. At first, however, the Tsarina was almost as unsuspecting as her children, and failed to grasp the extent of the revolutionary movement, though the crucial events were occurring only a dozen miles away. She was informed of the first incidents through reports from Protopopov, Minister of the Interior; but the reports were false, and also she received them at second-hand, because they were given on the telephone to the groom of the chamber, Alexis Volkov. (This is the man who was confronted with Anastasia in 1925.) Afterwards, when Volkov brought graver news, to the effect that even the Cossacks in Petersburg were no longer dependable, the Tsarina answered: 'No, that's impossible. Cossacks are not traitors.'

Both Dr Botkin, however, and the mistress of the robes, Narishkina, who were constantly with her in the children's sick-room during these critical hours, realised that this was no chance disturbance, but revolution itself. And when the Tsarina at last began to understand the truth, she still remained calm, and asked no questions. Her chief reaction was to say: 'I knew it. The Emperor could not protect the holy man, he was too weak even to punish the murderers. This is the judgment on us.' So powerfully was she reminded of Rasputin that in this hour of trial she still connected her mysticism with her belief in the divine right of the crown. When Narishkina courageously remarked that the revolutionary leaders' demands were at that time still moderate, being directed not against the Emperor but towards the establishment of a cabinet responsible to the people, Alexandra answered haughtily: 'There is one thing I learnt from Gregory Yefimovich: to see our Russian democrats as they are, not as one would like them to be. . . . It is not our selfish wishes but the holy church which has imposed on us the duty of handing down undiminished to our successors the rights of the imperial throne. There is no danger or threat which could move me to ask my husband to break the oath he swore before God.'

When Alexandra became aware of the whole terrible reality, she did, it is true, follow Narishkina's counsel, and at the eleventh hour advised her husband in a letter to give the country a ministry responsible to the people. But it was too late, the letter never reached him—Nicholas II had already renounced his throne. He understood the extent of the upheaval even less than his wife did; and from now on all her efforts were to be met with the fatal answer: too late.

Events moved very fast. At first the Tsar thought it was sufficient to send troops against the rising in St Petersburg. When, however, the news became more and more ominous, the only thing he could think of was to board his imperial train in order to return to Tsarskoe Selo and his wife and family—that resolute wife who had always mastered every situation. On the way, however, the train was stopped by the rebels in the middle of the night. General Russky, commander of the northern front, who was travelling with him, brought him the fateful news. They tried to travel by another route, but only reached Pskov, where they soon received answers to the questionnaire sent by General Alexeiev, chief of the general staff, to all the other army commanders, as to their views on the decisions the Tsar should take. All the telegrams spoke of abdication, renunciation of the crown, and one bore the signature of his uncle and enemy, the Grand-Duke Nikolai. The Tsar made the following entries in his diary:

*Monday*, 27 *February*.

'For several days now there have been disturbances in Petersburg; unfortunately the army too is involved in them. It is dreadful to be so far away and receive short unfavourable reports.

'The sermon did not last long. During the day I went for a walk along the road leading to Orsha. The weather was sunny. After dinner I decided to travel to Tsarskoe Selo at once, and boarded the train at one in the morning.

*Tuesday*, 28 *February*.

'Did not get to bed till a quarter-past three, because I had a long talk with N. J. Ivanov. I am sending him to Petersburg with a strong force to restore order there. Slept till ten. We left Mogilev at five in the morning. Sunshine and frost. Passed Vyazma and Rzhev during the day, and Lichoslavl at nine.

*Wednesday*, 1 *March*.

'At night we returned to Malaia Vishera, since it turned out that Lyuban and Tosno have been occupied by the rebels. Travelled via Valdai and Dno to Pskov, where I spent the night. Saw Russky. He, Danilov and Savich had a meal with me. Gatchina and Luga are also occupied. It is a shame and a scandal. I didn't succeed in reaching Tsarskoe. My heart and mind are there all the time. How hard it must be for poor Alix to go through all these troubles alone. May God help us all!'

On the evening of 2nd March, in the presence of two delegates from the Duma who had meanwhile arrived, the Tsar signed the deed of abdication for himself and his son in favour of his brother Michael, having no idea that Michael would refuse to accept the succession. In the morning he had thought of abdicating only in favour of his son, but changed his mind on being told by his personal physician that the sick boy could not carry so heavy a burden till he was grown up. With this signature the dynasty's fate was sealed.

*Thursday*, 2 *March*.

'This morning Russky came and read me his extremely long telephone conversation with Rodzianko, the Octobrist President of the Duma. According to him the situation in St Petersburg is such that for the moment a Duma ministry will be powerless to do anything because it is being resisted by the workers' council representing the social democratic party; he says my abdication is necessary. Russky passed this conversation on to headquarters and Alexeiev reported it to all commanding generals. At two o'clock the answers came in from them all. This step must be taken to save Russia and maintain calm in the army at the front. I gave my consent. A draft of the manifesto was sent from headquarters. In the evening Gutchkov and Shulyin arrived, with whom I discussed the matter and to whom I handed the signed and revised manifesto. At one o'clock in the morning I left Pskov with grim feelings at what I had just experienced. All round me treachery, cowardice, deceit.

*Friday*, 3 *March*, 1917.

'Slept long and soundly. Woke far beyond Dvinsk. Clear frosty weather. Discussed the happenings of yesterday with my suite. Read a lot of Julius Caesar. Arrived at Mogilev at eight-twenty. The whole staff was on the platform. Received Alexeiev in the carriage. Went to my quarters at half-past nine. Alexeiev came with the latest news from Russky. It appears that Misha has declined. His manifesto ends by fawning on the constituent assembly which is to be elected in six months. God knows who can have let him sign such a piece of shamelessness.

'In Petersburg the disturbances have ceased—if only it goes on like that.

*Saturday*, 4 *March*.

'Slept well. Dear Alek came at ten. Then I had a conference. At twelve I went to the platform to greet dearest Mama, who had arrived from Kiev. We sat together and talked for a long time.

'Today I at last received two telegrams from dearest Alix. Went for a walk. The weather is horrible: cold and snow-storms. After tea I received Alexeiev and Fredericks. At eight I went to Mama's for dinner and sat with her till eleven.

*Sunday*, 5 *March*, 1917.

'Violent storm last night. Clear frosty weather. Went to divine service at ten. Mama came later. She lunched with me and stayed till a quarter to three. Went for a walk in the garden. After tea I received N. J. Ivanov, who has returned from his command. He has been in Tsarskoe and seen Alix. Said good-bye to poor Count Fredericks and Voyeikov, whose presence has for some reason upset everyone here. They both went off to the count's estate in the Pensa province.

*Monday, 6 March*, 1917.

'The last day in Mogilev. At a quarter-past ten I signed the farewell message to the troops. At half-past ten I entered the house of the duty adjutant, where I said good-bye to the staff officers and the government officials. At home I said good-bye to the officers and Cossacks of the convoy and the combined regiment—it was heart-rending for me. At twelve I went to Mama's, lunched with her and her suite in her carriage, and stayed with her till half-past four.

'Said good-bye to her, Sandro, Serge, Boris and Alek. Poor Nilov wasn't allowed to travel with me. I left Mogilev at a quarter to five. Was accompanied by a crowd of people who seemed deeply moved. Four members of the Duma are escorting me in my train.

'We are travelling in the direction of Orsha and Vitebsk. It is freezing, and there is also a strong wind.

'How harsh and painful it all is, how deeply sad I feel!'

The Tsar had offered no serious resistance to the demand for his abdication, despite the clairvoyant words of Rasputin, which must still have been ringing in his ears: 'If I die, within six months the Tsar will have lost his throne and the Tsarevich his life.' If Alexandra had been with him, he might not have given up the struggle, might have fought the last and perhaps hopeless battle, supported by her firm resolve and by the loyal troops still available. But Nicholas II had never had the strength to make up his own mind without advice from others, and it was this lack of decisiveness, rather than a failure to understand the Revolution, which proved fatal. He had never wanted to rule, yet he had loved his people and felt the misfortunes of his country. But the deepest feelings he was capable of went all to his wife, his children and his church; so now that the tragedy had burst upon him and was inescapable, his family was required to help him bear the bitterness of the time.

* * *

The abdication was a dreadful blow for my mother. At first she refused to believe the news, and for some days was quite stunned. She had never dreamed my father's weakness would be so great. As I heard later, she tried retrospectively to make the abdication invalid; and my grandmother, too, the Empress-Dowager, went to see my father a day after the terrible event in Mogilev, where he had once more gone—it was their last meeting. But then one day a red battalion came from St Petersburg, surrounded our palace in Tsarskoe, and an officer declared my mother was under arrest; at this she resigned herself to the inevitable. She did not lose her calm or her courage, though; her strength of character was still great enough to enable her to comfort us and her entourage.

I believe my father ought to have offered greater resistance, he was just too good-natured and too weak to be Tsar, and not forceful enough. There should have been a man of iron on the Russian throne; I can't help thinking of Peter the Great. Today I even believe it would have been better if the Tsar had been my father's uncle, who was commander-in-chief before him; for he was the opposite of Papa. He would never have been weak and inactive.

It was in one of our rooms that Mama was told of her arrest, which applied also to us children and to any of the palace residents who wished to remain with our family. During these days Mama stayed with us most of the time, because for one thing we felt the need to cling together; also we still had the measles, Maria especially being very ill.

My father arrived by train at Tsarskoe next day, having been informed of his arrest while at headquarters. There was a motor-car waiting for him at the station, but when he drove up to the palace, they had to call the officer on duty, who had the gates opened with the order to admit 'Colonel Romanov.' This was the rank Papa had when his father died.

Mama would have liked to dash off to meet him, but he forestalled her, so my parents met in one of our rooms, with only Volkov present. He saw them kiss with smiling faces, and then they came over to us. It was not till they went to their rooms that they began to weep, as we were told by my mother's lady-in-waiting, Anna Demidova, who was in the room; she was to be one of those who lost their lives at Ekaterinburg. Despite her grief Mama did not reproach Papa. Her love was strong enough to bear even this burden.

* * *

On the morning of 9th March, Nicholas II reached Tsarskoe, he and his family being prisoners of the Provisional Government. His diary reads as follows:

*Thursday*, 9 *March*.

'Arrived safely at Tsarskoe; it was half-past eleven. My God, what a difference: guards on the road, round the castle and in the park; some ensigns on the drive inside. Went upstairs and there saw my beloved Alix and dearest children. She looked well and healthy, they were all in bed in the darkened room. They are in good spirits, except for Maria, who has only recently gone down with measles. We had breakfast and lunch in Alexi's nursery. Saw dear Benckendorff. Went for a walk with Valya Dolgorouki and worked with him in the garden, for we are not allowed out further than that.

'Played patience after tea. In the evening I went to see all my entourage in the other wing and found them all together.

*Friday*, 10 *March*.

'All slept well.

'Despite the situation we are now in, I feel heartened and comforted by the thought that we are all together.

'Received Beckendorff in the morning, afterwards went through some of my papers, sorting and burning them.

'Was with the children till half-past two. Took a walk with Valya Dolg., escorted by the same ensigns; they were more amiable today. Worked hard shovelling away snow. The weather was sunny. We spent the evening all together.

*Saturday*, 11 *March*.

'Received Benckendorff in the morning, and heard from him that we are to stay here a long time. That is a pleasant feeling. Continued burning letters and papers.

'Anastasia has ear-ache. The others have already had it.

'From three to half-past four I went for a walk with Valya Dolg. and worked in the garden. Unpleasant weather, windy too, a little below freezing point.

'At six forty-five we went to the field church for divine service. Alexi had his first bath. Visited Ania and Lili D.[1] and later the others.'

* * *

Although the storm-clouds had loomed up so threateningly, they seemed to disperse once more. Spring had come, the sun began to shine more brightly in the grey sky, the flowers began

[1] Lili Dehn, close friend of the family who was later to testify for Anastasia's identity.

to bloom. Such days can help one to forget a little about the most grievous troubles. Papa had ceased to be a ruler; he could live now as a private citizen, even though a prisoner. He tended lovingly the little vegetable garden he had himself laid out, he put his letters and documents in order, gave Alexi lessons in history and geography, and chatted with us children as in happier times.

He also showed more cordiality towards other people than was his wont. When Easter came, he went to service with us in the castle chapel, distributed Easter eggs to everyone as usual, and embraced not only us but our guards, imprinting the kiss of reconciliation on their cheeks. I sometimes wondered afterwards whether this composed bearing was a sign of courage, or whether Papa had already become insensitive, indifferent, to the danger daily threatening us from outside.

* * *

One of the emissaries of the Petersburg soviet, who went to see the prisoners at Tsarskoe palace, has described the peaceful atmosphere of those days:

'When we entered the hall, we were surrounded by a mass of respectful, if inquisitive, servants. They included a large and powerfully built Hajduk with a huge bearskin cap; Negroes in crimson velvet jackets embroidered with gold, turbans and slippers with turned-up points; also couriers with cocked hats and red capes, which showed large imperial eagles on them.

'The footmen who accompanied us through the inner apartments were wearing snow-white gaiters and soft patent-leather shoes. They walked noiselessly up the carpeted stairs. On the upper floor we went through an endless succession of blue, yellow, pink and red salons; now we were treading on thick, swelling rugs, and now over glittering parquet floors. Outside each door stood footmen in the most varying costumes appropriate to the function of the room. Some wore the traditional black dress-coats, and other fantastic uniforms with white, black or red shoes, stockings and gaiters. Everything was as in "the good old times." These countless rooms in the vast palace showed no trace of the gale of revolution which was sweeping across the whole immense empire.'

* * *

Then Kerensky came for the first time. He was received by my parents, who were in our schoolroom at the time. Olga, Tatiana and Alexi were there, but Maria and I were still ill. According to everything I heard about this visit, he behaved as if he were master in our house.

As a member of the Provisional Government he had given instructions that we were to be deprived of all freedom of movement, so that we could not go into the village, the village church, or outside Tsarskoe at all. We might not even enter the part of the park which directly adjoined the castle. We were told exactly which paths we had to take when we went for walks, and we had to be back in the house before dark.

In the course of the summer the restrictions were tightened still further. For one thing Papa had all his papers taken away, after he had burnt some documents—Mama had destroyed hers before—and soon afterwards his personal freedom was limited even inside the castle. For some while he was separated from Mama, and we saw him only at meals, where the food we ate was ordered by our guards; and then we could only talk of indifferent matters. This arrangement too had been made by Kerensky.

During our stay at Tsarskoe he came to see us quite often, to make sure his instructions were being carried out. On these visits he sometimes saw Papa alone, but sometimes Mama and we children were also there. He was now somewhat politer than the first time, enquiring whether we had any complaints against the soldiers and promising to remedy any abuses. Having examined Papa's confiscated papers, he had evidently become convinced that my father had committed no crime against his country.

As Papa told us, Kerensky believed he had tried to conclude a separate peace with Germany; so the Provisional Government was occupied with this question, which I shall talk of later.

Yet one cannot imagine how my parents were humiliated by this man; he quite forgot who they were, and we were doubtful of his honesty. I try to recall his appearance. His face was pale, his expression arrogant and vain, his voice loud and affected. He usually wore a short coat and a shirt with soft collar. Still, my father was grateful to Kerensky for one thing: he did not impose the greatest humiliation, which Papa felt most of all. He did not make Papa take off his epaulettes; that only happened afterwards in Siberia.

* * *

This was the time when an abortive attempt was made to bring the Tsar and his family over to England. Among its chief sponsors was King George V, whose mother was a sister of the Tsar's mother and who had remained a close friend of his cousin's; understandably, the attempt was kept a strict secret within the court. King George sent a telegram to Buchanan, his ambassador in St Petersburg, with the message that a British warship was being placed at the Tsar's disposal and would be waiting for him and his family in the port of Murmansk. A purely humanitarian action on the King's part, it was thwarted by the opposition of his government, who succeeded in delaying matters, so that eventually, after the growth of the revolutionary movement, the plan could not be carried through.

The entry in the Tsar's diary for 23rd March speaks of preparations for departure for England. Hopes of being allowed to travel freely were offered him by the Lvov-Kerensky government, and a code letter found among his papers contains a promise by Prince Lvov to bring him to Murmansk.

Subsequent comment on this plan from the Bolshevik side (*The Last Days of the Romanovs*, Bykov) is as follows:

'The order for the Tsar's arrest was originally connected with another and more important plan. Even before the plan was settled, however, Miliukov was commissioned by the Provisional Government to contact the English ambassador, Buchanan, and discuss with him the possibility of the Tsar's going to England. Having made previous enquiries in London, Buchanan was able to inform Miliukov that the British Government was ready to receive the former Tsar and his family in England and that a British cruiser would be sent to take them over. In the note delivered to the Russian foreign office, it was stated *inter alia* that the King and His Majesty's Government would be happy to offer the Russian Tsar a home in England. The task of getting the Imperial family across the border was assigned to Kerensky, who was very ready to assume the rôle of the last Tsar's rescuer. All preparations for conveying the Romanovs overseas were kept rigorously secret, and very few people knew about them. By ordering Nicholas' arrest, the Provisional Government was only trying to lull the attention of the masses, so that they could later be faced with the *fait accompli*. On the very day the decision for the arrest was taken, Count Lvov, the head of the Government, sent the following telegram to General Alexeiev at headquarters: "The Provisional Government has decided to allow the former Tsar free transit for a stay at Tsarskoe Selo and for a subsequent journey to Murmansk."

'Even today it is still not known whether the promised cruiser really did wait at Murmansk.

'After their formal renunciation (before the Petersburg soviet) of the plan to ship the Romanovs abroad, the Provisional Government continued to discuss this question in secret diplomatic negotiations through the intermediary of Miliukov. When he retired from his post in April, the negotiations were pursued, according to Kerensky, with even greater zeal by Teretchenko, Miliukov's successor. But in June the Provisional Government suffered an unexpected disappointment: they were officially notified by the London cabinet that "entry into British territory by the former Tsar and his family will not be possible till the end of the war." The Romanovs were apparently kept informed of the progress of the secret negotiations, but the longer these lasted, the more they despaired of ever reaching England.'

* * *

As the influence of the Tsarskoe Soviet increased and was brought to bear on our guards, we were exposed to further humiliations. The guards now followed us step for step on our walks, and they would not let us be alone for a single minute. If Mama sat down on a bench, they would sit down by her and even insist on talking to her. If they met Papa, who was accustomed to saluting both officers and privates, they did not return his salute. Once Alexi had a little toy gun taken away from him, whereupon he burst out sobbing, until the harmless toy was returned to him. Another time we were sitting together in our room one evening, when the soldiers suddenly rushed in and accused us of communicating with the outside world by means of light signals. In fact all that had happened was that I was sitting by the window with some needlework and my shadow had blotted out the light first from one direction and then the other.

A lack of discipline became more and more apparent. Some of the soldiers would now break into the rooms which were not guarded, jeering at all our belongings, also plundering and stealing them; though there were others who showed signs of a touching humanity. The saddest thing for my parents was probably that most of their officers and suite had left them. The only ones still with us in those days were old Count Benckendorff, Prince Vassili Dolgorouki, the mistress of the robes Narishkina, the Countess Hendrikova and Dr Botkin. Our governesses, Alexandra Tegleva and Elizabeth Erzberg, and the two foreign tutors, Monsieur Gilliard and Mr Gibbs, had also stayed with us, although they were not allowed to give us any lessons then. They even followed us to Tobolsk.

But we had come to our last days at Tsarskoe. Although we had no idea that all was now lost, we did feel that some change was in the offing. Shortly before our departure Kerensky paid one more visit and explained to my father that the Provisional Government was afraid of disturbances in Tsarskoe and so a quieter place had been chosen for our residence. As we found out later, this was because the country was already on the edge of the abyss and the pressure of the soviets on the government was growing stronger and stronger. It had therefore been decided to remove us from Tsarskoe and send us as far away as possible from Bolshevist Petersburg, somewhere where our safety could be better guaranteed.

This time Kerensky adopted a remarkably accommodating tone, even addressing Papa as 'Majesty' and giving him *carte blanche* to choose the people he would take with him. He did not, however, give any information about our future residence, which was kept secret from us till the very last minute; in fact we did not learn of it till we had started the journey. He only said we should probably be travelling south. When he felt Papa's eyes upon him, he no doubt lacked the courage to tell him the whole truth. Papa was very sad about this.

A painful time began for us children, since hard as things had already been, this meant saying good-bye to everything which made our home—and how much we had to leave behind! Even today I am often sick with longing to see again all we had at home, to walk through all the rooms again, or run up the stairs as we did so often when going to wish Mama good morning.

We left in the early morning of an August day, being taken to the station under guard in motor-cars. Two trains had been reserved, the first for us and our immediate suite, the other for the remainder, and both trains had a military escort. It was the first time we had travelled in Russia in an ordinary train, and to deceive the population, I suppose, the engine carried a Japanese flag. I wonder what happened to our royal train, in which we had travelled so many miles.

Of course we wondered where we were being taken. From Kerensky's hints we all thought we were heading south for the Crimea and our beloved Livadia. After all, the Revolution would not yet have made itself felt there, and Papa could give himself up to his hobby, the growing of rare flowers.

But on one of the next mornings Mama woke up and drew the curtains (which at first had not been allowed) to see dreary steppes ahead. This filled her with dark forebodings, and the name of the next station confirmed her worst fears: our destination was Siberia.

Though I have forgotten so much, I can still remember my parents' downcast expressions in that train, their utter despondency on realising we were being sent to Siberia—no, I shall never forget how they looked then. We children did our best to put a brave face on things so as not to make it even harder for Papa and Mama, but I don't know if this helped them at all. Our only consolation was that we were all together.

The journey passed without incident. Our train stopped at small stations, sometimes in the open country. We were quite often allowed to leave our carriage and walk for a stretch, while the train slowly followed. So we at length reached Tyumen, where we boarded a steamer, which sailed first down a small river and then entered the great river Tobol. One afternoon, four days after our departure from Tsarskoe Selo, we saw the citadel of Tobolsk, which lay on a mouth of the river further on. But we had to stay on the ship for another week until the house allotted to us, the Governor's residence up till the Revolution, had been put in order.

I found everything very strange in Tobolsk, this remote little convict town; but I had always been a cheerful girl, so I tried to make the best of things. Perhaps the most depressing moment was when we left the ship, with thousands of people pressing around to gape at us. We really ran the gauntlet then, and it was made worse by the fact that we all had to carry our own luggage. Only Mama and Alexi were allowed to use the one miserable cab in the place.

Our house was a two-storey stone building in a street renamed 'Freedom Street' at the time of the Revolution. Now in summer it was warm and bright, but everything was worn out, and in several of the rooms the furniture had torn covers. After our wonderful Tsarskoe we found this pretty disagreeable.

I have forgotten exactly how the rooms were allocated among us. The ground floor, I think, was reserved for the guards, our governesses and the staff. The dining-room was also there. On the upper floor Papa had a study and reception room, then came the drawing-room, and next to that our parents' bedrooms and ours. Alexi had a room on the other side of the corridor, where there was also a dressing-room and a bathroom.

A second house, opposite ours, belonging formerly to the merchant Kornilov, was occupied by everyone else who had travelled with us or followed us there, including the adjutant-general, General Tatishchev, Prince Dolgorouki, Mr Gibbs, Dr Derevenko, Countess Hendrikova, and also Baroness Isa Bukhoeveden, one of my mother's ladies-in-waiting. She had had to stay behind at Tsarskoe with appendicitis, and after our arrival at Tobolsk was apparently not allowed to see us. Not realising this, Mama and we children felt rather cross with her, and Mama wrote to her friend Anna Vyrubova that perhaps the Baroness had a guilty conscience.

In the first six weeks our life was bearable. This was mainly thanks to the chief of the guard, Colonel Kobylinski, who had already filled the post of Castle Commander at Tsarskoe. He tried to lighten our lot as much as he could. At this time he was responsible only to the Provincial Government and not yet to the workers' and soldiers' councils, though by now these were already making their influence felt in an unpleasant fashion.

It had been decided, for instance, that my father should be kept under strict surveillance, with sentries posted in and outside the house and a watch kept on the surrounding streets. But the worst thing was that our house was invested with a big fence of planks and multiple wire, so that we could not make any contact with the outside world. We were only allowed free movement in the house, the courtyard, and a small vegetable garden which had been extended by a bit of the street; two hours in the morning and two hours in the afternoon were allotted for these walks in our very confined territory. Once a week we were allowed, under guard, to go to the early morning service in the town church, though even here we did not meet anybody else; the local population were forbidden to enter the church. As a matter of fact, they were friendly and sympathetic towards us, and if any of them went past our house and met one of us, they would always greet us or bless us with the sign of the cross. Mama, however, was satisfied with the new arrangement, since at Tsarskoe, the services had always been held in the palace, whereas now she could go to a proper church. The evening service at Tobolsk, though, was also held in the house.

The last days of summer went by in a calm, regular existence, calmer than in Tsarskoe. But it was a Siberian calm, life was monotonous, you saw always the same faces, had the same worries and thoughts, which of course were shared by everyone.

To help overcome the monotony, my parents made a firm routine for us and themselves. In the morning Papa breakfasted with my sister Olga in his study, where afterwards he read or made entries in his diary. Then he went downstairs to get fresh air and do some work in the garden. The other three of us girls breakfasted with Alexi in the dining-room. Then we had lessons, after which we also went downstairs to do gym and help Papa chop and saw wood. We also built ourselves a small terrace above the orangery, with steps leading up to it, and there we enjoyed sitting in the sun. One of our servants, whose name escapes me, also worked with us in the courtyard and the garden. Mama was the last to get up, though she woke very early. She stayed a long time in bed, however, and drank her coffee in the bedroom, which she usually did not leave before lunch; she was always complaining of her heart. Sometimes she expounded the catechism to us children, did needlework or painted.

Lunch was at noon, and we still had our old chef. There was soup, fish, meat, preserved fruit and afterwards coffee. For supper, too, we sometimes got fruit, whenever it was obtainable in the town. After meals Alexi had to rest while we others went downstairs again; but Mama rarely joined us on our walks. Before tea, which we drank in Papa's study, Alexi got a history lesson from Papa, and before supper he worked another hour with Monsieur Gilliard and Mr Gibbs, but he was very often ill again. At this hour we sisters were doing our 'home-work' for the next day's lessons. We all came together again for supper, at which we were joined by Dr Botkin, General Tatishchev, Prince Dolgorouki and others. Afterwards people talked and played games. Sometimes English and French plays were produced, in which we children also took part. I myself, to help while away the dreary hours, tried hard to enliven the little company with my jokes and to make people laugh, even though I was in no real mood for it and realised like everyone else the grave dangers ahead of us. At eleven we all said our good nights, except for Alexi, that is, who had gone to bed earlier.

Quite early in the autumn a greater harshness in our treatment became apparent. Two commissars had arrived from Petersburg, whose obvious function was to restrict the influence of our Colonel Kobylinski. They were two old revolutionaries, who had earlier been exiled to Siberia and had now attached themselves to the new regime. The elder of them was quite a nice fellow, who always behaved honourably towards us and also showed consideration when Alexi was ill. We did not know his name at that time, but I found out later that it was Pankratov. We enjoyed listening when he talked to us and told us tales of his Siberian exile. But the other commissar was coarse and ill-mannered. He encouraged the soldiers not to return my father's salute, he instituted a system of passes for anyone setting foot in our house, so as to stop any strangers being brought in, and showed his hatred by thinking out all sorts of other petty annoyances for us. Many of the old soldiers had remained loyal, however, and pitied our lot.

If we children ever looked through the boards of the fence, he would come up at once and stop us, and he had it in for Alexi particularly. Once when a military band marched by, my brother ran up to the fence and pressed his eye against a hole. He got a thrashing for this 'piece of spying,' and only Pankratov saved him from the other commissar's fists.

We girls, I must admit, had good reason for looking through the fence. Dr Botkin's children, who had come to join their father, had for some time been living in the Kornilov house opposite our own. We knew Gleb and Tatiana Botkin, who afterwards married Monsieur Melnik, from Tsarskoe Selo, but we had seen even more of them in the Crimea. Once before the war Mama had them come to us when we were lying at anchor in the *Standart* at Sebastopol, and their father had fallen sick on the ship. Since then we had been playmates of theirs, particularly Maria and I, who were nearest to them in age. Gleb was always having new ideas for games. His best game was the story of a teddy-bear living on a planet entirely inhabited by animals; these adventures were preserved by him in a great many picture books. He was brilliant at drawing, and also wrote the stories himself.

Mama had asked our doctor to have his children join him at Tobolsk, so that they could take lessons with us, and he readily fell in with this wish. But when Gleb and Tatiana arrived, to our great dismay Commissar Pankratov refused Mama's request for permission that they should do so. We could only wave to them out of the windows, and when we wanted to say anything to them, had to do it through the fence; but in this way we could at least make contact with them whenever they passed. Gleb was even kind enough to go on drawing pictures for Maria, Alexi and me—naturally pictures of animals who had been through a terrible revolution. In return I embroidered him a wallet for Christmas.

At the beginning of October the days of Kerensky, who had meanwhile become head of the government, drew to a close, but we heard nothing about it for a long while, until one day the soldiers' councils took over the power and immediately cancelled all our remaining privileges. Now we began to feel the iron hand of the 'new people.' My father's suite and the servants, who till then had lived opposite, were now billeted in our house. There were fears, so we gathered, that monarchists were planning attempts to set us free; plots were suspected everywhere. The next thing to happen was a house-search, during which Papa had his gun taken away. Soon afterwards he was also made to take off his epaulettes, although this humiliation, which applied to all officers, was opposed by Colonel Kobylinski. It saddened Papa very much, but all the same he went on wearing the epaulettes when he was in his room, and the next day, when we went to church, he hid them under his coat.

Mama was particularly upset that we were soon forbidden to go to the town church; instead, the services had to be held at home, and in the presence of the guards too. The reason for this was that the deacon performing Mass at Christmas used the old form of prayer which included a wish for the Tsar's long life. It was only with great trouble that Kobylinski succeeded in getting us permission at least to go to church on the chief holy days.

The worst thing was a question which till then nobody but our colonel had bothered his head about, although it concerned us all: our money was giving out. Just think of it—the Tsar, one of the wealthiest princes in the world, without money! All the letters Kobylinski wrote to the government remained unanswered, the Bolsheviks cared even less, and the money my father had abroad was out of reach. This last fact, of which he once spoke in Ekaterinburg, was to play a significant role in my later life.

Our chef, consequently, often came back empty-handed from the shops, declaring that they refused to sell any more goods on credit; often he had to resort to downright begging. Some of the servants had to be dismissed, while others volunteered to go on serving us without pay. The housekeeping was rearranged on a basis of great simplicity. For lunch we now only had soup, meat (often horse-meat) and fruit; and for supper macaroni, groats, rice or pancakes, with some vegetables, usually cabbage or turnips. Sugar too was so short that we were all rationed to three lumps a day, and we only had butter when it entered the house in a gift parcel. And Papa, who was so passionately fond of cigarettes, also got some tobacco. There was a great shortage of everything else besides, particularly linen, which could not be renewed at the high prices. All these restrictions and humiliations made our life as prisoners thoroughly miserable, and wore down the nerves of our most loyal followers. How were we to find the strength to bear it?

* * *

From the Tsar's Diary:

*Monday, 2nd October.*

'A warm day, slight rain about four o'clock. All the inhabitants of our house who want a walk must now be escorted by soldiers if they are going into the town.

*Saturday, 21st October.*

'From our window this morning we saw a funeral procession carrying the body of a soldier from the 4th Regiment. There was a small choir of schoolboys at the head of it, singing very badly. We had divine service at eleven. Sat with Kestritki till tea-time. Evening service at nine, then we made our confessions to Father Alexis. We all went to bed early.

*Saturday, 4th November.*

'Very pleased to get a letter from my sister Xenia this morning. It has been snowing hard. I shovelled the snow away, to have a clear path for walking, and during the day we brought wood into the shed.

'No agency telegrams have arrived for two days, probably things are very bad in the big towns. Evening service at nine.

*Friday, 10th November.*

'Another warm day, after which the thermometer went down to freezing point. I finished the first volume of "1793." In the evening I read to the family some of Turgenev's "Memories of a Hunter."

*Saturday, 11th November.*

'It has been snowing hard. For a long while now there have been no papers from Petersburg, nor telegrams. This is very tormenting in such hard times. The girls played on the swing and jumped down into the snow-heap. Evening service at nine.

*Tuesday, 14th November.*

'Dearest Mama's birthday and our 23rd wedding anniversary.

'A thanksgiving service was held at noon; the singers were out of tune and time, probably they hadn't had any rehearsals. The weather was sunny and warm, though there was a strong wind. During afternoon tea I glanced through my earlier diaries, a pleasant occupation.

*Friday, 17th November.*

'The same unpleasant weather with strong winds.

'It is sickening to read descriptions of what happened at Petersburg and Moscow a fortnight ago. Much worse and more deplorable than anything that has gone before.

*Saturday, 18th November.*

'The incredible news has come in that three truce officers of our 5th Army met the Germans outside Dvinsk and signed a provisional armistice agreement with them.

'Never in my wildest dreams did I expect anything so appalling. How could these scoundrels of Bolsheviks have the effrontery to carry out their pet schemes and offer peace to the enemy, without asking the people for their opinion, let alone at a time when the enemy has occupied most of the country?

*Monday, 20th November.*

'It has grown colder, and the day was clear. There were disturbances among the soldiers because no pay had been received from Petersburg for three months. The matter was quickly settled, however, by the necessary sum being temporarily borrowed from the bank.

'During the day I chopped wood. Evening service at nine.

*Tuesday, 21st November.*

'There was no service for the feast of the Presentation of Mary in the Temple, because Pankratov hadn't felt like arranging one for us. It was warm, and we all worked in the courtyard.

*Sunday, 26th November.*

'We went to church at 8 a.m. Today is the feast of the Knights of St George. The town produced a meal and other diversions for the knights in the Community Hall. But some knights among our sentries refused to relieve their fellow-soldiers who weren't knights, so that the others were obliged to do their full sentry duty—on a feast-day like this. Oh, freedom!

'We walked a great deal today, the weather being mild.

*Friday and Saturday, 1st and 2nd December.*

'Both days have passed in the same monotonous way. It was a cold sunny day. In the afternoons after our walks we meet at . . . (illegible) and learn our parts thoroughly. Evening service at nine.

*Sunday, 3rd December.*

'Alix and Alexi didn't come with us to church, because it was too cold, 29 degrees below freezing.

'During the morning we rehearsed our play in the hall, where a sort of set had been built with the help of screens and various pieces of furniture. In the evening everything was cleared away again. We walked as long as it was light. While the others played Bezique, I read out loud some of Turgenev's "The Evening Before."

*Wednesday, 6th December.*

'We spent my name-day very quietly, not as in former years. A service of thanksgiving was held at noon. The soldiers of the 4th Regiment on duty in the garden congratulated me, and I returned congratulations for their regimental party. I received three special cakes, and sent one to the guard. In the evening Maria, Alexi and . . . (illegible) put on a cheerful little play.

*Thursday, 28th December.*

'A splendid warm sunny day. Just below freezing. We stayed out a long while both morning and evening. We were indignant to hear that our dear Father Alexi has been denounced and is under house arrest. This was because our names and titles were mentioned during the Mass on Christmas Day. There were many soldiers from the 2nd Regiment in the church. As usual, the trouble came from that quarter, probably encouraged by Pankratov and Company.

*Sunday, 31st December.*

'Not a cold day, but a biting wind. Alexi got up in the evening, since he was able to put on his boots. We left each other after evening tea, without waiting to see the New Year in.

'Oh Lord our God, save Russia!'

The date of this last entry is about six months before Nicholas II's death.

* * *

That winter we spent at Tobolsk was very changeable, now terribly cold, now quite mild again; but there was usually an icy wind blowing over the steppe. Yet despite all privations we did still have the necessities, whereas the life that lay ahead of us at Ekaterinburg was more like a Hell on earth.

None of us had any idea that this move was coming, when in April a new commissar arrived, the other two having been replaced. The new man's name was Yakovlev, as I later found out, and it looked as if he had been charged with a special assignment, which was causing a lot of excitement to everybody. He put up first at the Kornilov house opposite us, and then came over to talk to my father. After he had inspected the whole house, Papa took him to Alexi, who at the time had Mr Gibbs watching at his bedside. For with all the misfortunes that had befallen us, a new one had now occurred: Alexi was again seriously ill. As once before, both his legs had been paralysed by a fall, and he was in frightful pain; he had already been in bed for a fortnight. We sisters did not set eyes on Yakovlev, nor did Mama see him until his second visit, at which he appeared interested in Alexi alone. On the morning after that he informed my parents, who received him in the *salon*, that he had received orders from Moscow to remove the whole imperial family from Tobolsk at once; but that as Alexi was ill, he had been given new instructions to travel with the Emperor alone. So that was why he had paid so much attention to Alexi.

I can no longer remember the details of what happened after this. I only know that Tatiana, who always got on specially well with Mama, talked of never having seen her so upset before. Papa went out for a walk, an unusual time for him, and Tatiana was with Mama in her bedroom. We kept hearing Alexi call for her, for she had promised him a visit after lunch, but she seemed to have completely forgotten him. With frightening suddenness Mama found herself faced with the hardest decision of her life: she felt she could not leave Papa on his own, lest he should be forced into something against his better judgment, as with the abdication; on the other hand, she did not want to leave Alexi either when he was so ill. It was a terrible conflict of duties for her, and it took her a long time to make up her mind. On Tatiana's persuasion she eventually decided it was more important to accompany Papa, and only then did she go in to Alexi, who had been calling for her all this time. With great self-control she told him that she had to go on a journey with Papa and Maria but that all the rest of us would follow as soon as he was better.

It was probably the greatest sacrifice she made for Papa during the twenty-three years of their marriage. Their decision to take Maria along was due—since they loved us all alike—only to her soothing, friendly presence, something my parents needed especially just then.

Meanwhile it had been decided that besides Maria my parents should be accompanied by Prince Dolgorouki, Dr Botkin, Mama's lady-in-waiting and a few others; but their destination still remained a mystery. Some expressed the fear that Papa was to be taken to Moscow for condemnation on Lenin's orders. Colonel Kobylinski, on the other hand, who discussed it with Tatiana Botkin, was quite optimistic and believed they were being taken via Moscow, Petersburg and Finland to Norway, so that we should all be saved. Alas, he was sadly mistaken.

The next day the carriages were outside the house before four o'clock in the morning. They were all two-horse Siberian *telegas*, except for one, which had three horses. My parents wanted to board this one, but Yakovlev would not let them, so Maria got into Mama's carriage and the commissar joined Papa. Otherwise he was very polite, and once or twice even brought his hand to his fur cap in a military salute.

We three girls left behind accompanied our parents as far as the steps leading up to the door, and there said tearful good-byes. Then the carriages drove off at top speed. We gazed after them a long while, before going slowly back into the house. On the opposite side of the road, in the Kornilov house, our friend Tatiana Botkin was watching the carriages from behind a curtain; her father, of course, was also in the departing company. It was all infinitely sad. I even think the soldiers guarding us must have felt sorry for us, for they became much friendlier all of a sudden.

Kobylinski had chosen two trustworthy men among the military escort to give us reports on the journey, so we received news by telegram in the next few days. The first telegrams said that everything was going well, but then there was suddenly one saying that our parents were in Ekaterinburg; and when the escort returned, we heard that apart from Prince Dolgorouki, who had been thrown into prison, the whole party was now in the house of Ipatiev, the former big merchant—the house which was so soon to attain a gruesome notoriety. Yakovlev and his men had also been put under temporary arrest by the soldiers' council, and only obtained their release with great difficulty. We did not know what to make of all this, and were terribly worried.

* * *

The mysterious story of Yakovlev and his mission has never been fully cleared up. It was almost like a tragedy where there seems to be an eleventh-hour hope of the final catastrophe being averted. Yakovlev was apparently a former naval officer who had been condemned to death for some political offence but succeeded in escaping abroad; he lived in Germany and Switzerland before the Revolution, and then returned to Russia. He was evidently a special confidant of Lenin's, who in fact gave him the warrant for the prisoners' transfer. But they were only handed over with reluctance by the workers' and soldiers' council in Tobolsk, who did not trust him; and he was even more suspect in Ekaterinburg, where the prisoners were taken away from him because the revolutionary soldiers imagined that the Tsar was being kidnapped. As Anastasia states, he only just managed to secure his own release.

This time, however, the kidnapping had political rather than humane motives, as was recognised at once by the Tsar and Tsarina, even though Yakovlev said nothing to them about the significance of his mission. The day before they left Tobolsk, the Tsarina declared that the Tsar was probably intended to sign the peace in Moscow. 'The Germans are demanding it because they know that no peace has any validity unless it is signed by the Tsar. It is my duty not to allow this, and not to leave the Emperor.' And the Tsar said: 'They want me to sign the treaty of Brest-Litovsk. I would sooner cut off my right hand.'

So it seems they both regarded Yakovlev as an agent of Germany who was only pretending to be a Bolshevik and was in fact to take them into European Russia. They could not know that the treaty of Brest-Litovsk had long been concluded already. (General Hoffmann, who later interceded for Anastasia, played a leading part in its conclusion.) Their intransigent attitude towards Germany may date back to the abortive peace-feelers made by the Grand-Duke Ernest Louis of Hesse, who travelled to Russia in the winter of 1916 to encourage the Tsar to make a separate peace, and possibly to advise the Imperial family on a flight to England, because the Russian Revolution was obviously imminent.

Certainly the German Emperor asked King Christian X of Denmark to intercede with the Bolsheviks to secure honourable treatment for the Tsar and his family. Yet there is little plausibility in a second version of 'Yakovlev's mission,' whereby the Germans were trying to give the Tsar or his heir the chance of winning back his throne, breaking with the Allies and forming a pact with themselves. It is equally doubtful whether Germany could have 'demanded' the surrender of the Tsar, his family, and all Russian princesses of German stock, although in individual cases such intervention might have been possible through the troops on her Eastern front. Basically, the German standpoint seems to have been that the Tsar's fate was a matter of Russian 'internal politics.'

So the mission must have had different motives. Presumably the Bolshevik government thought for a few days that it would make a good impression in other countries if the Tsar and his family were removed from Russia. Their own position in the country was by no means firm, and the armies of the counter-revolutionaries were gathering in menacing strength. But only a few members of the Government were told about the plan, which could not be carried through unless the party headquarters in the rest of the country were ignorant of it; otherwise these would rebel, failing to grasp that it was dictated by the requirements of foreign policy. Moscow, therefore, was indeed to be the first stage on the road to freedom. But the game was lost as soon as the soldiers' council in Ekaterinburg, beginning to suspect the facts, took Yakovlev's prisoners away from him.

Yakovlev himself went to Moscow after this episode, and was not heard of again till the civil war, when he was supposed to have been shot somewhere in the Urals-Volga sector for trying to go over to the White Russians. Although the Bolsheviks then branded him as a traitor, the more likely inference is that they were uncomfortable about his knowledge of the Moscow kidnapping plan, and also that the Bolsheviks' radical wing now had the upper hand. At any rate the Tsar's fate was already sealed, and from now on things took their inevitable course.

* * *

The time without our parents became doubly tormenting for us. We had heard little from them since they had been in Ekaterinburg, although a few letters reached us from Mama, Maria and the lady-in-waiting, Demidova. We could gather from these that their new life was hard. At their arrival they had been searched in the most shameless manner, and apparently had some of their valuables seized. Mama wrote in our prearranged code that we should be very careful when taking the jewellery we still had with us.

In Tobolsk we had little male protection left. Colonel Kobylinski was ill, and besides, he now had little influence with the commissars, who had meanwhile again been changed. The only men who could help us were General Tatishchev, Mr Gibbs and M. Gilliard; and this was very important for Alexi, since all attention was now concentrated on him. The commissars talked about our departure being hastened, and though we looked forward to being soon reunited with our parents and Maria, the commissars' behaviour made us terribly apprehensive, for it suggested they had special plans connected with the heir apparent.

One of them, who evidently had a good deal of influence, was particularly rude. He would plague anybody he thought was too devoted to Alexi—Nagorny, for instance, who was still my brother's most loyal servant. But we girls also often had cause to be infuriated by his boundless impertinence. He forbade Olga to lock her door at nights, threatening that he would break it in for her. The nuns who came to divine service were subjected to physical searching, and a Red Guard was posted beside the priest.

Once he was satisfied Alexi was fit to travel, this commissar fixed our departure for the following morning. It was about four weeks since our parents had left us, and we were now in the second half of May.

I have forgotten the details of our leaving, for everything was done in a great hurry. I only know that our suite was much reduced. It included General Tatishchev, Countess Hendrikova, Baroness Buxhoeveden, Mr Gibbs, M. Gilliard, Miss Schneider and Nagorny.

We travelled as far as Tyumen on the same ship as had been used when we came from Tsarskoe. After stopping there for some time, we got into a passenger carriage, part of our suite being crammed into a goods waggon. The horrible commissar was still in charge of the journey, and again showed his power by his odious orders, before he left us at Ekaterinburg. For instance, the cabin on the ship for Alexi and Nagorny had to be locked from the outside, while we sisters were not allowed to bolt our cabin door. It was pure tyranny.

We arrived at Ekaterinburg in the early hours, but could only leave the train later in the morning; evidently the commissars receiving us were not to be dragged out of bed in the middle of the night just for our sakes. There was a fine rain falling, and the streets were dirty. Behind the soviet delegates stood some cabs for our conveyance, and we had to carry our own luggage again, which was particularly tiresome for Tatiana, since she had to use one of her hands to hold her beloved dog. When Nagorny tried to help her, he was pushed back; but he was at least allowed to sit with Alexi in the cab. There was always one of the commissars sitting in the cab in which my sisters and I rode. We were unable to say good-bye to anyone, because the guards thrust everyone back, and so this was the way we saw many of our suite for the last time.

We drove through the town's desolate streets till we reached the Ipatiev House where my parents and Maria were held, the house which was soon to see the terrible fate of my whole family. It stood on a hill overlooking the town, at the corner of Vosnessenski Prospect and Vosnessenski Lane. Because of a slope the lower of its two storeys could hardly be seen till you reached the building. In any case there was a provisional fence round it to impede the view from outside, while a second and higher fence was put up afterwards even closer to the house.

I can't remember now where we first embraced our parents and Maria, but there were commissars and Red Guards standing all round, watching our every movement. I do know that we all wept for joy at the reunion but also in distress at the new severity of our imprisonment. Mama and Maria were very thin, and all three looked care-worn. I suddenly saw that Mama's hair was beginning to go grey, a thing I had never noticed before.

The news we had had in Tobolsk of our parents' life in the Ipatiev house was by no means exaggerated; we were to experience far worse. Although our household consisted of no more than Dr Botkin, the lady-in-waiting Demidova, a manservant, a cook and a kitchen-boy, the family proper only had two rooms at their disposal, both on the upper floor: one for our parents and Alexi, the other for us four sisters. But there were so few beds that we girls had to sleep on the floor. The other rooms were shared by our last loyal followers and the Bolshevik guards. The remainder of our escort was put in prison or else had to leave Ekaterinburg, except for Dr Derevenko, who alone was allowed to visit us now and then.

Two kinds of guard had been assigned to us: the sentries outside, all Red Guards, who were usually relieved after three days, and the guards inside the house, chosen from factory workers in the town and its neighbourhood. Among these were many deserters who had thrown in their lot with the Bolsheviks, and they guarded us as if we were dangerous criminals, or even animals—we were completely at their mercy. Despite their disgusting behaviour we did not betray our feelings, but tried to bear all the trials that were imposed on us. I am sure, though, that some of the soldiers must have felt sorry for us.

Usually we got up between eight and nine, and met in one of our rooms for morning prayers. Then we drank tea together, with any black bread left over from the night before. About noon we went out into the garden with Papa, where there were some trees and bushes, poplars, limes, lilacs and acacias. At first we were allowed twenty minutes for our walk, but later the time was reduced to five minutes a day, and we weren't allowed to do any gymnastic exercises or work in the garden. Mama never went into the garden, but remained on the steps near the fence surrounding the house. Alexi was still partially paralysed, so Papa carried him outside, and he sometimes sat by Mama for a while in his wheel-chair. Although he was already quite a big boy, my father never found it hard to carry him. Alexi was very thin by now, whereas Papa was still very strong. Nor did he like to see anyone else handling Alexi.

Sometimes Papa spoke to one of the sentries, but either the man didn't answer or else he would keep the cigarette in his mouth as an added insult and tell Papa rudely that he should remember he was a prisoner. There were only a few of the guards who still had some decency. Most of them were equally insolent to us girls also. They would follow us to the toilet, on the pretext that they had to keep watch on us everywhere, draw caricatures of Rasputin on the walls, and generally do everything to make our lives a misery. Once when one of us climbed on the window-sill to get some fresh air through the fanlight, the sentry immediately fired a shot in her direction, accusing her of trying to signal to the outside world. Mama was terribly upset by all the brutalities we were subjected to by the soldiers. Worst of all was the chief of the guard, a drunkard and a thief and really vicious. All these men were in clover, stealing gold and silver articles, then clothes and boots, and plaguing us over the most insignificant trifles, just to make us feel their power.

Usually we did not get our lunch till the early afternoon. It came from a canteen and was brought by women or girls who handed it to the guard at the door; they weren't allowed to set foot inside the house. It consisted of some sort of soup and a meat dish, not at all the right diet for our invalid brother. It was only now and then that the nuns from a convent brought us milk, butter, pumpkins, cake, ham and white bread. Later the cook was allowed to prepare our meals himself. We ate all together, including the staff. We did without a tablecloth, for we hadn't brought any with us, nor were we given one. Everything was very short, sometimes there weren't even enough spoons.

We never had our meals without the Red Guards in attendance. They let us talk to each other, but only in Russian. They were in our rooms almost all the time, and would burst in at any hour of the day or night. Their chief once attended one of our meals. He sat down at the table with his cap on his head and a cigarette in his mouth. We were having cutlets. Suddenly he took a plate, pushed Papa's plate aside, helped himself and began to eat. For supper we had the same fare as for lunch. Afterwards there was tea, and then we went early to bed, unless the guards made us play the piano for their amusement.

Apart from the brief walk, we spent all day in our room, while Papa mostly read in his. Mama too would either read or else sew and do embroidery with us. We also sang a lot, usually hymns, and on Sundays a priest came from the town church to read Mass. These quiet hours were our only recreation.

In those days Papa told us more about his life than he had been in the habit of doing. He talked a lot about recent events in Russia, which were a mystery to us, for after all he had always had the best of intentions and like Mama was very good to the people around him. Yet they all deserted us one after the other.

Once when he was in a particularly sad mood, and seemed to have a presentiment of his own death, he told us four sisters that in 1914, before the outbreak of war, he had deposited five million roubles for each of us with the Bank of England in the name of an agent.[1] Unfortunately, I can no longer remember the name my father mentioned then, I think it was a German-sounding one-syllable name with an 'a' in it. On the giving of this name the money would be handed over to us. When Papa revealed this, only Mama was in the room with us, not Alexi. This matter afterwards caused a terrible quarrel with my relatives, which is not settled even now.

In the beginning of July there were again changes among our guards. This time not only the commissars were replaced, but the workers belonging to the 'inner guard,' who had lived on our floor, were also removed. The soldiers who came instead were almost all Latvians, who walked around the whole time with guns and cartridge-pouches. Their chief, I think, was called Yurovski, he had been a photographer and a medical orderly. This fellow looked truly cruel, and he was always thinking out new ways of humiliating Papa. I heard afterwards that he and the

[1] See translator's note page 262.

two other commissars belonged to the Cheka, which was now spreading terror throughout Ekaterinburg. Yurovski was to be the murderer of my parents, brother and sisters.

Now something strange happened. On the Sunday before that terrible night the priest held a Mass in one of our rooms, as he had done several times before, and he brought his deacon with him. All our people were gathered there, Dr Botkin, Demidova, and the manservant. Alexi was there in his sailor's jacket, sitting in his wheel-chair, Mama had taken a chair near to him, I stood by Papa, and my sisters were next to me. Yurovski had insisted on attending the service with one of his minions, to stop the priests saying anything personal to us, which was strictly forbidden. The two Latvians had taken their seats in a corner, and with their glowering faces they seemed to me like emissaries of the Devil.

When the Mass was nearly over, we approached the priest to kiss the Cross. As usual the deacon said prayers after the liturgy. But when he came to the place where it says 'The souls of the dead are at peace among the saints,' he began to sing the words; and the priest joined in the singing. I don't remember now how it happened, but I know that suddenly we all fell on our knees, which is normally only the custom at funerals. Perhaps it was a presentiment of what lay ahead of us. We all felt great relief, Mama and Alexi especially had such happy expressions on their faces. Then the priests left us in silence, as they had come. Only Yurovski was left standing there, as if wanting to remind us of the harsh reality.

* * *

The murder of the Tsar and his family was worked out in every detail beforehand, the political preparations being made in Moscow and only carried out by the Ekaterinburg soviet, who certainly did not act on their own initiative. The Kremlin's radical wing led by Lenin and Sverdlov, had gained ground since the failure of the Yakovlev mission, and it was they who decided to wipe out the whole Romanov dynasty.

First victim of the decision (shot at Perm) was the Grand-Duke Michael, the Tsar's brother, who in 1917 had declined to accept the throne renounced by his brother. His death was followed during June and July 1918 by the deaths of many other members of the Imperial family, irrespective of their age and sex. In every case the method of execution and subsequent concealment of evidence were the same as those soon to be used with the Tsar, which proves that the orders coming from Moscow must have been uniform. After the Grand-Duke's murder the German Emperor, his Secretary of State von Kühlmann, and Count Mirbach, German ambassador in Moscow, all interceded, far more vigorously than before, in attempts to save the Tsar and his family; but these efforts inevitably failed, because the victims were doomed from the day of their transfer to Ekaterinburg. The Soviet diplomats in Berlin and Moscow could only lie to their German colleagues, and Count Mirbach, most troublesome of the latter, was silenced with a bullet.

The men chosen to carry out the grim task were Golostshekin, Beloborodov, and Abraham Yurovski. The former maintained contact with Moscow and gave all the orders. An old follower of Lenin and Sverdlov, some-time dental student at Moscow University, he was a man who shrank from nothing, a shrewd perverted butcher. Beloborodov, a former book-keeper, was now president of the Urals area's executive committee; while Yurovski, the former photographer and medical orderly, had been playing his part in this trio since the arrival of the three Grand-Duchesses at the Ipatiev house; brutal and ruthless, he was the best possible person to carry out the actual murder. All three belonged to the Ekaterinburg Cheka.

On 4th July Beloborodov sent the following telegram to Golostshekin, who was in Moscow to make final preparations: 'To the President of the General Executive Committee Sverdlov, for Golostshekin. Avdeiev (the former commissar at the Ipatiev house) removed, his assistant Moshkin arrested. Inner guard completely re-formed—4558. Beloborodov.'

This shows that the murder was prearranged, and that the men at Ekaterinburg who were to organise it and carry it through acted on Kremlin orders. A week after the Tsar's murder the town of Ekaterinberg was seized from the Bolsheviks by the White-Russian Siberian army and a Czechoslovak legion made up of former Austro-Hungarian prisoners-of-war. A Tsarist public prosecutor was appointed to hold an inquest on what had happened, and while going through the files in the office of the Ekaterinburg soviet, he came across the original telegram.

Bykov, then a member of the Ekaterinburg soviet and later president of the soviet executive committee in the Urals area, confirms the facts:

'After Golostshekin's return from Moscow, a session of the (Ekaterinburg) soviet took place on 12th July, at which a report was heard on the views of the Central Committee (at Moscow) as to the shooting of the Romanovs. The soviet came to the conclusion that it was too late to carry out the Moscow plans for a trial, since the front was moving too near the town, and the postponements caused by a trial might lead to new complications. It was resolved to ask the military commander at the front for information on how many days Ekaterinburg could still hold out, and on the situation at the front in general. Apparently the Czechoslovak legion was already south of the town and attacking from two sides: the strength of the Red Army was inadequate, and the town might fall in three days. In these circumstances the Urals soviet resolved to shoot the Romanovs without trial. The shooting and disposal of the bodies was to be undertaken by the commander of the guard with the help of reliable worker-communists. At a special session the soviet decided on the method of execution and the way the bodies should be disposed of. The decision to destroy the bodies was taken in view of the possibility that the counter-revolution might stir up trouble with the "relics" of the former Tsar.'

All was prepared, the fruit was ripe for the terrible harvest. On the morning of the 16th July brand-new revolvers were taken from the Cheka headquarters, while large quantities of sulphuric acid and petrol were obtained for disposal of the bodies. A lorry was to drive up at an appointed time, the driver would leave the engine running during the murder, and then pull up at the back of the house. A place in the forest where the bodies could be burned had already been fixed. But Yurovski was still not satisfied; he checked once again the reliability of the men on the inner guard, and chose the ten men who were to be his henchmen. There was only one Russian among them, although four of the others spoke the language; the remaining five were Latvians.

Yurovski was even more concerned about the outer guard. They had already been changed very often, but he did not know any of the men in the present guard except Medvedev, their leader, also a member of the Cheka. He ordered Medvedev to relieve the sentries of their revolvers, and lest they should be worried about the night's shooting, to inform them, but not before ten that evening. 'Tonight we'll put away the Tsar's whole family,' he privately told Medvedev, who understood and gave his men plenty of schnapps so that they should sleep till the evening. Sometimes the assassin is more afraid of his victim than the victim of his assassin.

That evening the murderers assembled at the Ipatiev house in the commander's office. There was general agreement that the rooms in the upper floor, where the Tsar and his family lived, were unsuitable for the execution, so it was decided that the victims should be taken down to a large vaulted cellar-like place near the lumber-room, with a double window protected by strong iron grating. It was fairly bright during the day, but now had only a meagre lamp to light it.

* * *

The days had passed like any others. On the Tuesday, the last day before that appalling night of terror, Papa went for his usual walk in the garden with the four of us girls. So far as I remember, we did not notice anything out of the ordinary which might have given us some hint of the murder planned; except that there seemed to be some excitement over at the house opposite in Vosnessenski Lane, where some of the sentries were living: apparently they had got drunk. Once we even heard firing in the far distance, but it wasn't the first time, and as we were cut off from all news, we attributed no further significance to it. After all, civil war was going on everywhere, nor had we any hope left of being rescued. We returned to the house, and occupied ourselves as usual. I took up my needlework, I think my mother and sisters did the same. At ten o'clock we went to bed.

Suddenly, in the middle of the night, we were all woken. They shouted to us that we should get up and dress at once, because there were disturbances in the town and there would probably be shooting; that was why they wanted to take us down to the lower floor. I think I put on a skirt from a suit with a blouse. I had sewed my pearl necklace into the skirt, but did not wear the coat, although it had diamonds concealed in its buttons. Nor, I believe, did my sisters. It was summer, and we were supposed to be only going downstairs. I can still remember that I put on light shoes.

When we got downstairs and were taken into a large room, I felt terrified. My sister Olga was the calmest. Papa carried Alexi. Mama was half fainting with fear, and being almost unconscious, she perhaps took in least of the appalling things that were happening to us all then.

As soon as we were all in the room, the soldiers began firing at us with revolvers. Yurovski was there, too; he stood in the middle of the room and fired at Papa. I can remember standing behind Olga, trying to hide behind her shoulder, and I know I saw Papa, her and Alexi being hit. But I don't remember anything after that, I had lost consciousness.

* * *

The execution scene has been reconstructed down to the last detail on the basis of a great many examinations and statements from guards and other witnesses. Yurovski and his assistant Nikulin led the way from the first floor through the courtyard and the hall down to the cellar. They were followed by the Tsar and his wife, their daughters, Dr Botkin, Demidova the lady-in-waiting, the manservant and the cook. Strangely enough, the murderers had taken pity on young Leonid, the kitchen boy, and sent him off beforehand to the guards' house. They showed no pity, however, for the other child, the heir apparent. The Tsar had to carry him downstairs, but Yurovski allowed him to be seated on a chair; so that there were three chairs needed in the macabre scene. Some of the party also took cushions, Demidova even had two. At the rear of the sad little procession marched Medvedev and the Latvians living on the ground floor whom Yurovski had fetched from the Cheka. They all had the new revolvers, two had rifles, and Yurovski had a Mauser rifle as well.

Protocol, as the Bolsheviks understood it, was maintained even at the execution. The Tsar sat in the centre, with his son on his right, and Dr Botkin standing next to them. The first bullets were for the former monarch and his heir apparent. Behind them sat the Tsarina, with her four daughters standing round her. The others stayed by the wall.

Yurovski took a step forward and delivered a terse death-sentence: 'Nikolai Alexandrovich, your followers tried to set you free. They failed, however. Now you are going to be shot.'

'What!' cried the Tsar uncomprehendingly.

'This,' answered Yurovski, raising his revolver. The Tsarina and one of her daughters crossed themselves.

At the same moment Yurovski fired at the Tsar, killing him on the spot. Now Medvedev and the Latvians also fired, and one victim after another fell: first the manservant, who had ducked at the shot and died in this position; then the Tsarevich, groaning and still thrashing about him in the very throes of death, so that Yurovski fired two or three more shots at him. The Tsarina, three of the Grand-Duchesses, Dr Botkin and the cook died instantaneously. One of the Grand-Duchesses, probably Anastasia, rolled on the ground screaming, and defended herself desperately against one of the murderers, who came up to her and rained blows on her. Demidova was left longest in agony, for she first tried to escape and then to protect herself with her cushions: she died only after receiving many stabs from bayonets. Then the moaning and groaning of women's voices was at an end. There was a strong smell of blood and powder.

Yurovski and his henchmen were hardened characters, and completed the second half of their crime with the same cold-bloodedness though with a haste suggesting a guilty conscience. In this haste some things got overlooked, for instance whether all the victims were really dead. There were not enough men available, Medvedev had to send for ten more from the outer guard to cover up the traces. Not that the murderers needed fear they would be called to account; but the Russian people might be angry at the news, and the enemy was at the gates of the town. To keep up appearances, the house was still guarded for four days, just as if nothing had happened.

Stretchers were improvised from two sledges in the coach-house, and there were tarpaulins in the lumber-room. The still bleeding victims were packed together, everything they had on their person was removed —rings, bracelets, two gold watches—and handed over to Yurovski, who thus exacted a reward for his butchery.

The lorry to take the bodies into the wood had its engine roaring away outside in the courtyard. The gruesome load was carried up out of the cellar by the servants' steps. It was still night and pitch dark. The Cheka men, the Latvians and the extra soldiers just called in, were all jostling each other and talking louder than they were meant to. Some of them did not hide their revulsion, and even were sick when cleaning the bloodstains off the floor. During the pandemonium things happened that were not foreseen. No one kept a check on the number of bloodstained bundles that were thrown on the lorry. The nightmare scene lasted for a good twenty minutes.

Then the gate in the fence was opened, and the lorry set off on Vosnessenski Lane to the Cathedral Square, heading for the wood. Liuchanov, the driver, had trouble finding his way in the darkness, and also broke down two or three times; it was with difficulty that he eventually reached the destination ordered, the pit of an old mine, about thirty-five feet deep, near which the bodies were unloaded. The mine was called 'The Mine of the Four Brothers,' after four ancient pines which stood round it. On the following day the bodies had petrol and sulphuric acid poured on them, and they were cremated in a ghastly funeral pyre; then the ashes were thrown into the pit. A few days later, when the White Russian troops entered Ekaterinburg, they found remains of bones, scraps of cloth, stays and jewellery, which had either resisted the fire or else had been trodden into the earth. Not all the traces, in fact, could be destroyed.

The house where Tsar Nicholas II spent his last days was called Ipatiev after its former owner. Three hundred years earlier, by a strange coincidence, Michael Romanov had been fetched by the nobles of the Russian empire from the Ipatiev Monastery in order to assume the throne; so this name connects most strangely the first and last of the Romanov Tsars.

When the news of Nicholas' death reached the Kremlin, his successors again employed their now well-tried device of falsifying history. Sverdlov entered the council-room of the People's Commissars and asked Lenin for permission to speak. When this was granted, he declared in a calm voice: 'I have to inform you that a report has come in, telling us that Nikolai has been shot in Ekaterinburg on the decision of the Urals soviet. He was trying to escape, and the Czechoslovak legion was advancing. The Praesidium decided to approve the measures taken.'

With all the documents and evidence available today on the crime of Ekaterinburg, it is established incontrovertibly that there was never any question of the Tsar's attempting to escape, and that there were very slight prospects for any rescue coming from outside, since there was no appropriate organisation, and the actions of individuals were clumsy and either suppressed immediately or betrayed later on.

When the Tsar and his family were still in Tobolsk, individual monarchists did make attempts to establish contact with them. But these attempts failed because people were either working in isolation or else fell into the hands of a Bolshevik spy. Anna Vyrubova, the Tsarina's friend, was still so much under the mystic influence of Rasputin's name that she unsuspectingly sent her followers straight into the hands of the enemy. Tatiana Melnik, daughter of Dr Botkin, has this to say:

'One must do our monarchists the justice of admitting that they made preparations for their Majesties' escape. But the plans they worked out were made without even knowing Tobolsk or its geographical position. The Petersburg and Moscow organisations sent off some of their members to Tobolsk and Tyumen, where they lived under assumed names in great poverty. All of them fell into the same trap; joining the organisation of Lieutenant Soloviov (Rasputin's son-in-law), who—being related to a man who had enjoyed the respect of their Majesties—had won the monarchists' confidence. From Tyumen he passed information to Petersburg and Moscow. No one arriving in Tyumen escaped him, he stopped them all, allowing them to stay only one night in Tobolsk. If the travellers refused to obey him, he handed them over to the soviet officers, with whom he was on excellent terms.'

Even Bykov, a member of the Ekaterinburg soviet, admitted that the prospects of the Tsar escaping from there were even smaller than they had been in Tobolsk:

'It was not till they reached Ekaterinburg that the Romanovs were virtually treated as prisoners. They were very closely watched, by a guard made up of workers from the factories in the district. One glance at a plan of the Ipatiev House will make it obvious that with the guard system prevailing the Tsar and his family were in a completely hopeless situation . . .

'On the other hand, since the first days of the Romanovs' removal to Ekaterinburg, many monarchists began to converge on the town, from feeble-minded ladies, countesses and baronesses of all shades, to nuns, priests and representatives of foreign powers. The letters Nikolai received from them consisted very largely of congratulations and condolences. Doubtless these people's abnormality was often shown in such screeds, for they described their dreams, visions and similar nonsense . . .

'The White Guard organisations acted fairly openly. Supported by the bourgeoisie (who had plucked up courage because of the nearness of the front), they prepared for a rising in the town to free the Romanovs from the Ipatiev House. But the extraordinary commission (the Cheka) succeeded in tracking down these organisations and arresting some of the activist White Guards . . .

'The soviet, however, had to guard the Romanovs not only from White Guard plots; there were other plots being brewed. The left-wing social-revolutionaries and anarchists of the Ekaterinburg organisation doubted whether the Bolsheviks would shoot the Tsar, and decided to attend to that themselves. These two organisations worked out a plan for an attack on the Ipatiev House, during which the Romanovs would be shot . . .'

Certainly attempts were made in Ekaterinburg to set free the Imperial family or at least to lighten their lot. A former high officer of the Tsar's, Sidorov, made contact with the Tsarevich's doctor, Derevenko, and organised the delivery of food and letters to the prisoners. Most of the loyal officers, however, broke through to the Czechoslovak legion, so as to hasten the fall of Ekaterinburg and in this way carry out the Tsar's liberation. In the town itself the Cheka held ruthless sway, as has been recorded by a German doctor who was a prisoner-of-war. Many townsmen were shot merely on slanderous accusations that they were planning to help the Tsar to escape. The situation was so threatening, the tension before the entry of the White Russians so appalling, that attempts at rescue were out of the question from this quarter.

But even if a rescue of the whole Imperial family proved impossible, it soon turned out that the most carefully planned murders can go wrong. Things happened so fast that night that a body was missed; and immediately, with all the resources of the Red Terror, a gigantic search operation was launched from the Baltic to the borders of Rumania, throughout Siberia, in European Russia, in all territories, in fact, that were subject to Red domination. Notices were put up on walls, army orders issued, innocent people cross-examined, arrested and shot, on the mere suspicion of being accessories. There was terrific excitement, indicating that the search was being made not for a dead body which might be used to start a cult, but that the person saved was still alive, someone round whom the counter-revolution might rally, even if it should be a woman. And in only a few days' time the possibility of its being a woman became a probability. Witnesses of the most varied character, from Red Guard men to prisoners-of-war, came forward and declared that it was the Grand-Duchess Anastasia, the Tsar's youngest daughter; that instead of going with the rest on the grim drive to the 'Four Brothers' Mine,' she had survived and been brought to safety on a Siberian farm-cart.

Testimony of Anatol Yakimov, Red Guard man and one of the Tsar's guards, at the inquest on the Tsar's murder held before Alexeiev, officer in the White Russian Kolchak army:

'About four o'clock in the morning I and the other sentries were woken by Kleshchev, who was shouting in great excitement: "I must give you some news. Come into the other room. Tonight the Tsar has been shot." We asked him how it had happened, and he related how Medvedev, followed by Dobrynin, had come up to them to tell them that they must remain on sentry duty after two a.m. because the Tsar was going to be shot. Kleshchev looked through the hall window leading on to the garden, while Deriabin watched the window from which the room of the murder got its light—a window opening on to Vosnessenski Lane. It was about one in the morning by the old time or three by the new, when people entered the ground floor and Room I; Kleshchev could clearly see them crossing the yard and going through the hall door: Yurovski and Nikulin in front, followed by the Tsar, the Tsarina, their daughters, Botkin, Demidova, Trupp and the cook Charitonov. . . . Through his window Deriabin could see Yurovski saying something and making a movement with his hand . . . and at that moment shots were fired. All revolver shots. After the first of them the moaning and groaning of women's voices could be heard. . . . When they were all lying on the ground, their bodies were examined. One or two had another shot fired at them or else were stabbed to death. Of the Tsar's family, I remember that Anastasia was the only one mentioned as being stabbed with a bayonet. . . .'

Declaration on oath by Franz Svoboda, former Austrian prisoner-of-war, on 12th December, 1938 (Svoboda came to Ekaterinburg in May 1917, and after winning the confidence of the Cheka commandant, he managed to make contact with the Tsar and his family in the hope that they might yet be liberated):

'Yurovski and Vagenov planned the murder secretly . . . all the preparations for the operation and the guards were made beforehand with my friend H. Getting the signal after one o'clock in the morning, the driver of the lorry took it to the back of the house, after which we heard shots being fired inside. I couldn't get in, because the sentries outside were barring the entrance with fixed bayonets; but a bit later we were able to because they ran into the house themselves. These sentries had been summoned by Yurovski to carry out the rest of the operation.

'They fired at everything that was still moving, and looked for jewels, though without removing anybody's clothes. I noticed that the Tsar's daughters were wearing white and were without coats or hats; their clothes, of course, were completely fouled with blood. I saw a soldier in the act of turning over a female body, when she screamed and the soldier hit her on the head with his rifle-butt. This man was one of those Yurovski had called in to clear the slaughterhouse. Even during the shooting, but especially just after it, men from outside began to come into the house, including my friend H.

'So far as I can recall, the bodies of the Tsar, Alexi and Dr Botkin lay by two chairs in the centre of the room, the Tsarina and one of her daughters near the window on the right, with the other daughters along the back of the room.

'Yurovski came along with some other Russians and gave orders for the bodies to be put on the lorry. In the house there was a fearful confusion.

'My friend and I had a clear view of the bodies being dragged out. The Tsar and Tsarina were the first, hastily covered in blankets. A member of my company reported to H. that he had seen a girl's body move. He and I and H. then took blankets and rolled the body up in them as carefully as the circumstances allowed. This was when I saw for certain that it was the body of the girl who had been hit on the head with the rifle-butt when the soldier tried to turn her over and she screamed. And at the same moment I recognised that the girl was Anastasia.

'We brought her to the lorry, thus wrapped in blankets, and found that neither its driver nor any other guard was watching it. H. came up with a low, sledge-like cart, which he had luckily left at the back entrance near the lorry.

'When we reached the lorry with Anastasia and saw there was nobody behind us, we fortunately had the chance to put her in my friend's cart instead of the lorry, jump into it ourselves and ride off. In the haste and tension not a word was said. H. did not go far, only about two hundred yards; then he stopped at the house of one of the Russians, and we got Anastasia into a bed.

'I ran back so as not to attract attention by being absent in case there were special orders being given. When I got back there, the lorry left. I stayed another two hours. Yurovski returned, and gave orders that the house should be properly cleaned up. I had another look at the room so as to be able to make sketches of it afterwards. Then I went off myself.

'After two or three days there was talk in Ekaterinburg of Anastasia's complete disappearance, and the whole town was searched. I remember too that orders were given for the surrounding district to be searched as well, but without result.

'I lived with farmers under cover in the town and surrounding country, until the Kolchak army arrived, and even when I was nearing Vladivostok with them, the search for Anastasia was still being carried on.'

Svoboda was by no means the only person who knew that the massacre at Ekaterinburg had a survivor. People kept coming forward to report details from first-hand knowledge. Search operations undertaken by both sides could not remain secret. The news that one of the Tsar's daughters had escaped must have very quickly reached the lines of the advancing Kolchak army, which now also began to hunt for the survivor.

A certain A. Rohsé, a member of that army, who today is living in Germany, stated in November 1956:

'I herewith make the following declaration, in so far as I remember the events of the year 1918:

'I, Arthur Rohsé, born in East Prussia on 28th May, 1897, was in 1918 a first-lieutenant of the special detachment in the army higher command of the First Siberian Army (Admiral Kolchak's White Russian army). After the capture of Ekaterinburg—about three days after the murder of the Tsar and family (which took place during the night of 16–17th July)—I received orders from the staff of General Kappel, the commander of the First Army, to assemble an armoured train for purposes of safe transport and arrange with transport command that it should be ready to move at a moment's notice. These were special orders delivered to me as "strictly confidential." The train consisted of four fully manned armoured coaches, two in the van and two in the rear, and an ambulance coach which I was to put in the middle. I guessed that the operation was concerned with the rescue of one of the Tsar's daughters who by a fortunate chance had escaped from the massacre. There was a good deal of talk about a female body being missing. (The bodies had been thrown into a pit in a nearby wood.) The ambulance coach was under the direct supervision of Privy Councillor Dr Niefyodov of St Petersburg. The armoured train was to be dispatched in the direction of Orenburg. I asked Dr Niefyodov what this special operation signified, and on whose behalf it was being undertaken. He told me it was strictly confidential and of the greatest importance. The Brigade Commander, Brigadier-General Dubensky, told me afterwards that the operation was concerned with one of the Tsar's daughters.'

Declaration by Ludwig Berg, welfare-worker for Russian emigrés in Berlin, 12th April, 1928:

'Piatakov, commissar of the detachment which had been ordered to shoot the Tsar and family in Ekaterinburg, told a Russian Bolshevik after the murder that when the bodies were being loaded on a truck for removal and subsequent burning, there had been one body missing.

'This Bolshevik (I will not give his name because he is still a Soviet official today) revealed the above fact in 1927 at a party in Berlin.'

Report by the former prisoner-of-war, the customs officer K.J., on the statements of the Red Guard man Serge Michailovich Komarov, published in the *Hannoverscher Anzeiger* of 13th March, 1927:

'. . . I remember a conversation I had in spring 1920 with a Russian who had been in the Red Guard and had been guarding the imprisoned Tsar and family in Ekaterinburg up till the night of the murder. He avoided taking part in the actual murder, but afterwards had to help remove the bodies. It then turned out that although all the rest of the Tsar's family had been murdered, one body had disappeared without trace, the body of one of the daughters. . . . Investigations had taken place, but even by the time the Red troops moved out of Ekaterinburg nobody had found out where the missing body was. Komarov believed that one of the guards, perhaps specially interested in one of the Tsar's daughters, had removed and secretly buried her. No one else, he thought, could have entered the room of the murder at the time, but after the murder there were both time and opportunity for the removal of a body.'

Letter from Alois Hochleitner of Langenbielau in Silesia, to Mrs Harriet Rathlef, dated 6th March, 1927:

'. . . I was taken prisoner by the Russians in July 1916, and in 1918 tried to reach the German and Austrian troops, but was picked up by Bolshevik patrols and brought back. I was taken into the Red Army as M.O. and army surgeon, and came to Ekaterinburg on 17th May. . . . We heard of the murder of the Imperial family about two days after it had happened, from marines who were brought in as patients. The story went that at one of the random searches of the family weapons had been found on their persons, and this was the reason for the decision; also that two of the Grand-Duchesses had inexplicably disappeared. A whole succession of special orders were promulgated concerning the harbouring of unauthorised persons, and there was also an order relating to army deserters, by which the death sentence was reintroduced.'

Part of a notice addressed 'to the population and the Army' read as follows: 'During the execution of the sentence pronounced by the Ekaterinburg soviet on the Romanov family, certain persons in the firing squad acted insubordinately and made off with female members of the family, also taking along valuables . . .'

At any rate is is established that one or more members of the Tsar's family survived, since the murderers themselves knew that at least one of their victims was missing. The search for such a victim was very thorough and went to fantastic lengths. Houses were searched everywhere, and so were hospitals, especially female blocks, which were constantly subjected to the strictest checks.

Declaration at Hörnungsholm, 13th October, 1952, by Count Carl Bonde, one-time head of the Swedish Red Cross mission to Siberia (Count Bonde was in Siberia in 1917 and 1918 as emissary of the Swedish foreign ministry to inspect prisoner-of-war camps for the Red Cross and also to represent German interests. Until October 1918 he was at Omsk, and heard a good deal about the murder at Ekaterinburg as well as rumours that one of the Tsar's daughters had escaped):

'In my capacity as head of the Swedish Red Cross mission to Siberia, I was travelling in a special train during 1918. At some place, the name of which I have forgotten, the train was stopped and searched for the Grand-Duchess Anastasia, the daughter of Tsar Nicholas II. The Grand-Duchess was not on the train, however. No one knew where she had got to.'

Such testimony has assumed particular importance in Anastasia's subsequent struggle to establish her identity. The Bolsheviks would never have conducted so extensive a search, including the use of posters, had they not been convinced that one of the Tsar's daughters had disappeared and been afraid of the consequences. The testimony, moreover, seems to refute the declarations of the former language-teacher, Pierre Gilliard, who at first thought that the unknown woman appearing in Germany was probably the Grand-Duchess Anastasia, but from the year 1926 onward inexplicably went over to her adversaries' camp.

Anastasia's description of the night of the murder is different from Gilliard's in that she gives only a short interval between the time when they were all taken down to the basement and the actual murder. According to her, however, Gilliard is in no position to describe the scene of the murder exactly because he was not there. It is also very understandable that she can no longer remember everything, because she very soon lost consciousness. Gilliard was only in Ekaterinburg for a short time, at the end of May, after arriving there with the three Grand-Duchesses and the second group of the Imperial suite. He says himself: 'We stayed a few days in Ekaterinburg. I went through the town and looked at the Ipatiev House from outside. It was on the 14th or 15th May (old style)'—that is, on 27th or 28th May. The murder did not take place till 16th July.

Gilliard has made a great many other claims in support of his change of mind. Among other things he states that the murder was carried out by prisoners-of-war and had been favoured by German agents. Bykov's statements show that this was not alleged even by the Bolsheviks, and it elicited immediate protests from the former prisoners-of-war.

It is still more striking that in Gilliard's book, *Le tragique destin de Nicholas II et de sa famille*, first published in 1921, the murder scene ends with the words: 'Anastasia Nikolaievna was only wounded and began to scream when the murderers approached her; she fell under blows from their bayonets.' In his book *La fausse Anastasie*, which appeared in 1929, all he writes in describing the scene is: 'The prisoners were driven down into the cellar on some pretext or other, and were there murdered. The bodies were not given proper burial, but were taken on a lorry the same night to a wood about fifteen miles away, where there was a derelict pit.'

* * *

I can't think back to that night without shuddering, that night when Papa and Mama and all the others were killed; their screams still ring in my ears. I know I prayed passionately, but it was always night around me.

And it was always night when we were travelling, although I really had no idea whether I was still alive. I wasn't fully conscious, I could only feel a cart shaking me. My head ached dreadfully, it was covered with wet cloths, and my hair was sticky with blood. I must have had a high fever. My only wish was that this terrible shaking, which was making my head burst, would stop some time.

Now and then I must have cried out in pain and despair. I heard the voices of people I didn't know, who were looking after me without my being able to ask them. I could now feel that I was lying on straw, and I smelt the vinegar and onions they were rubbing me with to bring me round. Sometimes they lifted me out of the cart and carried me for part of the way so as to lessen my agony. One has to experience it first to know what riding in an unsprung Russian farm-cart is like.

How long I travelled like this—I cannot tell. It may have been weeks, it may have been months. We came into very lonely regions and had to rest in the woods; we also travelled on many roads. I was constantly numbed by the pain in my head. My arm was also raw from a wound, my face and mouth hurt me.

I remember that in the straw of the cart there were many bottles, which were always filled with fresh water; that was for my head. It was only treated with cold water. Later, when winter came, I was always wrapped in sheets on which snow had been put, so as to reduce my fever. Simple people often know better than doctors how wounds must be treated.

But when we travelled too long through deserted country, we had no water left, I suffered appallingly from thirst, and our food ran out, too. They thrust sodden black bread into my mouth to stop me starving. I think the people with me often gave me their last crust and went hungry themselves because of me. When we got back into inhabited areas, we would often stay for days with strange farmers, in whose rooms I could rest and recover from the shaking of the cart.

My escort consisted of four people, two men and two women. While the men were walking, the women often sat with me in the cart. Sometimes we stopped in the woods, and the men went ahead to look for quarters. They told me their name was Tchaikovski, the women, too. One of the men's Christian name was Alexander. He was of medium height, had light-brown hair, handsome, clean-cut features, a narrow nose and a small moustache. The whole face was impassive and severe as if it had been carved from stone; he looked as if he never smiled. The other man was called Serge. I find it very hard to describe him, but like Alexander he was probably in his twenties; he was also of medium height and very good-natured.

They always spoke Russian with me, but talked to each other in Polish, and I never understood then what they were saying. They were simple peasants. The older woman was called Maria and looked about forty but was apparently the mother of the three others. This woman also had very good features and dark hair. The younger woman's name was Veronica, she looked far more rustic, and had a broad ruddy face. Both women were always good to me and did everything they could to keep me alive. May God reward them for it.

When I had recovered consciousness enough to open my eyes and recognise the people with me, I didn't get the impression that they were soldiers, for the men were clothed like Russian peasants, and neither of them had a soldier's cap on his head. The women too looked like all Russian peasant women and wore scarves round their heads.

Afterwards, though, in Rumania, when we had got some money, all four dressed much better. The women no longer wore the head-scarves, and the two men always wore good suits. Alexander Tchaikovski had such a good figure that in his new things he looked more like an officer than a former private. About the rôle he had played as a private, which has a very close connection with my rescue, he did not tell me till later, when I was feeling better and for the first time asked after my people and what had really happened.

But all I can tell about my rescue is what I heard from him. There are also large gaps in my memory of what happened in the next few months.

Alexander Tchaikovski said he and his brother had belonged to the Red Guard who were our jailers in Ekaterinburg. After the terrible slaughter he noticed that I had moved and was not dead but only wounded. In a moment when he wasn't being watched, when the bodies were being taken out of the Ipatiev house, he pulled me out of the heap of the murdered. He felt so sorry for me that he quickly wrapped me in a blanket and secretly carried me away at great risk to himself.

Yet I cannot remember having seen Alexander Tchaikovski among the soldiers guarding us when we were at Ekaterinburg. Of course they were always being changed, it is true. I only know that at the end there were a lot of Latvians in the guard. They were the worst and most brutal men I have ever seen.

What Tchaikovski told me about the horrible fate of my family upset me terribly, so that I became very ill. I had a serious nervous fever, and was laid up for a long time. Tchaikovski also told me that he had concealed me in the straw of a farmcart and then escaped in the cart with his brother, mother and sister, so as to avoid pursuit by the Bolsheviks, who were looking for a vanished Grand-Duchess. They owned a small farmhouse near Ekaterinburg, which no doubt is where they got their cart from. It was from here that the appalling journey started.

And so for months I was travelling the woods and roads like the gipsies, sick and unwashed, with the wretched feeling that something terrible had happened, always in dire fear of being pursued and discovered. When I look back on it even today, I am still overcome with an agony of terror. On the other hand, I can remember the indescribable sense of relief I felt on hearing from my rescuers that we had crossed the Rumanian frontier. It must have been at a river, it was very cold already and the snow was lying. We had been travelling all that time. The Tchaikovskis told me that we were now safe, and that a relative of theirs, a gardener, would take us in.

* * *

Understandably enough, in view of the secrecy with which it had to be carried out, there are few witnesses for most of this remarkable flight to Rumania. The Bolsheviks were searching for the missing Grand-Duchess, and when the little party stayed the night with farmers and not in the woods, they could not disclose who they were. The nearer they got to the border, the more they had to take account also of the political confusion. Conditions in the Ukraine at the end of

1918 were still quite chaotic, with Bolsheviks and various Ukrainian nationalist groups all fighting each other. So that useful evidence is available only on the last lap of the long journey.

There was, however, a prisoner-of-war trying to get back to Germany who says he met a farm-cart in the neighbourhood of Ekaterinburg, and went a short way along with it; on it he saw two women sleeping in the straw, of whom one, allegedly a Grand-Duchess, was wounded. But it is over fifteen hundred miles from Siberia to Rumania, and the statement says nothing about the direction taken: as usual with the statements of such witnesses, there are contradictions and obscurities in the dates, although these can be explained by a telescoping of happenings in 1918 and 1919.

More valuable evidence for the route is the declaration made by the German Lieutenant-Colonel Hassenstein, then communications officer at Nikolaev on the Bug. He speaks of an ox-drawn turnip-cart crossing the pontoon bridge there which was held by the Germans. Tsarist and also democratic Russian officers (the Cadets' Party), both opposed to the Bolsheviks, informed him that Anastasia, the Tsar's youngest daughter, was on this cart accompanied by two moujiks, and that the party was trying to reach the west bank of the Bug through the German-occupied part of the Ukraine. Hassenstein interceded on their behalf with his superior, General von Gillhausen, and some time afterwards found in his quarters a note from one of the Russian officers, generally called Kilya or Kolya, saying: 'All is well. Thanks. Kolya.'

On 12th May, 1955, Hassenstein made the following affirmation:

'This communication could only refer to his above-mentioned request. It was therefore quite obvious to me that my approach to General von Gillhausen had been successful, so that the vehicle with the Tsar's youngest daughter had been readily allowed to cross the pontoon bridge. . . . Because of the above facts I have always been convinced that the Tsar's youngest daughter crossed the Bug at this time, a belief to which, as I can prove, I have always adhered.'

At the end of November 1918 the refugees certainly stopped in the Ukraine in the Nikolaev-Odessa region (between the Bug and the Dniestr), and from there headed for Rumania. There is further evidence for this from another witness, who after an article in one of the Bucharest papers reported to the police there and deposed the following statement (witnessed by the police officer on duty, A. Stroian) above the initials A. C. C.:

'From 1917 to April 1918 I was in Russia, working for the Ministry for War Industry and also the French military and technical mission. . . . When I returned to Rumania, I had to have an operation, and shortly afterwards, on 27th November, 1918, I went into the Filantropia Hospital, from which I was soon discharged again. One day I was sitting on a bench in Victoria Square, near the above hospital, when an old friend came up to me, a man of Polish origin whom I had met in Russia, where he had served in the Bolshevik army. I knew him under the name Stanislav. He was of medium height, had light-brown hair and a scar near his left eye . . . I never knew his surname. . . . When I had promised (to keep my mouth shut), he began to tell me how he had a seriously wounded person with him, whom he wanted to take to Bucharest, to get her into a hospital there; but it mustn't be a military hospital and the secret must be kept. . . . Then my friend Stanislav told me the truth with tears in his eyes: "I have under my protection a woman from the Tsar's family who escaped when that hulking brute of a metal-worker, Yurovski, killed the rest of them. . . . I want to save her from the Bolsheviks, who would kill me too if they knew what I'd done." . . . On that I asked him how he had done this. He told me in reply . . . that out of all the members of the Tsar's family he had saved one daughter and brought her in a small cart as far as the Nikolaev-Odessa region. She had head and face wounds from the butt of a rifle. . . . I expected him to write to me at the address I had given him in C., but never heard from him again.

'*PS.*—When Stanislav and I met in Victoria Square, it was November 1918. He was very neatly dressed, wore a stiff round hat, coat with cloth buttons, and shoes, not boots.'

Still more valuable evidence was obtained in May 1927 by another Bucharest police station. After long enquiries they traced a man called Sarsho Gregorian, an Armenian working in a church at Jassy, who stated that on 5th December, 1918, he had helped to get the wounded Grand-Duchess Anastasia across the Dniestr. The police report, translated and signed by Superintendent Héroua, is as follows:

'. . . Sarsho Gregorian states that . . . before crossing the Dniestr on his way from Russia to Rumania, he stayed at a monastery near the Rumanian border. Also staying there was the Grand-Duchess Anastasia, youngest daughter of Tsar Nicholas II, who had been saved during the night of the murder at Ekaterinburg by a Red Guard soldier, one of those guarding the Ipatiev House where the Imperial family were interned.

'One night while the refugees were at this monastery, waiting for a good moment to cross the Dniestr, the Bolshevik army drew near, and they were all obliged to flee. Sarsho Gregorian with his wife and three children crossed the river, as did the Grand-Duchess Anastasia, at a point called Rezina; on the other bank they met a Russian officer, apparently a colonel, who took them all in his car and brought them to Orhei. From there the Grand-Duchess was taken to Bucharest; and on 6th May, 1919, when Sarsho Gregorian was at Kishinev, a messenger arrived bringing him the sum of 5,000 leis from the Grand-Duchess Anastasia in gratitude for the help he had given her in the flight described above.'

* * *

My rescuers, of course, did not travel over this vast distance without expenses. Our cart got completely worn out by the bad roads, and a new one had to be bought several times; the tired horses, as I remember, also had to be changed for fresh ones. These expenses could only be covered by selling the precious stones which Tchaikovski had found in my clothes. If I hadn't had these valuables with me, we should not have escaped with our lives.

For this fortunate circumstances I have Mama to thank, since already in Tobolsk she had made us girls sew jewellery into our clothes and underclothes, naturally so that nobody else knew of it—not even her maid, the lady-in-waiting Demidova. Even before our banishment to Tobolsk my mother had had the crown diamonds which were at her disposal taken to the Kremlin, as well as valuables—diamonds, gold and lace; but we possessed other personal jewellery. I had unset stones, including many emeralds, and a pearl necklace. The necklace had been sewn in all along the side of my skirt lining (as skirts were worn then) without being taken apart. It was very beautiful, the pearls were rather yellow; I had sewn them up in white linen. I held the necklace in my hand for the last time in Bucharest, before it was sold by Tchaikovski. I think we lived off it while we were there.

* * *

Obviously the sewing of precious stones into the clothing of the Tsar's daughters did not remain a complete secret, for the lady-in-waiting Zanotti and the governess Tegleva afterwards stated before Sokolov, the examining magistrate of the Kolchak army, that two of the Tsar's daughters had worn lined under-bodices, which had a large number of unset stones sewn into them, chiefly diamonds, emeralds and amethysts; Anastasia's had the precious stones belonging to the Tsarina and also a pearl necklace with a big sapphire and diamonds, while Tatiana's had stones belonging to the Tsar's daughters.

Investigations were also made concerning the pearl necklace, and in the summer of 1927, when the world once more became interested in the dispute about Anastasia's identity, the Grand-Duke Andrew of Russia (brother of the Grand-Duke Cyril) had a visit in Paris from a certain S. M. Chokolov, who had been in Rumania in 1919 and was described as completely reliable. When consulted, Superintendent Héroua, the former police chief at Bucharest, wrote of a pearl necklace offered for sale by an unknown young man in Kishinev. There may, of course, be two different necklaces referred to, but from the young man's description it is also possible that he is identical with Tchaikovski and was offering Anastasia's necklace.

Chokolov's statement (dated 20th July, 1927), addressed to Superintendent Héroua at Teleshevo, is as follows:

'I happened to be visiting the jeweller Atazkaia in Kishinev, and noticed a string of pearls someone had given her to sell. She offered them to me, but I declined. However, she sent their owner to my address (Ssadovaia 15), and a young man of between twenty-five and twenty-eight, smartly dressed, with hair combed straight back, clean-shaven except for a small moustache, introduced himself to me as the owner of the necklace. Unfortunately none of us can remember his surname, but it certainly was not Tchaikovski. He told me he had come from Russia, but had only brought this string of pearls with him, and was going to Bucharest. He wanted to sell them.

'I advised him to do so in Bucharest, where he would get a higher price, but he said he was afraid to take them himself because his papers weren't quite in order; he might be discovered and arrested, when the necklace might be stolen from him. He showed me a string of pearls of medium size, very regular and of a particular yellow tint. The string was about an *arshin* long (about two feet), and must have contained a hundred pearls or so. It was sewed into a roll of white stuff so that it could be tied round the waist. As we were on our way to Bucharest ourselves, he asked me to take the necklace with me, to which I agreed. A few days later, probably at the beginning of May 1919, we went on to Bucharest, where I delivered the pearls to him, having arranged to see him in his hotel. I also remember meeting him again in Bucharest a few days later, when he informed me that he had sold the necklace for between 80,000 and 90,000 leis.'

* * *

I don't know how long my nervous fever lasted after Alexander Tchaikovski told me about the terrible happenings in the Ipatiev House. My memories of this period which I spent in Bucharest have become blurred, and although I can recall a whole succession of details, the whole picture escapes me like a dream one can't piece together after waking.

I was told that we should live with a gardener, a relative of my rescuers; it is possible, although I do not remember it. Once, when someone asked me afterwards, the name of the street came to me: 'Svienti Voyevoda'—Svienti means 'saint,' and perhaps I remembered this name because I recalled another saint who had been murdered in Russia. It must have been somewhere outside the town or else near a railway station. I never went out that winter, because I was ill, very ill.

During this period something happened which I cannot look back on without deep melancholy, but which I must still mention, because it has always made me very reserved with my relatives and has since turned them into my enemies. I had a child by Tchaikovski and afterwards married him. He was always kind and considerate to me. I refuse to judge him harshly and think of him with bitterness, for he saved my life. A peasant is just a different sort of person from us, and often does not know what he is doing. Afterwards he lost his life because of me, and if that hadn't happened, I should not be here now. That at least is what I feel today—today when all has become still around me.

This new blow of fate struck me soon after our marriage. It was mid-summer, and one day I heard that Alexander Tchaikovski was seriously wounded, by a man firing at him in the streets of Bucharest. How it happened I do not know, nobody told me anything about it. I can only think that the Bolsheviks killed him in revenge for his having rescued me. Three days afterwards he died. I saw his dead body before I drove to the funeral, with his mother and sister; it took place at a Catholic cemetery. I don't know where his brother Serge was then, probably he also went in fear of his life. I did not see him again till afterwards when I decided to leave Bucharest. Apart from the wedding and the funeral I had never ventured out of the house.

* * *

It is understandable that Anastasia should describe in only a few words what had happened: just as she was beginning to get better, she found to her horror that she was pregnant. Yet she refused to reproach her rescuer. For months he had escorted her on the difficult journey and cared for her like a good Samaritan. In the long lonely hours, gazing his fill on her features, he may well have woven fantasies on which he would never before have ventured in his wildest dreams. When she slept or was ill, he may have stroked her hair and the poor injured head to soothe the pain; perhaps she even smiled her thanks without knowing it, for she was living in a strange shadowy world. If so, he may have taken this smile as encouragement, or found unintended meaning in the pressure of her hand. They lived as a family, to which the stranger suddenly belonged; he may have thought that only the bonds of fate were valid here. She, anyhow, can hardly be blamed for what happened.

So far as is known, Anastasia had no special feeling for Alexander Tchaikovski, did not voluntarily live with him, and did not even feel the normal first stirrings of happiness of a mother. Yet afterwards, even when making her wills, she kept on remembering the child. It was a boy, with his father's dark hair and his mother's blue eyes. He was christened Alexei, but Anastasia insisted that he should not be registered under the name Romanov. She also insisted on marrying Tchaikovski, lest the child should go through life with the handicaps of illegitimacy.

The wedding seems to have taken place in a Catholic church near where the refugees lived; but Anastasia was unable to follow the words or the actions of the priest. Nor can she say whether rings were exchanged and whether a marriage certificate was signed. All she can remember is having sat on a bench during the service; she thinks she wore a black silk dress and a black hat with a thick black veil.

The flight from Russia and what happened while Anastasia was in Bucharest might seem bold inventions even for a dramatist. An emperor's daughter still in her teens, grievously wounded, travels countless miles through Siberia and the war-stricken regions of the Ukraine and Bessarabia, till she collapses on a sick-bed, shattered by the news that all her family is dead. One of her simple rescuers takes advantage of her, and in great secrecy a child is brought into the world. She gets married at a foreign church in a rite she does not understand, after which her rescuer is shot down. Naturally, Anastasia's enemies treat this barely credible story as a piece of far-fetched romance, especially as all efforts to find documentary evidence for the period leave as many gaps as the failing memory of the woman who was knocked out with blows from a rifle-butt.

Who *was* Alexander Tchaikovski? It seems certain that he served under the Bolsheviks and was one of the guards posted in and around the Ipatiev House who were summoned by Yurovski directly after the murder to clean up the room. The investigations of Sokolov (the Kolchak army's magistrate) proved that while the bodies were still lying in the room of the murder, at least thirty Red Guard soldiers were ordered into the cellar for this work, so that in the prevailing commotion a survivor might well have been concealed. It was dark as well, since Yurovski wanted to have the bodies taken to the wood and the 'Four Brothers' pit before sunrise.

Tchaikovski's brother Serge seems also to have belonged to the guard at the Ipatiev House, even if, with the continual reliefs, he did not take part in the operation directly. The lists drawn up by Sokolov, of soldiers involved in guarding the Tsar and family, contain two hundred names, among which two brothers Stanislav and Nikolai Mishkevich have been found. This suggests that the name Tchaikovski was an 'alias' which the brothers used to avoid detection.

The witness A. C. C., who later made his statement to the Rumanian police, says that his friend's name was Stanislav, not Alexander, and the description of his friend tallies with that given of Alexander Tchaikovski by Anastasia. Moreover, A. C. C. states that Stanislav was of Polish origin, and Anastasia says the Tchaikovskis talked Polish among themselves. Sokolov's lists only contain one Stanislav, with a brother Nikolai; the surname is Mishkevich, and against Nikolai's name there is a note saying 'Marine from Petersburg.' The remaining Red Guard men seem to have all been former workers at the Slokasov Brothers' factory near Ekaterinburg, which fits in with earlier statements. Anyhow, there seems a strong presumption that the brothers Mishkevich were Anastasia's rescuers. As worker in a local factory Stanislav would have lived in a little house there and also owned the traditional small horse which made the flight possible.

That Tchaikovski was only an assumed name is also suggested by the subsequent investigations in Bucharest, in which Queen Maria of Rumania showed great interest. The name was not found there in any files, civil or church register, at least not where it could possibly be connected with Anastasia. It may therefore be assumed that the gardener with whom the refugees stayed was a relative of the mother and had a different surname. The only road with a name like Saint Voyevoda is to be found in Old Bucharest, where there is a Sventa Voyevoci Lane.

As for the child, a man who came to Berlin in 1925 trying to find Anastasia—looking very like the descriptions of Serge Tchaikovski—made statements to the effect that it was in an orphanage in Galatz

(Rumania). This trail was followed up, but without finding the child, who must have gone by another name.

Anastasia declares with great conviction: 'If Tchaikovski were still alive, I shouldn't be here.' But this declaration of loyalty to her rescuer does not help one over the difficulty that everything is built up on assertions, conjectures and second-hand information; so that in the end it is a matter of personal belief. Why, then, did Anastasia not give her confidence to one of her own family, who would have been most likely to believe her?

Queen Maria, wife of King Ferdinand of Rumania and daughter of Duke Alfred of Saxe-Coburg-Gotha, was living in Bucharest at the time. She was a near relative, a generous and warm-hearted woman known to be sympathetic in situations not covered by ordinary convention. What is more, Rumania had been Russia's ally in the war. Surely the Queen could have helped Anastasia? All the agonies of loneliness, all fears of being caught by the Bolsheviks, would have been lifted at one stroke; all the tensions of a hurt soul would have been relaxed. Yet when Anastasia was asked afterwards why she did not do this, she could only answer that first she had been very ill, and then when she realised she was pregnant she dared not show herself in such a condition before the Queen.

It may not have been only the natural shyness of an eighteen-year-old, who would not even go to a doctor. Perhaps she also remembered her parents' dislike of Maria's sister, Victoria Melitta, who had got a divorce from the Tsarina's brother, the Grand-Duke of Hesse. Or perhaps she could not bring herself to put the claims of humanity above social condemnation; certainly she had grown up in an environment separated from the ordinary world by almost insuperable barriers. But in that case how is it that hardly six months later she hit on almost the same plan, seeking refuge with her mother's sister, wife of Prince Henry of Prussia, who held far stricter opinions?

This contradiction is only explicable in terms of her whole psychology, the continual agitations she had experienced, and the new conflicts facing her. It is highly characteristic of a person who on a sudden impulse accepts something she has only just rejected and then defiantly goes ahead with the new plan: in this respect, indeed, Anastasia seems to take after her father. At any rate the consequences of her new journey, from Rumania to Germany in the winter of 1919–20—this time a journey she made herself—were to expose still greater contradictions in her character and deepen the mystery about her still further.

* * *

I had nothing more to keep me in Bucharest. Alexander Tchaikovski was dead, and my baby had probably been taken away from me because I was still not quite well. But if I only had to think of myself, why should I stay in a country where everything was strange to me, a country that was so near Russia, where after Tchaikovski's murder I lived in continual fear of being discovered and meeting the same fate as he? This fear, against which I simply could not struggle any longer, was from now on my constant companion. It had come over me for the first time that dreadful night in the Ipatiev House, when we all had to go downstairs to the cellar. It followed me on the long cart-ride through Siberia. Since then it has never let go of me, but sometimes it comes on me with particular violence, and then I know there is no stopping where I am. Then I know that I must move on, even if by night and to a strange country.

Of course everything has become strange to me since I had to leave Russia and my home, but there are degrees of strangeness, and Germany was not quite so strange as Rumania, for I had been there in earlier days on journeys with my parents. And as I knew, my mother's sister lived there, an aunt from the branch of the family which had seen most of me. I was still a child then, but she would remember me, I thought. She would be as kind to me as my own mother, a refuge in my need.

When I felt sufficiently recovered to be able to travel, I asked Serge Tchaikovski, Alexander's brother, to act as my escort and go with me to Berlin, where I would write to my aunt. We still had some money from the sale of the jewels, and I gave the rest of them to my protectors so that they could care for my child. Male protection was what I most needed, because I had no identity papers and we would therefore have to cross frontiers on foot. I was well aware of the great dangers involved in such a journey, for if I were discovered, I should be arrested, cross-examined and perhaps expelled, and all the trouble I had taken to remain hidden and keep my origins secret would be in vain.

Tchaikovski agreed, and we set out on the journey. But what a journey it was! The few memories I have of it are grim and depressing. It was a continual attempt to run away from my own fears, almost like the flight from Siberia a year and a half before. Till we came near frontiers, we used the railway. They were ordinary trains, dirty, unheated and ill-lit. People spoke in languages that were strange to me, and even when I could understand them, I did not take part in any conversation for fear of being discovered. Tchaikovski was touchingly concerned about me and always at my service, even when he was not in the compartment with me. Police or soldiers put me in a terrible agitation whenever I saw them, and I several times insisted on getting off the train at once, even though it prolonged our journey.

I have forgotten which frontiers we crossed and where—we always did it in the dark. We avoided the roads. It was winter, but different from our winters at home. I was often so exhausted that Tchaikovski had to carry me. But this brother of my husband was a very considerate escort, kind and sympathetic, going to any trouble to make the journey as comfortable for me as possible. He always found something to eat, although that was difficult at the time and he had to pay a lot of money for it. I was most frightened during the nights, for I often had to wait alone in a frontier town at some small inn, till Tchaikovski had discovered the way we could get over the frontier. I suffered appallingly during those nights.

The longer the journey lasted, the more I felt my strength failing. I had dreadful pains in my head and my mouth; the blows from the rifle-butt on the night of the murder had knocked in my front teeth. Now I must have caught cold as well through staying out in the open so long, and everything was sore and inflamed. I had to grip my head with my hands, because it felt as if it were going to burst. And as well as all my other pains I had such distress of spirit. I could not help continually looking back at all I had lost; I forgot about where I was and where I was going. Is it surprising that I even stopped looking out of the window? We had now been travelling for weeks, but it always seemed just the same: the same bleak grey landscape, the same black woods barely covered by the snow; and my thoughts, too, travelled always over the same ground. Everything was so wearying. Had my escort not told me one evening that we had reached our destination, I probably shouldn't even have noticed it. The last day was the most dreadful of all.

'Where now?' Tchaikovski asked me. I didn't know, still less did he. Berlin was quite unfamiliar to us. The station was bright, and there was a stream of people coming and going. Outside many cars were passing, their lights reflected on the wet asphalt. Tchaikovski tried to find out where we could stay, but it was very difficult for him to make himself understood, because he spoke hardly any German. In the end he got the address of a hotel, which was only a short way away. The streets we drove through were rather dark. The hotel must have been as bad as all the hotels we had stayed at on the journey. We took two rooms, quite a long way from each other. Afterwards I was asked where I had stayed, but how am I to remember that when I was so completely exhausted? I don't even remember which district we were in.

I tried to go to sleep, but could not do so in this awful room. I walked restlessly up and down. My nerves were all churned up, and I was once more in pain. I must get out of here, was my only thought. I looked for Tchaikovski, but could not find him. His room was empty, and I thought perhaps he had gone off on some brief errand. But when he did not return after a while, I left the house and began drifting aimlessly through the streets. I found myself thinking about Tchaikovski again, I just could not grasp that he had gone away without informing me. On the journey he had looked after me so devotedly—had he now betrayed me? But what was to become of me if I did not find him again? Suddenly a terrible thought came to me: I had not noticed the hotel's name, did not even know the street it was in. Should I ask someone—but what should I say, and suppose in the end I were asked my name? It was awful. But I was too exhausted by now to think about it for long. I walked and walked, as if to the end of the world; like an automaton my steps took me forward.

Now I wondered even more what on earth was going to happen to me. If Tchaikovski did not return, I was wholly without help. From a park I came to a canal, with a road on each side of it, joined by a bridge. There were trees along the canal banks, which were quiet and deserted. Because of the weather, I suppose, there were not many people about, nor did I see any boat on the canal. I leaned over the side of the bridge and looked down into the water, which was black and had a slight mist drifting over it. The sight of this water disturbed me greatly. I never thought about its being cold if I jumped in, I thought instead that it would completely envelop me with its white mist and then everything would be over: the pain in my head, my despair and my loneliness. Then I should no longer need Tchaikovski, nor Aunt Irene; and after death I should meet my parents again, meet again my sisters and little brother. I don't know how long I stood like this, nor do I remember whether I dropped from the bridge or from one of the canal banks. I believe I was no longer in this world when I glided into the water. Afterwards I have thought much about this unfortunate step. It was certainly the stupidest thing I could have done, and all the developments which followed, all the misery that faced me, come back to this one step. But it must be appreciated how completely despairing and bewildered I felt.

When I came round, there were a lot of people standing round me. I must have been still lying near the canal, and obviously they had given me artificial respiration, but I was almost numb with cold. I simply could not grasp that I was still alive.

I was wrapped in blankets and taken to a hospital which seemed to be quite near. When I woke next morning, doctors and nurses were standing by my bed. They all looked at me enquiringly, and as if they were not kindly disposed towards me but the reverse. This gave me a terrible shock, and I at once closed my eyes again.

I wondered why people did not feel any pity for me. Does somebody who despairs of life not deserve pity? Of course they could not know all I had been through, but was that a reason for regarding me with cold aloofness, even with disapproval? I remembered that the day before, when I was fished out of the water, there had been a policeman there, too. Probably they had been through my pockets to find my name, so now they were all suspicious at having found no papers on me, and must take me for the worst type of woman. I recognised the danger threatening me. As soon as I opened my eyes again, the questioning would start. If I told them the truth, they would not believe I was the daughter of the murdered Tsar. But if they found out that I was a Russian, they would hand me over to the Bolsheviks. After all the terrible ordeals I had been through during the last years, had I come to Berlin for that? In such circumstances I could not even send for Tchaikovski to confirm my statements—even supposing he was findable.

Of course I could tell them, I thought next, that they should apply to Aunt Irene, to a Princess of Prussia; after all, we *were* in Prussia. But then I should have had to tell Aunt Irene everything, about Tchaikovski, my marriage and my baby. And what would happen if she showed no understanding for me and disowned me? I should be mortally ashamed, and then the rest would be after me properly. I had no alternative but to remain silent, I decided not only to keep my name secret, but not to speak at all, come what might. It was my sole salvation, since it seemed I was to go on living.

When I opened my eyes again, the doctors and nurses were once more standing at my bed; was it the same day or had weeks passed? I had lost all sense of time. They were the same suspicious faces as before, the same mistrust was expressed also in their questions, which were impersonal and unsympathetic and now made me feel really defiant. When the questions became more pressing, I began to tremble and tried to hide under the blanket, but I did not betray my name to them. The blanket was pulled from off my head. I saw some of them shrugging their shoulders uncertainly and whispering things to each other which seemed to be very serious. Again I felt the agonising fear come over me. But if I now tried to run away, they of course wouldn't let me. I must just lie here and go on playing the part I had deliberately chosen.

* * *

The attempt at suicide opened a difficult new chapter in Anastasia's remarkable life. The complete psychological breakdown which inspired it also drove her into a fatal if understandable attitude of defiance towards the outside world: hence the stubborn refusal to give her name. For many doctors and officials a name is more important than anything, and they are an easy prey to ideas suggested by their own convictions. They felt in this case that anyone so recalcitrant after attempting suicide must have something to hide. Other people jumped into canals and got pulled out, but they always came to their senses again and said who they were; for of course they must eventually be taken to some place that used to be their home. The unknown woman would not give her name, so she couldn't have come to her senses; nor in all probability had she a home: she must be an adventuress, a criminal or a lunatic. If she had been trying to carry off some big swindle, she would have needed style; and the wretched patient obviously had no gifts in this direction; so presumably she had lost her reason. Nothing simpler than to examine her to find out whether this was so. Nobody thought of the idea that she might be mortally afraid of betraying herself if she talked.

After a few weeks the doctors at the Elisabeth Hospital sent their obstinately silent patient to a mental hospital, while the police started on their search operation:

'Berlin. 28th February, 1920. Unknown girl's attempted suicide. Yesterday evening at 9 p.m. a girl of about twenty jumped off the Bendlerbrücke into the Landwehrkanal with the intention of taking her own life. She was saved by a police sergeant and admitted to the Elisabeth Hospital in Lützowstrasse. No papers or valuables of any kind were found in her possession, and she refused to make any statements about herself or her motives for attempting suicide.'

Note from the records of the Berlin Police, 23rd December, 1926:

'The researches of the Criminal Investigation Department and the Welfare Office, and the observations of Detective-Inspector Grünberg, have established the following facts about the alleged Grand-Duchess Anastasia: Her presence in Berlin can be traced back to 27th February, 1920. When and where she stayed before this could not be ascertained. On the above date she jumped off the Bendlerbrücke into the Landwehrkanal, was pulled out unconscious and taken to the Elisabeth Hospital in Lützowstrasse as an unknown woman. There she refused to give any information about herself, and on 30th March, 1920, she was taken to Dalldorf Mental Hospital, suffering, according to the doctors, from mental alienation of a depressive character.'

* * *

In Dalldorf a time of appalling suffering began for me. Whenever I look back on it today, I am still amazed that I did not really go mad. Nobody who had not been through it can imagine what it is like to be a sane person confined with real lunatics in an asylum for two and a half years.

I shall never forget the shattering things I saw here. Such memories stay with one for a lifetime, in fact I think they make one unfit for the society of normal people.

When I left the Berlin hospital after a while, I guessed that something dreadful was ahead of me, but I had no chance to prevent it, and everything was far worse than I had anticipated. The questions about my name, my origins and my profession began once more; I was photographed, filmed and weighed; I had my finger-prints taken like a criminal; my head, face, hands and feet were measured.

I remained true to my plan of making no statements that would betray me. Because I was so often silent or evaded the questions, and also spoke German with a foreign accent, the doctor obviously assumed that I did not understand everything, so they began to address me in many different languages. At first, I think, I let it all pass over me with a certain indifference; I was too depressed and apathetic, and could not see any point in objecting. But when I was asked questions about why I had tried to kill myself, whether I heard voices or saw faces, something rebelled inside me, and I no longer said anything at all. Let the doctor think what he liked. What right had a complete stranger to hear what had driven me to despair? On another occasion he even thought I was a criminal who had been in some jail. Now he was given a taste of all the bitter irony that was bottled up inside me; but I did not reveal my name to him.

I was put in a public ward. I think it was on the first floor; it had bars. How dreadful to look at the world through bars without having committed any crime or being ill! The women in the ward with me were all simple folk, and not vicious, though some were certainly very sick. The worst thing was that they were always wanting to talk, so that each could air her own particular obsession, and this depressed me terribly: I wished I were dead. To avoid the sight of these pathetic creatures, I stayed in bed almost all the time, turning my face to the wall and building myself a sort of partition with the pillows, so that I would be completely shut in on myself—for I felt I had to guard against becoming like my neighbours. During this period I refused all occupation. The food revolted me. Every day there was the same mashed potato, the same greasy gravy, a cup of coffee and a roll. Often I left everything, and they began to consider feeding me forcibly.

Afterwards, when I had grown accustomed to my new existence, I took more part in everything, although I still stayed in bed most of the time, and did not go into the garden like the others. But I looked at papers and books and even discussed political questions with the nurse. Once a nurse brought me a newspaper in which there was something about Russians being deported to the Bolsheviks. I was very shocked over this, but also realised how right I had been to conceal my name. Better be here, I thought, than handed over to the men who had murdered my family.

Another nurse, one Miss Walz, once showed me an illustrated magazine with pictures of our captivity at Tobolsk and the night of terror at Ekaterinburg. Of course this shattered me still more, and I had the greatest difficulty in controlling myself and not saying anything. Actually, as I learnt afterwards, this nurse claims that I once said: 'If people knew who I was, I shouldn't be here!' Another nurse, Miss Buchholz, even asserts that in my first year at the hospital, when she was on night duty, I confided to her who I was and told her my name was Anastasia. That may well be so. I was questioned so long and talked at so often, that I may some time have forgotten my normal precautions. Altogether I have forgotten a great deal about that dreadful period, even though there are some things I remember quite well.

The first time I knew I had betrayed myself was during my last months at Dalldorf. A woman had been admitted for medical treatment and put in the same ward as I. She had the bed next to me, I think. She kept staring at me, following me with her eyes, in a way I found uncanny. One day she came up to me in great excitement, shouting at me, 'But I know you!' I did not admit to anything, in case she was a police spy, and as she was soon discharged again, I thought no more of this incident. But soon afterwards I was visited by some Russian emigrés, who absolutely insisted on seeing me. One of them had brought a picture of my grandmother. When I looked at it, I was so overcome that I forgot all caution and exclaimed: 'That's my grandmother!'

Later I heard that the woman who had professed to know me had been working in Russia for some time before the Revolution. Apparently she had been a dressmaker or a governess who had worked for the ladies of Tsarskoe Selo, although not actually employed at court. Her name was Klara Maria Peuthert. Now she sought out my compatriots and told them she had found the Grand-Duchess Tatiana in a lunatic asylum—she mistook me for my sister.

This Klara Peuthert was a strange woman, and despite her importunity there was something good-natured about her. She too, in my opinion, was sane enough, and only in Dalldorf because of her fits of temper when thwarted; so her neighbours got a doctor to send her to the asylum. I felt a certain bond with her because of this, and as she was the only person in our ward you could talk to sensibly, we got into conversation. Probably she had no idea of what she was starting by spreading her news, nor did I know the sort of person she was. I was too young to cope with such people and such experiences: I had just turned twenty-one, and despite all the cruelties I had suffered, my upbringing was such that I only looked for the good in others. This gave me trouble all my life, till I changed my attitude and looked for the evil. At any rate I was soon to have unfamiliar experiences with Klara Peuthert and the Russians she sent to me at Dalldorf.

* * *

Detective-Inspector Grünberg of Berlin's Criminal Investigation Department, who handled Anastasia's case after the attempted suicide, continued to take a personal interest in her. On 30th November, 1926, he wrote as follows to his superior, Councillor Goehrke, at Berlin:

'. . . A bed-neighbour of hers was a certain Klara Peuthert, a woman in her forties now living in Schumannstrasse. She is known to have previously spent a long period in Russia, though no further details about her life there are ascertainable. Though she now looks a slut, she must have once seen better days, and apparently was governess in aristocratic houses. Because of a family likeness she thought she recognised the young woman in the next bed as one of the Tsar's daughters—concerning whose miraculous rescue there had long been rumours circulating—and after her discharge from the mental hospital she informed Russian emigrés of her discovery. A certain Baron Kleist (living at Nettelbeckstrasse 9) heard about it and afterwards took the young woman to his house; during the Tsarist regime he had been police chief of a large district in Russian Poland. It should be noted that he went to immense trouble to solve the mystery, and made no secret about his original conviction that the alleged Grand-Duchess was genuine. It is true that he may have had ulterior motives, as was hinted in emigré circles: if the old conditions should ever be restored in Russia, he hoped for great advancement from having looked after the young woman.'

* * *

Soon after the first visit at which I was shown my grandmother's picture, some Russians came to see me again, including a woman who at first only struck me as particularly well-dressed. One of the gentlemen with her had been to see me before. It was an appalling hour. I was so ashamed of my situation and surroundings that I at once pulled the blanket over my head and refused to speak to them. I was trembling all over my body and also began to cry, I felt so humiliated. But my visitors kept on trying to persuade me to reveal my identity, and from under the blanket I could only say I had never asked them to come, and implore them to leave me again. I shall never forget the way the blanket was then pulled off my bed. I felt a hand on my arm, the woman forced me to get up and asked me to stand in front of her just as I was.

At first I had had no idea what they wanted with me, but now I recognised the person who had handled me so roughly: it was Baroness Isa Buxhoeveden, my mother's former lady-in-waiting. One of the gentlemen with her, as I later learnt, was a certain Baron Kleist, a Russian living in Berlin, and the other a Captain Schwabe, who had formerly been Colonel Markov's adjutant in a cavalry regiment at Sebastopol and was now also a refugee in Berlin.

As I stood there, I suddenly heard the Baroness say: 'It's certainly not Tatiana. By her height it could only be Anastasia; but it's not her either.' I was beside myself at this remark, for I had seen the Baroness only five years before, so that she must have remembered me. I was so nonplussed that I could not utter a single word. I just jumped back into bed and left my visitors standing. An attendant showed them out again.

Afterwards I learnt how it had all come about. When the rumour got around that I was in Dalldorf asylum, Baroness Buxhoeveden happened to be staying with my Aunt Irene, wife of Prince Henry of Prussia; just at this time Colonel Markov, leader of the Russian royalists in Germany, came with Captain Schwabe to inform her that I had turned up in Berlin. But instead of talking about me, they kept on thinking it was Tatiana, and since Aunt Irene had not seen us girls for ten years while the Baroness had been with us as late as 1917, my aunt asked her to go to Berlin to identify me. I realised afterwards why I had been made to stand in front of my bed. Isa Buxhoeveden wanted to know whether I was tall or short, and as I was short she knew I could not be Tatiana.

She asserted later on that it was only after this fact was established that I said I was Anastasia, while before I had professed to be Tatiana. This is completely untrue. In fear of being handed over to the Bolsheviks I told nobody my name except for that one nurse. I can only think that Isa Buxhoeveden was so shocked at meeting the daughter of her Empress in this dreadful asylum that she refused to admit the truth. We children never liked her much, as I mentioned earlier, but Mama was always good to her and never let her feel that she preferred other ladies in her entourage. It was only in Tobolsk that she spoke critically of the Baroness. After leaving Russia, Isa Buxhoeveden was for many years given the most generous hospitality by my mother's sisters and brother. Her behaviour has always remained inexplicable to me.

After this visit Russian emigrés often came to see me—I can't remember now who they all were. The first woman to whom I confided my story was Zinaida Tolstoi, who visited me with her daughter. I had known her from the old days, for although she had never been with us at court officially, she used to come as a friend of the family and was very attached to us all. Afterwards, when I had been discharged from the asylum and had a bad attack of pneumonia, Mrs Tolstoi nursed me over a long period. She herself was ill at the time with some nervous complaint, yet she even watched every night at my bedside and altogether did a great deal for me.

Then came a woman who spent whole days trying to get me to leave the asylum and go to an emigré family who would take me in. At first I kept on refusing. I had never pressed to be discharged nor expressed any wishes in this direction. But at last I gave in. Through being constantly in the company of lunatics, and through the way I was treated by the doctors, who thought I too was mad, I had reached such a state of fear, suspicion, indifference and depression, that I told myself there could not be anything worse. Today I regret this decision, and have regretted it a thousand times. For had I stayed in the asylum, I should have died long ago and so been spared all the humiliations, torments and disappointments I was afterwards exposed to.

* * *

From the statements of the Dalldorf nursing staff, who were in daily contact with her, it is clear that from a medical standpoint the holding of Anastasia was unjustified. The matron declared: 'This patient never gave the impression of insanity; her only abnormal feature was her refusal to give details about herself and her terror of recognition. She was always well orientated about everything and knew the names of the different blocks and nurses.'

All the nurses questioned emphasised the patient's friendliness, politeness and gratitude for small favours. According to one of them, 'In her whole behaviour she suggested a real lady. Sometimes she was even on the haughty side, but generally most amiable, although rather reserved.' Another nurse, Erna Buchholz from Libau, a former language teacher who spoke Russian and was described by the doctors as skilful and trustworthy, states that the patient 'talked Russian like a native, not like a foreigner who has learnt the language later in life. And when talking German she gave certain words the harsh Russian stress on the final syllable. In my presence she never spoke anything but Russian and German. Nor have I ever heard her utter a word of Polish. . . .'

Of particular importance is the opinion given after several weeks of personal observations by Dr Bonhoeffer, a specialist in psychopathology, on 16th March, 1926, when Anastasia had been in a nursing home for eight months with a tuberculous infection of the arm. In essentials it applies to the period at Dalldorf, the case-history for which was at Dr Bonhoeffer's disposal, and it sheds particular light on the partial amnesia from which she again suffered in the four years between the two periods.

'Any thorough psychological examination was rendered difficult by the patient's habit of saying after a short time that the pain in her arm had worn her out; whereupon she would lie back in bed and close her eyes with an exhausted expression . . . you cannot get any coherent account of her childhood and later experiences. She often evades detailed questioning by telling you it is too painful to talk about her memories and she feels too ill—or else expressing this through a look of despair on her face. She declares she is not only physically ill, but no longer up to anything mentally; she has no interests left, and it is not worth going on living. In fact, after talking for a long time there is congestion of the face, and her features become distended. But in her conversation and behaviour she has always been attentive, polite and amiable. Her choice of words to express herself is often unusually felicitous. Her pronunciation is foreign, with a Russian accent, which nevertheless has a special *timbre* of its own. There is at present no sign of the South-German intonation mentioned in the Dalldorf case-history.

'In combination with other facts about her memory, there seems a strong probability of an auto-suggestive amnesia originating in the wish to suppress unpleasant experiences. The question whether hypnotic influence over the patient by a third party is a possibility, must be answered in the negative; and the same applies to conscious pretence.'

One day, after questioning her about what she remembered of Dalldorf, Dr Bonhoeffer explained to her that she must now do everything to strengthen and exercise her memory so that she could again think normally and retain knowledge of her past experiences. Then he left her, and directly he had closed the door behind him, she exclaimed in disgust: 'I go to the most frantic trouble to forget everything, and then this man comes and stirs up my whole memory again. I refuse to let him.' This refusal was to cause her a great many difficulties throughout her life.

The intervention of Russian emigrés certainly produced a turning-point in that life, though by no means a favourable one. At the beginning of March 1922 the wife of Baron Kleist applied to the management of the Dalldorf Institution for permission to take the patient to her home in Berlin. This application was granted on 25th May by Berlin police headquarters, after consultation with the medical authorities. The police records noted that '. . . Various attempts are being made in Russian circles to establish the unknown woman's identity, since there is some question of her being the Grand-Duchess Anastasia. It has not yet been established whether she is in fact the Grand-Duchess, but there are many who do not doubt her identity.'

*   *   *

It may sound strange, but the day of my discharge from Dalldorf was by no means a joyful one. Though I had lived here behind bars with lunatics for over two years, I felt neither joy over my freedom nor over the fresh air of the sunny May morning—despite my being such a nature-lover. After all the trouble I had seen, I had simply lost the capacity for feeling joy. It is hard to imagine that long ago I was once so merry and light-hearted a girl.

My visitors of the last weeks had all hurried along to fetch me: Baron Kleist and Captain Schwabe with their wives, and Mrs Tolstoi. I was even told that Isa Buxhoeveden had felt an obligation to come, but I did not see her; presumably she kept in the background somewhere.

Outside by the porter's lodge there was a taxi which was to take me to Berlin. It was surrounded by curious spectators, and the patients too looked out of the windows in curiosity. I found this so distressing that I asked a nurse to put a thick black veil over my face. I wanted nobody to see me and not to see anybody myself.

Baron and Baroness Kleist, who were giving me hospitality, lived in a simple flat in West Berlin, for they also had lost everything. But the flat was comfortably furnished, and the only depressing thing about it was that it was near the canal into which I had thrown myself. Anyhow, I was soon to experience far more depressing things than that.

When I moved in to the Kleists, I believed they did not know who I was, but were trying to help me out of pure kindness; nor did I know anything about *them*! It was only afterwards I learnt that Kleist had been in the administration somewhere in Russia's western provinces, but had been obliged to leave the service.

The Kleists immediately took me out into the country near Berlin, from where we often drove into the city. Sometimes we saw the Schwabes, who asked me to become godmother to their daughter. Although Schwabe always told me he had been a captain in one of the Russian Guard cavalry regiments, I do not believe this, for he is only a year older than I am; so when the Revolution broke out, he must have been about seventeen, which is certainly too young to have been a captain in a Guards cavalry regiment. In any case he at first behaved like a real officer, and I thought of him as a true friend. He was married to a woman much older than himself, whose chief idea was to make a lot of money in the shortest possible time.

I once told Schwabe that I was very fond of uniforms, so he appeared in uniform at the christening of his child, which I found very nice of him—though I was somewhat surprised that they should have asked me to be godmother and have given their daughter my name—Anastasia. Also I found it very tactless of them to be always turning the conversation to Russia and my father. Even so, it never occurred to me that they might know who I really was. These people, who were absolutely convinced then of my identity and regarded it as their privilege and good fortune to name their child after me, afterwards showed hostility towards me. I don't know what harm I did them, but apparently they no longer felt there was anything to be gained through me.

From the first day of my stay with the Kleists a lot of visitors came. They were all Russians, wanting to see me, waiting for me to say something, and without my being yet aware of it, scrutinising me keenly to find out whether I really was the Tsar's daughter. In the beginning I was very reserved and reticent, but later—especially when Mrs Tolstoi was there—I told them some things about my girlhood. Only fragments, of course, because I had forgotten so much and always found it very hard to collect my thoughts. Although at first people were very polite and sympathetic to me, many of them wanted also to hear something of the latest happenings in Russia, and I did not feel able to talk about that when there were more than a few people present. I had suffered such awful things that I did not want to be reminded of it. For this reason I had also decided always to speak German, because Russian had become disagreeable to me, although I of course understood it. Some of the Kleists' visitors did not appreciate this and even considered me unpatriotic. They soon showed their true face, and I hardly think they were better patriots than I.

I had quite forgotten that Kleist knew my birthday, and still thought nobody realised who I was. Once when I had been living with them for some time, his wife asked what she should call me. As I did not wish to reveal my name, I reflected a minute and then asked her to call me Anna, after the first part of my name—and Anna I remained. At my birthday party there was a lot of dancing, and I kept on being asked to dance myself. At first I declined the invitations because I felt so weak, but I was so fond of dancing that I eventually accepted.

But my fears had been justified, for immediately after the dance I became so ill that I had to be carried out of the room and the doctors despaired of saving my life. A lot of Russians came with flowers; I suppose they thought they would find a dying woman.

Not all of them were allowed to enter my room; they had to stay in the sitting-room. Kleist did not like this at all and said his house was no hotel.

There were so many flowers in my room it might have been thought I was already dead. Mrs Tolstoi never left my bedside, except at night when she was relieved by her niece, who slept on the floor by my bed. During the day the Kleists also spent all day in my room, and there were often so many people coming that the German doctor became very annoyed, saying I needed absolute rest; but he failed to get the visitors to leave me. Once Mrs Tolstoi brought me a marvellous bouquet of roses from Colonel Markov, who was afterwards to cause me such harm.

Although the doctor said my illness was already at its peak, nobody believed that I should live. I was given morphia. Then I was again asked who I really was. In normal circumstances I should not have told them, but then I thought my last hour had come, and besides I was under the influence of the drug—so I at last said that I was the Grand-Duchess Anastasia.

The crisis passed, and by the next day I was already feeling much better. On that day Kleist came and told me he had received a very disagreeable letter from Mrs Tolstoi, which said among other things: 'A Grand-Duchess cannot have a child by a private soldier.'

Some years later Mrs Tolstoi wrote to me that she had never said any such thing; she had quarrelled with Kleist, and it was all his fault. But she certainly disappeared at that time, for I heard and saw nothing more of her till 1926, when she again assured me of her friendship and asked if she might visit me. I was not specially keen on seeing her again, but she kept on writing me the friendliest letters. Anyhow, at the time when Kleist informed me of her letter, I was overcome by despair. How dreadful to have written something like that, and how incredible of Kleist to have told me about it. From then on his attitude towards me changed. Soon I could no longer bear it and demanded to be taken back to Dalldorf, but Kleist refused to do this. Sometimes before that I had felt like returning to Dalldorf, for I found the Kleists' circle a torment; only this time I was firmly resolved to go.

Also it had happened more than once that the refugees dared to tell lies about Father Gregory (Rasputin) and his family, declaring that he had exerted a fatal influence on Russia. They also spread malicious stories about the Grand-Dukes. At first I pretended not to hear, although my heart was thumping with indignation and I had to fight to keep back the tears. But then I found it too much to bear and I just could not control myself any longer, so I got up and went out of the room—whereupon they laughed and pretended to be insulted. Eventually I told them I would not have that kind of talk and threatened to make a scene at table. After that the tactless remarks ceased.

In Dalldorf, as I have already related, I got to know one Klara Peuthert. She was the woman who had taken me for my sister Tatiana and told the emigrés about it. She had come to Berlin as a refugee and had then been in the asylum for a while under observation, before being discharged again. True she was a simple woman, common and sometimes rather coarse; but there was something sincere in her very simplicity, which I preferred to all the hypocrisies I had met with among the Russian refugees. Perhaps this was why I took rather a fancy to her. This Klara Peuthert kept on coming to see me, although she was far from kindly treated by the Kleists. One day she suggested to me that I should move to her place. She said she had a quiet home where I should feel much better. But we were both afraid of the Kleists and decided not to tell them of our plan. On the arranged day she returned, and I left the house secretly with her. But as I was still very weak, I found this flight a great strain and it was not at all good for my health.

It was evening when we reached her place. She had a single room in a badly built house. It was a real Berlin workman's tenement and the room was very primitive. It smelt, and the furniture was threadbare—not very attractive accommodation, in fact, but at least I had escaped from the Kleists.

We talked about the Russian emigrés. She said she knew Russians better than I did, and they certainly did not care whether I was thrown on the streets, or didn't know where to turn in my need. I let her talk, only wanting to be left in peace and having no wish to start arguing with her about my compatriots. I think all I said was that I had preferred my company in Dalldorf to the people I had been moving among lately. She obviously took this remark the wrong way, for of course it was she who first dragged me out of my hiding-place. She became cross with me, and as uncivil as she had previously been friendly and obliging. Even if this did not make me actively suspicious, I still wondered whether Klara Peuthert was really as innocent as she made out, or whether she also had some special reason for being so interested in me.

Directly I moved in with her, she became terribly nervous, and scared the Kleists might come to look for me. I couldn't do anything myself, so I put myself fully in her hands. Eventually she decided to send me to live with another family, but these people were frightened too, and she had to come out surreptitiously by night and take me back to her house again.

But she was justified in her fears, for soon there were a lot of people wanting to see me: Baroness Kleist, her daughter, and Jaenicke, a civil engineer; one of the Schwabes also came, but I don't remember whether it was the Captain or his wife. They all asked Klara Peuthert about my whereabouts and even threatened her with the police. Although she had told me about all these visits, she did not tell me that in the end she had given in to them.

Three days after I left the Kleists, Klara Peuthert went for a walk with me, and as we had gone out before, I did not feel any suspicion; once she had even had me photographed by a man who spoke English with me. When we were walking down the street where she lived, we suddenly met Jaenicke. He was one of the first to visit me at Dalldorf; he had come with Schwabe. He had frequently visited me at the Kleists and always brought flowers with him—altogether I found him most agreeable. As I also liked his wife, I thought in them I had found true and disinterested friends. I did not know that this meeting had been prearranged and that Jaenicke even had a police officer at his house. He asked me to come with him, and I agreed. I hadn't been long at their house when the officer appeared, a certain Grünberg This meeting was to assume a strange significance in my life.

In the circumstances, since I had only been three days away from the Kleists, a detective had no difficulty in finding me. But Inspector Grünberg had not come to interrogate me about my running off and my stay with Klara Peuthert. Instead he suggested I go with him to his estate at Funkenmühle near Teltow, saying that after two years at Dalldorf my nerves would benefit from the good country air. He told me that he had a garden, and the forest was not far away; his wife would do everything to make my stay as pleasant as possible.

At first I refused point-blank. After all it was very strange to receive such an invitation from a police inspector, my personal inspector, as it were, since I now knew that he had handled my case. First I had been left for years in an asylum without anyone bothering about me, and now the police of all people were taking an interest in my shattered nerves. After the behaviour of everyone I had recently come into contact with, I had every reason to be suspicious of this proposal; nor did the Jaenickes want to let me go, even if they had private reasons for that. But Inspector Grünberg insisted that the police had nothing to do with the invitation, it was a personal wish of his to help me; he was well off, so it would make no difference to him if I were to live with him. He brought Schwabe along and talked to me for so long that I at last agreed. I drove out to Funkenmühle with the two of them and Mrs Jaenicke.

At first I had no regrets. It was really lovely out there in the country, and as promised, Inspector Grünberg's family did everything they could to make my stay pleasant. His wife especially took great care to see that I had peace and was well fed; right to the end she looked after me with great kindness.

I felt in Heaven. I sat a lot in the garden, which was well kept. After a long time I again took up a drawing-block and drew the animals which leapt around in the meadow. I found myself thinking of Gleb Botkin, who could do it so much better than I, and whom I had last seen at Tobolsk; I wondered where on earth he was now. Sometimes Grünberg sat near me and watched me, and then he would talk. Once he noticed that I was holding the block rather clumsily. When I was still a child, I had the fingers of my left hand crushed; one of them was badly injured and still bears a scar. At the time the incident caused great excitement: a footman had shut the carriage door too soon, crushing my fingers, so that I fainted with the pain. Grünberg's remarking on the bad finger led to my gradually telling him still more about my life at home and all the experiences I had been through since. I now felt confidence in him, and was convinced that he really had good intentions towards me and wanted to help me. Then came the remarkable incident with Aunt Irene.

* * *

Extracts from Grünberg's reports of 19th June and 30th November, 1926:

'. . . Feeling that there was a historical mystery here comparable to that of the Man in the Iron Mask, I decided, in agreement with Baron Kleist, to take the young lady for three weeks to my estate at Funkenmühle near Neuhoff-Teltow. Staying two years at Dalldorf had completely shattered her nerves. Moreover, she had been wounded in the head (skull battered by blows from a rifle) which led to a certain mental derangement; and in addition there was a mental instability in the family on her mother's side. She claims with great assurance to be the late Tsar's youngest daughter Anastasia, and had given descriptions of the Imperial family's stay at Tobolsk and Ekaterinburg, as well as of family life at court, which presuppose exact knowledge. . . . She also made precise statements about the night of the murder and the general massacre. When she fell on the floor, she saw only the room's wallpaper—which she describes quite exactly and correctly—before losing consciousness . . .

'She also related what she had learnt about her rescue. Among the Red Guard men who murdered the Tsar and family, there was a certain Tchaikovski, son of a Polish exile, who owned a farmhouse near Ekaterinburg. . . . She told of her flight from the Bolsheviks to Rumania, her stay in Bucharest, where she was then married in church out of gratitude to Tchaikovski and later also got a son by him called Alexis. . . . Then she travelled with her brother-in-law to Germany, covering the expenses by selling the last of the diamonds sewed into her clothes, in order to visit her aunt, wife of Prince Henry of Prussia, at Hemmelmark. . . . I did not get this narrative from her in the above coherent form, but only in rather disconnected fragments; and even then I had to proceed very gently, because recalling these horrible experiences made her tremendously excited, until she would completely collapse. . . . While she was on my farm, I wrote to Police Headquarters at Breslau, having already been in touch with the Superintendent there, and we planned taking an energetic action towards bringing about her recognition. In August 1922 we persuaded Princess Irene (Prince Henry's wife) to visit my guest, but under a false name . . .'

* * *

The day Aunt Irene came to Funkenmühle is one of the most painful memories I have of that period. I was ill at the time. A swelling on the chest was beginning to get bigger and bigger, and I had a temperature. Even so I did not feel like staying in bed, so had gone out for a walk; after all, I was in the country and a little exercise should do me good. On the way I found mushrooms, and not having brought a knife or a basket, I dug them up with my hands, even carrying them home in my arms. Unsuspecting and dirty, I entered the house with these mushrooms.

When Grünberg noticed me entering the dining-room, he came in there too. I was very surprised to see him on a week-day, because he usually only came out at week-ends; evidently he had not informed anyone in the house of his arrival. He was very nervous and excited, but did not say why he had come; instead, he shaded the lights in the room with paper. I showed him my mushrooms and explained that before supper I would just like to go to my room to wash and do my hair. He shook his head, went out of the room, and returned with two ladies. Because of the dim lighting I could not distinguish them properly. Grünberg introduced them to me, referring to them by quite indifferent names: I took them for friends or relatives of his. The two ladies, Grünberg, his wife, Mrs Jaenicke and I all sat down at table. During the conversation one of the ladies' voices sounded very familiar to me, and I suddenly recognised it as Aunt Irene's. I was deeply shaken and upset by this recognition, but at first I felt so hurt, helpless and angry at her sitting here before me under a false name, that I could not utter a word—indeed, I could hardly go on sitting at the table. As soon as I felt able to, I stood up, ran to my room, sat down on my bed, and burst into tears—so humiliating did I find it that she of all people, my own mother's sister, whom I had travelled all the way from Rumania to see, should have come to me now as a stranger under an assumed name.

Grünberg had no doubt expected the encounter to turn out differently. But I did not have long to reflect on this, for suddenly there was a knock on the door. I thought it was Mrs Jaenicke and called to her to come in. Instead of her I saw Aunt Irene standing in my room. She had noticed that I had recognised her in the dining-room, for all at once she called me by my name and tried to persuade me to come to her home. This was much kinder, but I felt so offended I refused. Then she asked me at least to talk to her, and put questions for me to answer. But I still could not utter a word, I choked, and the tears poured down my face; I had to look away so that she did not see I was crying. If only the circumstances had been different! But her coming was so completely unexpected, I felt so ill and wretched, and was so agitated, that I simply could not talk to her. If she had come a second time, I'm sure it would have been different. But she left me the same evening and never came again.

On the next day Mrs Jaenicke told me that the lady who had accompanied my aunt had been dreadfully agitated. I can't remember her name, but I was told that it was one of my aunt's ladies-in-waiting. While Aunt Irene was in the room with me, Mrs Jaenicke, who was about to come in, saw this lady-in-waiting standing outside the door and listening to our conversation through the keyhole. Mrs Jaenicke did not then know who the two ladies were, and when she heard she could hardly believe it. She told me that my aunt had been very irritable after leaving me, and that the other lady had argued with her in a manner quite unfitting for a lady-in-waiting. Afterwards I learnt that it was just this lady-in-waiting who intrigued against me and did everything she could to set my aunt and uncle against me and do me harm. The worst thing was, however, that Jaenicke, who kept on insisting I should go to my aunt, had apparently written to her asking for money. But I only heard this afterwards from Baroness Kleist. Understandably, it must have created a bad impression with Aunt Irene. I was very sad when I heard of this, and afterwards gave up the Jaenickes altogether.

I have been criticised since for behaving rudely to my aunt, and told that I have only myself to thank for her failure to recognise or acknowledge me. I was not discourteous, I was only very deeply offended that she should have had to resort to such anonymity. We were specially fond of Aunt Nini, as we used to call her when we were children, she often stayed with us in Russia for months at a time; and although I was only a little girl ten years earlier when she had last seen me, she still should never have treated me in such a way. Had she no pity for someone who had been through so much, and on top of that was ill? In the long years of struggle I was later to face in my attempts to get recognised, I always found it particularly distressing that Aunt Irene of all people refused her belief. I never lost a distinct hope that she would give up this hostile attitude, directly she talked to people who recognised me at once or (like her son, Prince Sigismund) had other proofs for the truth of my statements. But she died without this happening.

* * *

Clumsily prepared, the meeting between aunt and niece was bound to take a tragic turn. Grünberg had not told Anastasia beforehand what visitors to expect, partly from sound detective instinct but also out of genuine kindness; on the other hand, he could not very well expose Princess Irene when she came. As for her, it is again understandable that she did not give her real name, for she thought this was the only way of finding out whether the unknown woman was her niece or an impostor. This is an argument which the hyper-sensitive Anastasia still refuses to see; but a little less sensitiveness and more patience on both sides might have led to her immediate recognition. As it was, the result of the meeting was purely negative, and its initiator received a rebuke from his superior, who wrote under Grünberg's report: 'These futile investigations seem to me to have gone too far already.' The investigations, however, were by no means so futile, as can be seen from the comments of both Grünberg and Princess Irene. Grünberg writes:

'Her Royal Highness was placed opposite Anastasia at the supper table, so that she could observe her closely. The Princess did not think she could recognise Anastasia, admitting, however, that it was ten years since she had last seen the Tsar's family. After Anastasia had retired to her room, the Princess followed her, and made efforts to obtain some sort of information by talking to her. Anastasia was ill at the time, and also terribly headstrong and obstinate—as she still is today: she turned her back on the Princess and did not answer her. This was all the more incomprehensible in that she had immediately recognised the Princess, for the next morning she said at once that the lady had been her Aunt Irene. At any rate the Princess, quite justifiably, was deeply shocked by Anastasia's fantastic behaviour and has since refused to have anything more to do with the whole affair.'

Princess Irene, for her part, declared straight out: 'The hair, forehead and eyes are Anastasia's, but the mouth and chin are not. I cannot say that it isn't her.'

Even though the Princess was unable to form a clear impression about Grünberg's guest in the short encounter at Funkenmühle, she still invited Anastasia to her estate at Hemmelmark, showing that she was uncertain and hoped to reach a more definite conclusion in her own home. Then Anastasia refused the invitation, and the more time went by, the stronger the Princess' scepticism became. But until shortly before her death she certainly believed that the woman she had seen, though not Anastasia, bore a strong resemblance to her.

* * *

After my return to Berlin I went back to the Jaenickes. My health had greatly deteriorated, so I visited a number of doctors, but they all said something different and they all cut my chest about, where—as it was then supposed—I must have an inner hæmorrhage originating from one of the rifle blows on the night of the murder at Ekaterinburg. Afterwards it was found to be incipient tuberculosis of the breastbone, which also attacked the left elbow-joint. Consumption, alas, has been a common complaint in my father's family since the eldest daughter of Queen Louisa of Prussia married into the imperial house, to become the wife of Nicholas I. Anyhow, all the operations I had were so badly done that a really serious operation was needed, for which I had to go into the West-End Hospital at Charlottenburg, of which Dr Neupert was head. Another German doctor, whom I had met at the Kleists, undertook to cover all expenses, including the operation. They must have been rather high, for I was given a private room and the hospital was a good one.

Kleist kept on coming to fetch me back to him. Once when Mrs Jaenicke was not there, his wife and daughter came along to take me with them. Although I refused, the two of them began to pack my things. They were so persistent that in the end I gave up protesting, and when Mrs Jaenicke returned, I gave in. This time, however, I only stayed a week with the Kleists. My health was again so bad that I had to return to hospital. Fortunately I went into Dr Neupert's hospital once more.

I was so ill that he almost gave up hope for me, and when he had finished examining me, he said that all earlier operations had been quite wrong. He gave me only a fortnight to live, but nevertheless performed one more drastic operation. I survived it, and now he redoubled his care for me. I stayed a whole year in this hospital, and as they were all so good to me and gave me every attention, I enjoyed real peace for the first time in all these terrible years.

After my discharge I had to go back to the Kleists, and once more a dreadful time began for me. The German doctor, who till then had paid for my upkeep, stopped sending money.

In the early days a lot of money had been collected for me, though there was never enough left over to give me the chance of replacing my teeth, so that I could feel like a normal person again. Since Rumania all my upper teeth had hurt me. They had been loose and I could not bite with them, so at Dalldorf I had them taken out. An X-ray showed that because of a violent blow —from the rifle-butt at Ekaterinburg—the bones in my upper jaw had been split. Now the money for new teeth was refused me, even though many of the Russian emigrés almost went on their knees to me in their assurances that they were my best friends and would do everything to help me.

On my discharge from the hospital I was obliged, as I have said, to go back to the Kleists. It was no longer a pleasant place to stay. I had almost nothing but the clothes I stood up in, and although it was winter, my room was unheated. I had to do everything for myself, and had to wash in cold water the few articles of clothing I still had left. I did not even possess any cotton to mend my things with, but was obliged to darn the holes with thread I pulled from an old piece of cloth. It was all so horrible that it is a torture for me now even to speak of it.

Mrs Schwabe too was shocked when she came to see me in my ice-cold room. She told me that a lot of people would be glad if they could help me, but knew that nothing would reach me if they tried. Eventually a lady managed to obtain sewing work for me from the Baltic Red Cross, and then I began to work from sunrise till late at night. It was a great strain, for I had to do it with one hand and the light was poor. In this way I ruined my eyes, so that in the end I could not properly distinguish the different colours.

I had believed the lady who told me in Dalldorf that my so-called friends were acting from motives of sheer benevolence when they persuaded me to leave the institution. Now I recognised the real reason for their actions. I was always a mere object for all the people I stopped with, an object they could build plans around and use for their own profit. I was passed from hand to hand, and these people hated each other for envy whenever I happened to be with one of them instead of the other. Afterwards, when they saw that their plans weren't taking the form they had hoped, they dropped me. I shall never forget one of these Russians saying, when there was talk of a member of our family visiting me: 'Don't spoil my business.' They were interested in me so long as they hoped that some of our family's valuables might be deposited outside Russia, from which they would be given something in gratitude for their help should I be acknowledged. But since the papers had written that these valuables did not exist, they lost interest in me—I had ceased to be the precious object they used to see in me.

My health completely undermined by all these humiliations, I returned to Dr Neupert's hospital once more. But when I was discharged from there some time later, there was no one willing to give me a home. I did not want to go back to the Kleists, feeling my pride so hurt that I refused to stay any more with people who only wished to exploit me. The only person who had gone on visiting me was Klara Peuthert, and though she was a peculiar person, she did listen to my cares; in my distress I was grateful for any soul to confide in. When I was to be discharged, and nobody was fetching me, Klara Peuthert suggested I came to her again. In view of the Kleists' behaviour I had no alternative but to accept her offer.

I might have realised that things wouldn't go well for long with Klara Peuthert; yet I stayed for two months in that dreadful room. It was winter and cold, we had no fuel and hardly enough money to keep us alive; the only thing I received was some meagre assistance from the Berlin welfare office, and I never got my hands on this, because Klara Peuthert took everything herself to look after us both.

I could not help looking back on that other winter at Tobolsk and the time at Ekaterinburg. Even then I thought I had reached my lowest ebb and the end had come; it is true I was a prisoner there. But did I really have my freedom now? In those days I could still talk with my parents, sisters and brothers about our past, our experiences and journeys; the sun of my childhood was still shedding its last rays over that time. Anyhow, I was still with people who thought as I did and whom I could trust in everything. But where had I landed now? I no longer had even the essentials, just a worn-out sofa, on which I must spend my days listening to the chatter of the woman who had taken me in, a sofa on which I must spend my sleepless nights in brooding, until the grey winter light dawned even in this back-yard.

Had Klara Peuthert been hoping for something else from me, that she let the mask drop more and more from her face—a face which had once looked at me with kindness and even shown a sort of tacit loyalty? I suppose she also thought like the Russians, and hoped that since she had discovered me as the Tsar's daughter, she would be able to live off the allowance that would one day come in if I were acknowledged by my relatives. But as this did not materialise, in fact a newspaper one day published an article against me, her hopes too were brought to nothing. She demanded of me that I write a reply to this article; plainly she had selfish motives.

This article was obviously written by someone who knew all about me, for he wrote about my person, my room, the conditions in which I lived, and finally asserted I was nothing but an ordinary dressmaker.

Klara Peuthert must have scented a new bit of business for herself. She had always tried to impress newspaper people. Now she took me to a reporter's flat, where I was to write my reply and declare that I couldn't make dresses at all. I flatly refused, finding it beneath my dignity to argue against such attacks: everyone who knew me knew that I wasn't a dressmaker. But Klara Peuthert would talk of nothing but my writing about myself in the papers, and it now turned out that she had already received money for this from one of her friends, who was supposed to be particularly interested in my fate. She thought, no doubt, that in this way she would be better able to make me write. Since I went on refusing, she grew so excited that the quarrel burst the same evening. When I was already asleep, she pulled the blanket from off my body, dragged me out of bed and shouted: 'Get up. The police are outside. You're to go back to Dalldorf!'

I had such a shock I could not utter a word. Back to Dalldorf, what an appalling thought! I got up and began to dress. But on that Klara Peuthert took all the rest of my clothes away one by one, saying they were borrowed from her friends and I must leave them behind here. When I was only half-dressed, she opened the door and pushed me out. There was no sign of any police. There I stood, dropped even by this so-called friend.

I could not be humbled by a woman like her, and I am far from claiming that bad people are only to be found in the lowest strata of society: the same night I experienced the contrary. Next to Klara Peuthert there was a workman's family living, whose name I have forgotten. It consisted of a married couple and the man's brother. The men were coalmen, I think, for they returned black as sweeps from their day's work. They took me into their home at once, and I lived with them for several weeks. Although they were simple people, they showed themselves more tactful and sensitive than anybody I had met in Germany all this time. They shared every piece of bread with me and looked after me as well as they could—although Klara Peuthert, furious that they had taken me in, was spreading the most horrible slanders, even saying I had an affaire with the coalman. I tried again to earn something, by stitching handkerchiefs, which the wife took to the Baltic Red Cross, where they were sold.

Once I remembered something which made me cry. I thought of how on the evening of the night my family was slaughtered I had prepared a new piece of needlework, and how I had just started on it. It was a very colourful embroidery, I believe, and I was looking forward to finishing it, when Yurovski came with his men. . . . I wanted to give the proceeds from my work to my new friends as a present, but they refused to accept it, so I bought food with it and gave that to them. I was very proud to be able to show my gratitude to them with money I had earned myself, for they really took me in out of sheer kindness, without asking about who I was and whether they would some time get rewarded for it.

* * *

The Berlin police records for this period have the following note:

'. . . The alleged Grand-Duchess Anastasia stayed in various lodgings till the end of 1923. She went back to von Kleist for a while, but probably spent longest with the woman Peuthert mentioned above, who, according to Inspector Grünberg's statement, exerted a very strong influence over her. From 4th September to 11th November, 1924, she was in the West-End Hospital at Charlottenburg (Spandauer Berg 15-16) to be treated for tuberculosis, and gave her identity as Anna von Tchaikovski, *née* Romanovski, born in St Petersburg on 4th June, 1901. In the middle of January 1925 the District Welfare Office concerned itself with her case on the suggestion of the Officer of Health, Dr Graef, who diagnosed tuberculosis of the bone, a complaint which had frequently occurred in the house of Romanov. The District Welfare Office considered an intervention by the local welfare office absolutely necessary, since the alleged Anastasia was being badly looked after at the woman Peuthert's . . .'

Grünberg has these notes on the period:

'. . . After the return to Berlin, Baron Kleist again took her to his home, but she ran away from them (she did this four times with the Kleists, and each time they fetched her back). This, as she afterwards told me, was because she was afraid of her incognito being betrayed by the importunities of the Russian refugees, and of falling again into the hands—or rather claws—of the Peuthert woman, who had an almost diabolical influence over her, and what is more, described her everywhere as Anastasia, youngest daughter of the Tsar. It has never been clear what this woman was hoping for by clutching "Anni" to herself (that was the name she used to call her by). At any rate she was so possessive and domineering that Anastasia took refuge with the people on the same floor, a coal-heaver and his wife and brother (named Bachmann), who were living in little better than a public shelter . . .'

* * *

Although I did not want to go on living indefinitely with the workman's family in the Schumannstrasse, I should probably have stayed there longer had not Grünberg, the police inspector, again intervened in my affairs. It was, of course, easy enough for him to find me there, for Klara Peuthert lived in the same house, he only needed to ask her and he had my address at once. As it was winter, Grünberg did not take me out to Funkenmühle this time, but invited me to go with him to his town residence. He was very friendly now, as he had been the first time, and his wife even more so, welcoming me like an old friend. But all that did not last long.

Soon something happened which I by no means expected. One day I heard that a man had turned up at the Schwabes who, according to the description given me, could only have been Serge Tchaikovski. As it later transpired, he had searched for me first in Dalldorf, and had then followed my tracks till he eventually reached Klara Peuthert. There he saw a picture of me and on looking at it burst into tears. He knew me well, he told her, I was the Grand-Duchess Anastasia of Russia, he had brought me from Bucharest to Berlin, and then completely lost me. On the back of the picture he made a note, from which, however, there was nothing further to be gathered, except perhaps the confirmation that my name was Anastasia Nikolaievna. Underneath it was written Alexandrov and then Alexeiev Shorov, Petrograd. Probably these were again only assumed names.

Then the stranger went to Grünberg's town residence just when I did not happen to be there, and finally went to Schwabe, with whom he left a letter and a photograph for me. I was naturally very excited, for the photo could only be of Serge my dead husband, and it would have been a great help to me to trace my former rescuers. Besides giving news of Serge and his family, the letter might have information about my child. The stranger declared that it was at an orphanage in Galatz. Schwabe and Grünberg telephoned each other. On the same evening I and Grünberg went to see Schwabe.

Schwabe told me my brother-in-law had come to Berlin to look for me, but had gone away again. When Grünberg then asked after the letter, Schwabe said he had mislaid it and would try to find it later. He never gave it me. Then he promised to give the letter to Zahle, the Danish ambassador, who afterwards figured largely in my life; but that never happened either. I thought he had probably sold it to the Estonian Legation or to Koburg, residence of the Grand-Duke Cyril, with whom he was in correspondence; the Estonian Legation in Berlin was then also intriguing against me. A long while afterwards, however, I learnt that Schwabe had handed photograph and letter to the Berlin police headquarters.

Now Schwabe too had become my enemy. It was clear that he had only acted for his own advantage, in fact he made no secret of it. At first he had been very nice to me and behaved like an officer. Doubtless it was the influence of his older wife which changed him and made him do these horrible things. For he now began trying to persuade Grünberg not to give me any more hospitality and to have me deported from Germany. These conversations with Schwabe always made Grünberg very nervous.

* * *

The mysteries concerning Serge Tchaikovski's reappearance, if it *was* he, have never been satisfactorily explained. Evidently he made himself scarce on hearing that Grünberg was a police inspector, and the two never met; but it seems extraordinary that Grünberg failed to follow up so important a clue, either by obtaining from Schwabe the missing letter and photograph or by trying to trace the child in the orphanage. (It was left to Mrs Rathlef, Anastasia's next protector, to make enquiries in Galatz, which—so much later—proved wholly negative.) Probably Grünberg was already being criticised by his superiors for continuing his investigations, was coming to the end of his patience with Anastasia, and still hoped for easier success from the confrontation with Princess Cecilie which was soon to follow. The letter from Serge Tchaikovski was never heard of again, and the photograph was not handed to the police till several months later, by Kleist and another Russian emigré called Savich, who had had it from Schwabe and told an obviously cock-and-bull story about a visitor to Anastasia in Dalldorf. A report of their deposition was made in January 1926, without any explanation of why they were only going to the police now; and this sole reference to Serge Tchaikovski and the photograph was later found in the files of the Berlin Police Headquarters:

'One day while the alleged Anastasia was in Dalldorf Asylum, a man dressed in some kind of uniform came and asked to speak to her. When he was forbidden entrance, he wrote a few lines in Russian on a sheet of paper explaining that on seeing this she would receive him. She did so, and the two evidently talked in Russian. Mr Savich handed over a picture of the man in question which he had received from the former Russian officer Schwabe, living at Kurfürstendamm 114. Schwabe and his wife met the man and received the picture from him, but they did not know who he was. If it could be established who the photograph shows, the matter would doubtless be completely cleared up. Mr Savich asks for the picture to be returned, suggesting copies should be made and given to the authorities in question.'

* * *

I had scarcely got over this excitement when I was surprised by a new visit. I had long realised that, as with my first such visit, Grünberg had set himself to clear up the question of my identity. Considering our good relations I was offended by this. I had told him often enough who I was, and if he did not believe it, his investigations would not help either. I am an odd person. I have often spoken voluntarily of my family and my experiences, but if I ever feel there is any ulterior motive or compulsion, I may give very ill-tempered answers, when I do not refuse to answer altogether. This obviously drove Grünberg to despair, for he was now always complaining that it was my own fault if I did not get my relatives to acknowledge me. Yet he did not give up, and this time, instead of Aunt Irene, brought home Princess Cecilie.

As I was not prepared for it, this visit could have no other result than the unsuccessful visit of my aunt at Funkenmühle. Of course I knew the wife of the German Crown Prince. She and her husband had been with us at St Petersburg in 1911, when I was only ten, and I had liked them both. In other circumstances a bridge would surely have been found, but now it came to another of those terrible confrontations. I had to submit to prolonged scrutiny. I felt this was really beneath my dignity, and I believe I did not say one word. I know today, alas, that my behaviour towards the Princess was a particular mistake, for many years afterwards, when I saw her alone, we at once understood each other.

Although I still felt, despite the failure of this meeting, that the Princess by no means completely rejected me, Grünberg's patience was now at an end. He told me the Princess had refused to help me and he himself had reached deadlock owing to my stubbornness. Now he completely changed his behaviour towards me, giving me a time-limit for finding other accommodation and saying he would prefer not to keep me a day longer. Those were dreadful weeks I spent after that; it is a very long time since I have cried so much as I did then.

* * *

Inspector Grünberg was certainly no diplomat. After the failure with Princess Irene, he should not have repeated his mistake by disregarding Anastasia's pride and obstinacy. Having acted all along from disinterested kindness, he now abandoned the struggle too early. His views on the encounter between Anastasia and Princess Cecilie are shown in a letter he wrote on 19th June, 1925, to Mrs Harriet von Rathlef-Keilmann, who was soon to take up the same struggle far more effectively:

'. . . Following a sort of impulse, I searched for Anastasia; I discovered her staying with the Peuthert woman's floor-neighbours, and at the end of January (1925) took her to my house again. I made vain efforts to interest the Russian emigrés in her pathetic situation, but they are incredibly indifferent and also quite unreliable. First of all the lady-in-waiting N. N. was supposed to be trying to deny Anastasia's survival to the Dowager Empress (in Copenhagen); and afterwards it appeared that the Dowager Empress had no idea she was thought to be alive. Through the intermediary of Prince Oscar I next approached our Crown Princess, and about three weeks ago she came to see Anastasia in our house. She declared to me: "Hair, eyes and mouth show a striking resemblance to those of the Tsar's daughter. On the other hand, it is equally striking that she does not understand or speak a syllable of Russian or English."

'The noble lady informed me a few days ago that according to her view and that of the Grand-Duke of Hesse, the late Tsarina's brother, it must be considered quite out of the question that any member of the Imperial family is still alive. This brings me to a deadlock. Anastasia is certainly not a deliberate impostor, nor in my opinion is she a lunatic imagining she is the Russian Tsar's daughter. After living in the same house with her for months, I have reached the firm conviction that she must at least come from one of the very highest Russian families, and that it is quite probable she is of royal birth. For all her words and movements show such a regal attitude and sensitiveness that they could never have been picked up in later life.

'She hopes to achieve much, if not everything, towards her recognition if she can obtain the clothes she wore on the night of her family's murder and left behind with the Tchaikovskis in Bucharest . . .

'For some time her health has been deteriorating, in that tuberculosis with an open wound has been diagnosed in her left elbow; and she is also suffering from pleurisy . . .'

On 2nd October, 1953, Princess Cecilie, then resident in Stuttgart, referred thus to her former meeting with Anastasia:

'I, the undersigned Cecilie, Crown Princess of Prussia, make the following declaration on the identity of Mrs Anastasia Tchaikovski, also known as Anna Anderson, with the Grand-Duchess Anastasia of Russia:

'In the early 'twenties I and my near family, as well as our other royal relations, were much concerned about the news that the youngest daughter of the murdered Tsar and Tsarina had turned up in Berlin. At the suggestion (if I remember aright) of my brother-in-law, Prince Oscar of Prussia, I visited a young woman, then staying with a high police officer, to see if I could recognise her as the Tsar's youngest daughter, whom I had seen occasionally in her childhood. I was certainly struck at first glance by the young person's resemblance to the Tsar's mother and the Tsar himself; but I could not see anything of the Tsarina in her. There proved no opportunity, however, of establishing her identity, because it was virtually impossible to communicate with the young person. She remained completely silent, either from obstinacy or because she was completely bewildered, I could not decide which.

'Since Princess Irene of Prussia and the Grand-Duke Ernest Louis of Hesse, the Tsarina's sister and brother, would not have anything to do with Mrs Anastasia T., I held back myself. When these close relatives rejected her, I felt it was not my business to follow up the question of her identity. Yet I retained a personal interest in her fate . . .'

This statement on oath, read in connection with Grünberg's letter, makes plain the feelings of the warm-hearted Princess Cecilie after seeing Anastasia. Once in a small circle she even declared spontaneously: 'Her whole behaviour pointed clearly to her being one of the immediate family.'

Others besides Princess Cecilie were puzzled over what languages Anastasia spoke, and much of the scepticism about her identity was caused by the rumour that she knew no Russian or English but only German; she was even supposed to have a native South-German accent. But when Mrs Rathlef first met her in 1925 and addressed her in Russian, Anastasia, who made out she knew no Russian, gave completely appropriate answers (although in German) to everything that was said. Afterwards, when she was being treated by Mr Rudnev, he and Mrs Rathlef decided to talk only Russian in Anastasia's presence. At one point Mrs Rathlef deliberately told him that the patient was proving very stupid and obstinate, refusing to eat anything and giving it all to the cat. Anastasia reacted vigorously, protesting in German that she did not give the cat more than it needed and she ate quite enough herself. The others could not help laughing that someone supposed to know no Russian could defend herself so accurately against a complaint made in that language, and the doctor told her jokingly: 'But you understand Russian very well. From now on I'll always talk to you in Russian.' Anastasia started, pulled the bedclothes over her head, and said crossly: 'I didn't understand anything. Why can't you leave me in peace?'

As a child Anastasia knew Russian and English equally well. She did not speak good German during her first years in Germany, and although it improved later, she still has a non-German accent. In the last years before the Second World War she spoke English whenever possible. During the war she had to speak German, but after the war she reverted to English as her main language, and she has kept to this up till the present day. Living in her hut in the Black Forest, she of course talks to her neighbours and the postman in German, but as soon as she thinks anyone can understand English, she will not speak to them in anything else. Quite unwittingly, she sometimes brings in a Russian word.

A report by Dr Lothar Nobel of the Mommsen Nursing Home, written at the end of March 1926, gives a medical view on the question of Anastasia's languages:

'. . . I have been assured that in her childhood her immediate family spoke English almost exclusively, and that Russian was used only with tutors and servants. Yet the patient speaks no Russian. When asked the reason for this, she states that she went through so much misery and misfortune in Russia that she does not like the language and does not wish to speak it; she has made up her mind about this and will stick to it. I was often a witness, however, to the fact of her understanding Russian. She followed attentively a conversation in Russian between two other people and sometimes joined in with remarks in German, even correcting Russian words which were mispronounced. Reading Russian is a great effort for her, especially putting the letters together to make words. After long deliberation she can spell the word *Anastasia* in Russian script.

'Perhaps the avoidance of the Russian language is connected with the dangers of its use on the flight from Siberia and her fear then of being recognised; for this obsessive fear is constantly reflected in everything she says and the way she behaves. That is my explanation for her unco-operativeness in the hospitals she has been in previously and when she first entered the Mommsen Nursing Home. That was why she gave unsatisfactory answers or did not answer at all. Moreover, such a fear is responsible for her periodical melancholia, apathy, lack of energy and even death-wish. At these periods the patient is completely unco-operative, can scarcely be persuaded to eat, and only says "yes" or "no" to anything you ask her . . .'

Another doctor who treated her, Dr Eitel of Stillachhaus Nursing Home at Oberstdorf, noted on 22nd December, 1926:

'. . . It seems surprising at first that the patient does not now speak Russian. She says the last time she spoke it was at the beginning of the period she spent in the asylum (Dalldorf). At present she understands the language, knows individual words, and thinks she could speak it again after a few days' practice when her nerves were in a good state. It seems to be about the same with English, and she is now herself asking to have lessons in English . . .'

M. Gilliard, the former French tutor to the Tsar's family, who visited Anastasia in 1925 with his wife, took a different view of Anastasia's inability to speak languages she had learnt in her childhood:

'During our visit we first tried to question her (Anastasia) in Russian. We could see for ourselves that she understood it, although with difficulty, but was unable to speak it. We had no success when we tried English or French, so we were obliged to revert to German. We expressed our surprise at this, for the Grand-Duchess Anastasia knew Russian very well, English quite well, and French indifferently, but spoke no German at all. Mrs Tchaikovski was aware of the significance of the moment, for she knew we had come to establish her identity. So what could we think of the fact that if she knew one of the three above languages, she was not at pains to prove it to us by speaking any of them?'

There is another puzzle connected with Anastasia's ability to write. From childhood, as a matter of fact, she had always found writing very difficult, and she could neither read nor write when Mrs Rathlef first met her. Mrs Rathlef encouraged her, got her a notebook, and wrote down the letters for her to imitate. But it was no good, Anastasia said she had always written quite differently (probably with Russian letters). Once in the summer of 1925 Mrs Rathlef was sitting at her bedside when Anastasia, who had an illustrated magazine in front of her, took a pencil and wrote on the side of it first the Latin 'A' and then the whole name Anastasia. In the autumn, when she was feeling better, she tried several times to write her name. That Christmas she signed a postcard she had asked Mrs Rathlef to get her, to send greetings to the Gilliards.

M. Gilliard wrote to Mrs Rathlef in reply: 'My wife was very touched by the card you sent us. The signature certainly reminds one of the Grand-Duchess' writing at thirteen or fourteen. It is very important we should find out if the patient has seen the Grand-Duchess' signature on cards or books. If possible, you ought to get her to write a few lines.' Mrs Rathlef replied that to her knowledge the patient had never seen writing accepted as being that of the Grand-Duchess. Later that winter

Gilliard sent her a photograph of Anastasia as a child, with signature underneath, which she had presented to him at the time.

In the summer of 1926 Anastasia was so much better that she was able to travel to Switzerland. She now began to read English, though she had to use a book with very large print; with smaller print the letters swam before her eyes. On trips by steamer she listened with interest to conversations being carried on by the numerous English travellers. She kept on expressing the desire to speak English with someone. An Englishwoman was kind enough to oblige her by both talking to her and reading English with her. And now it suddenly turned out that Anastasia could read English altogether. Then her friend pushed a notebook over to her and invited her to take a dictation; on which she filled a whole page of the notebook, writing quickly and without hesitations, though with five spelling mistakes. Mrs Rathlef, who also reported this incident, was amazed that she could now suddenly write, having been unable to do so the whole year. She felt Anastasia was quite unaware that an inhibition had fallen away, partly because the Englishwoman took it for granted that Anastasia *could* write. From that moment on she really could: postcards have been preserved which she wrote in German, quite good and grammatical German, though with many spelling mistakes, and once she even wrote a letter four pages long.

* * *

Not feeling, I suppose, that he could very well leave me to my fate, Inspector Grünberg succeeded in getting me into another hospital. Before leaving his house, however, I met a lady who immediately showed an unselfish concern on my behalf. Her name was Harriet von Rathlef-Keilmann, and she came from Riga, but had escaped to Germany after the Revolution and was now working here as a sculptress. She kept herself aloof from the Russian emigrés, but had been told to try and help me by a certain Mr Sonnenschein, whom she knew through her conversion to Catholicism and who had assisted a number of other Russians; Grünberg had also been in touch with Mr Sonnenschein through another convert.

The first time I met Mrs Rathlef and the lady with her, Mrs Gisell, I had a general feeling that here were people who could take the troubles of others on to themselves. And troubles I certainly had. I felt dreadfully ill, had an open wound on my arm, and had still been unable to do anything about my teeth. Afterwards Mrs Rathlef told me she had been very worried about my appearance, I must have looked very frail and ill, and also much older than I really was because of the missing teeth. She also told me that even so she had at once seen a resemblance to my grandmother.

Next day, when the two ladies I had found so friendly came to fetch me, I felt very relieved to be going with them. It may sound hard and ungrateful after I had accepted Inspector Grünberg's hospitality for almost six months, but all the efforts he made for me were a great strain, so that in the end he got on my nerves badly. We parted on very cool terms. He must have been very disappointed that I made it so difficult for him to achieve his aim, but my passive behaviour must be largely put down to my weakened health. However, when I had packed the poor little bundle with my belongings and left his house, he did shake hands with me and tried his hardest to be polite.

I went to St Mary's, a Catholic Hospital in East Berlin. Although it was certainly no place for a convalescence, I was very well looked after, and I still remember gratefully the hard-working nurses, who showed self-sacrificing kindness to me in every conceivable way. The means which had been put at my disposal were very modest, so there was no alternative to going into a public ward with five others. But although this was outwardly rather like Dalldorf, I was, of course, much better off here; and at least my companions were not lunatics.

After my experiences with Klara Peuthert and the emigrés, I dared not get into any sort of conversation with the other women in the ward. It was not a case of my being haughty towards these simple women, but I had now become so suspicious that I preferred to remain alone—and besides I had such great pain that I scarcely left my bed. A first conversation could bring more questions in its train, and I was so weary of the continual interrogations and investigations that I preferred to avoid them all and keep quiet about myself. Nor could I be sure there was not some disguised spy of the Bolsheviks behind one of these questioners, who would then deliver me to my enemies—such cases had occurred time and again.

Yet how easily one forgets such precautions when one is not thinking or is faced by the authority of a doctor! Some days after my admission, I had to have my dressing changed in the theatre. This required the filling up of a new admission form. The doctor asked me for my particulars, which he entered on the form, and quite automatically I gave him the details he wanted. Born: 18th June, 1901; Father: Nikolai Romanov; Mother: Alexandra of Hesse; Brother and sisters: Alexi, Olga, Tatiana, Maria—all dead. It was only when the doctor asked me whether any of my grandparents were still alive, that I came to myself and refused to answer. He pressed the question, saying the Dowager Empress Maria Feodorovna was still alive and I should give her address as well. That was too much for me. I was appalled at having been so stupid, but also at their knowing so much about me here in the hospital. I was once told that Grünberg had informed Mr Berg, the hospital chaplain, about me, and he had reported it to the doctors; but it may also have been Mrs Rathlef who did this.

My memories of St Mary's Hospital are rather mixed. First of all, although my health was so poor, I did manage soon after my admission to see a dentist, and have the missing front teeth replaced. Mrs Rathlef bought me clothes, the first I had had for a long time which really fitted me, and in which, as she told me, I looked considerably younger. Although I could not use them much because I was in bed most of the time, I was still very grateful to her for them, and also for a lot of other material help with which she tried to lighten my lot. In the stony desert of East Berlin the July heat was unbearable, and the stuffy air in the room made it hard to breathe. But what was much worse—in this poor hospit l not a single piece of ice could be found to relieve the pain in my arm, which was glowing with fever and was inflamed right to the bone. Mrs Rathlef dealt with this problem too, by obtaining ice in the neighbourhood; also she brought light and appetising things to eat, as the heat made me unable to take the heavy hospital diet. I sometimes suspected that her friendliness had some ulterior motive, that she was wanting to be my only confidante and friend; I had perhaps become unnecessarily suspicious. Anyhow she jealously kept some of my acquaintances away from me, visited me almost every day, and every now and then brought along her own friends, whether I wanted to see them or not. One of these friends, Miss Amy Smith, was to play an important part in the question of my recognition.

In the long lonely hours at my bedside we of course talked about my past, especially my youth, just as the thoughts came. I spoke of my birthday, which this year had been so sad for me, whereas Grandma always used to give big parties for us children with a lot of cakes and chocolate. Then I recalled the young Prince Leuchtenberg, with whom we had played together, or Anna Vyrubova, my mother's friend, who had always taken part in all our activities. Once Mrs Rathlef told me that my father's brother, the Grand-Duke Michael Alexandrovich, had also perished in the Revolution. I learnt afterwards that Uncle Misha's widow, the Countess Brassova, was still alive; I was one day to find her on the side of my enemies. Then we came to talk of my other relatives who were still living, specially my mother's sister, Aunt Irene, and my uncle the Grand-Duke Ernest Louis of Hesse. This evidently gave Mrs Rathlef the idea of taking a new step towards getting me acknowledged.

Although the meeting with Aunt Irene had turned out so unsuccessfully, she suggested trying to get Uncle Ernie in Darmstadt to take an interest in me. As she made the suggestion quite openly, and did not act on the sly like Grünberg, I agreed at once, in fact I felt a passionate longing for my uncle to come to Berlin so that this troublesome question should finally be solved. I was utterly convinced that he would recognise me, for as I have already related he and his sons had been with us in Russia in earlier times. I also recalled that in the winter of 1916 he had travelled to Petersburg for secret peace negotiations, indicating a specially intimate relationship with my parents.

So Mrs Rathlef wrote the Grand-Duke a letter, telling him whom she had in her care and asking him on my behalf to come to Berlin and meet me face to face. Because of my state of health she did not then tell me that the answer sounded very unhelpful. However, she refused to be discouraged, and soon afterwards sent Miss Amy Smith to Darmstadt, as she could not get away herself, having to look after me. I waited anxiously for the result, counting the days like a child. I could think and talk of nothing else. If I had guessed the barriers that Miss Smith came up against at Darmstadt, I doubt if I should have ever survived this period.

* * *

From this period in St Mary's Hospital Mrs Rathlef has recorded many significant details:

'Anastasia was in an environment strange to her and among strange people; as I was her constant companion, she fairly soon came to feel confidence in me. After that she became more and more attached to me, waiting impatiently every morning for me to come and showing great reluctance to let me go home in the evening. Nevertheless, it was extremely hard to get her to talk about herself. Her bitter experiences among the emigrés had built up in her so strong a suspicion against the world in general that even with me she could only gradually free herself from it. She evaded all direct questions; anything like this seemed to terrify her. . . . Quite apart from all the suffering she had undergone during her captivity and escape, she was now being both courted and exploited by people completely alien to her, quite indifferent to her fate, and concerned merely—it was obvious—to serve their own selfish interests. Even if there were good and noble souls among them, she could no longer distinguish the good from the evil. She saw enemies in everybody, and often failed to understand actions sincerely meant for her good, so that people unselfishly working to help her were sometimes blamed no less than those who were doing the reverse; finally she would retreat into herself as the only way of escaping from an importunate world.

'So it was immensely difficult to surmount this wall of suspicion. Slowly, very slowly, I felt my way into her confidence, chiefly by learning very soon not to torment and burden her with direct questions. One had unobtrusively to get her talking, and then let her continue without confusing her by interrupting with questions. If she were led on to a subject which interested her, she would really begin to talk. This nearly always worked when you guided her on to the years of her childhood. Her whole interest was concentrated on this time, and on the life with her parents, sisters and brother. You could see how the memories would spring to her mind when she spoke of her father, her mother, her sisters and little brother. . . . She was indifferent to all other topics except where they could somehow be linked up with this one main topic.

'When she was talking then, she did so with the simplicity and straightforwardness that was reflected in her whole life. Above all, she never told a lie. All of us who have been concerned with her have this same impression of her utter honesty and frankness. In her whole personality she expressed a distinction, a nobility of mind, which deeply moved all who had anything to do with her. That she mixes things up, is because her memory has been affected; but during the whole year I have been with her, she has never contradicted herself. She is often uncertain in recalling things, like a person with poor eyesight groping for objects he can't recognise properly. But anything her memory does release is absolutely genuine; indeed, one is surprised by the precision of small details. . . . There is another reason as well why it was difficult and required a lot of patience to get her to talk: every time she related her memories in connected form, it brought her to a state of complete collapse. She was overcome by melancholia and driven to thoughts of death. . . . It was no pose when she said it would be better if she could die, because there was nothing at all she could do with her life. How often she has repeated to me such sentiments: "I cannot understand what God wants with me. Why did I have to stay behind alone, why was I not allowed to die with my dear ones?" . . .'

Anastasia was certainly a difficult person to help, but at least it was not her reticence and touchiness that were responsible for the failure of Mrs Rathlef's efforts *vis-à-vis* the Grand-Duke of Hesse; the Grand-Duke showed an obvious lack of goodwill, which—had it been present—might soon have settled Anastasia's problem once and for all.

His first suspicions were natural enough. In the course of the years the Tsar's relatives had been disturbed more than once by false reports of the existence of some survivor of the murder at Ekaterinburg. Olga Nikolaievna was supposed to have turned up in Poland, the names of Tatiana and Anastasia were also given. In 1920 an impostor came forward in Paris claiming to be the Grand-Duchess Anastasia, and in the same year another false Anastasia presented herself in America: both cases were very quickly exposed. After that there were reports all over the place that the Tsar's whole family was still alive and was either with the Dalai Lama in Tibet or far away on some Pacific island; such reports were based on the stories of opportunities for an escape which had in fact never materialised.

Another rumour went round and gained varying degrees of credence, to the effect that Alexi, the heir apparent, had been saved and was the only one still alive. Once he was reported in Poland, and it seemed that he had the same hæmophilia as the real Grand-Duke Alexi; he professed to have lost his memory and to speak no language but German. Another time a false Alexi was seen in Siberia, a boy of fifteen or sixteen. The population gave him a rapturous welcome and organised collections on his behalf. A telegram was sent to Admiral Kolchak, and he had the youth come to Omsk, to be identified by Pierre Gilliard, who—by a strange irony of fate—was staying there at the time. Gilliard asked him some questions in French; the boy claimed that he understood but would only answer the Admiral, not Gilliard; and at length this young pretender was exposed also.

Such things had been going on all the time, and now there was a new Anastasia coming forward years later; who was to say that she too was not an impostor? It was thus excusable for the Grand-Duke to be suspicious, but less so to reject out of hand the new evidence offered him.

Mrs Rathlef had a brainwave. There was a long historical tradition of disputed identities being proved by special physical peculiarities. So to Anastasia's dismay plaster-casts and numerous photographs were taken, showing her identifying marks, and Mrs Rathlef sent a list of these to the Grand-Duke with all the corroborating evidence, confident that this was bound to be accepted:

1. Bunions on the feet, specially marked on the right foot.
2. A radiograph of the head, with skull injuries visible.
3. A small white scar on the shoulder-blade from a cauterised mole.
4. The scar of a laceration or bruise at the root of the middle finger on the left hand: caused by a footman slamming the carriage door too soon.
5. A small indistinct scar on the forehead to the right, caused by a fall as a child, which was why Anastasia used to have her hair cut short and combed over her forehead.
6. A scar behind the right ear, established by the doctors to be a graze from a bullet.

Neither letter nor evidence made any impression at Darmstadt, and a curt reply said it was out of the question that any of the Tsar's daughters should still be alive.

Then Miss Amy Smith tried to approach the Grand-Duke through a family well known at the Darmstadt 'court.' But she was told that he refused to see her, being at his castle at Wolfsgarten—although that is extremely close to Darmstadt: perhaps he was not really informed of Miss Smith's visit. She was received by Count Hardenberg, the marshal of the Grand-Duke's household, to whom she handed over letter and evidence as well as giving her personal impressions. She told him that she had made repeated visits to St Mary's Hospital without ever feeling she was talking either to a lunatic or to someone playing a part. She also suggested that Anastasia's anxiety to see her uncle again hardly pointed to her being an impostor. But again such general statements fell on deaf ears; so Miss Smith came to points of detail.

'Who is Anya Vyrubova?' she asked, explaining that Anastasia had described this lady as an intimate friend of the Tsarina's. Hardenberg did not know her, and immediately telephoned Mrs Zanotti, a former lady-in-waiting at the Russian court now living at Darmstadt, who also denied all knowledge. Only the Grand-Duke knew what it was all about, and he noted on Mrs Rathlef's report that 'the name Vyrubova is familiar, but she was never a close friend of the Tsarina's. The Christian name is wrong; it ought to be Anna.'

A similar quibble was used over the name of the little prince that Anastasia remembered having played with. Mrs Rathlef, perhaps mishearing her, had called him Lichtenberg instead of Leuchtenberg, so the Grand-Duke wrote that the Tsar's children had never played with any such prince. He also flatly denied the giving of birthday parties by the Dowager Empress, and that the Tsar's children had ever called Princess Irene 'Aunt Nini.' Hardenberg, who evidently knew better, could not confirm these denials; but when shown photographs by Miss Smith, he was able to revert to his master's line. 'The queer and complicated thing is,' he said, 'that one finds Mrs Tchaikovski looks like neither the Grand-Duchess Anastasia nor the Grand-Duchess Tatiana, but a mixture of the two.'

Miss Smith: 'And if she is neither the Grand-Duchess Anastasia nor an impostor nor a lunatic, what other possibilities are there?'

Hardenberg: 'Oh well, the possibility that there is some mysterious stranger behind her who is hypnotising her.'

Feeling she was not being taken seriously, Miss Smith turned to another subject, the Grand-Duke's peace-feelers of 1916; at which Hardenberg abruptly dropped his frivolous tone. As Miss Smith describes it, 'he rejected so angrily and emphatically something Mrs Tchaikovski had said about the Grand-Duke that I guessed at once I had unwittingly touched on a sore point. My repeated requests and suggestions that the Grand-Duke should come to Berlin incognito to settle the case were always met with unshakable resistance. Count Hardenberg told me the Grand-Duke could not possibly travel to Berlin on this affair, because there might be press comment on it. I felt I was up against someone quite lacking in the humanity and sense of responsibility which would have made him anxious to clear up this strange and tragic case.'

When Miss Smith returned to Berlin with all her efforts thus frustrated, she found Anastasia once more very ill and in great pain, and tried to break the news gently by saying the Grand-Duke could not come straight away: 'You must just be patient.' But Anastasia understood, her eyes filled with tears. 'Oh, they'll all come when I'm dead,' she groaned, and turned her face away.

Hardenberg had suggested that Anastasia was under hypnotic influence. In fact, this suggestion is quite untenable in view of the thorough tests to which Anastasia was subjected by various doctors, all with negative results, to see whether she could be hypnotised. In 1927 her friends asked Dr E. Osty, a Paris specialist, to visit Castle Seeon in Bavaria (where she was then living), so that he might try to hypnotise her and so establish her real identity, as well as perhaps restoring her knowledge of Russian, English and French and full memory of her childhood. On 5th July, 1927, Dr Osty reported thus:

'. . . Two attempts to hypnotise her were made (on 30th June), one at 11 a.m., the other at 5 p.m., both in the presence of the Duke of Leuchtenberg and Monsieur Emanuel de Toytot. My attempts were no less persistent than they would have been with any reasonably co-operative person who offered involuntary mental resistance. The result was so completely negative that after these two attempts I considered it futile to continue, concluding that Mrs Tchaikovski was unhypnotisable.

'It can be stated objectively that:

1. Mrs Tchaikovski co-operated fully with my attempts to hypnotise her.
2. These attempts were abandoned solely on my own decision.
3. The result was a complete failure, because Mrs Tchaikovski is not capable of being hypnotised, or at any rate not by me.'

Dr Nobel of the Mommsen Nursing Home in Berlin gave a similar verdict in his report at the end of March 1926:

'To recapitulate, I should like to state that in my opinion no mental alienation of any kind is present. I at least, during a long period of observation (eight months), have never noticed any trace of insanity in the patient, nor any kind of auto-suggestion or outside suggestion by persons unknown. Although her memory has suffered, perhaps owing to the evident head injury, and although she is subject to moods of melancholia, these have, in my opinion, nothing pathological about them. One can scarcely decide how far the loss of memory is connected with the head injury, since no clear picture can be formed so much later as to the injury's seriousness. The form of amnesia is extraordinary and comes under no known category, since it applies equally to the whole of the past, except for the most recent times, where the memory is normal. It is hard to decide, of course, what part is played in this by the patient's will-power, but clearly she remembers better on some days than on others, both when questions are put to her, and when she is talking spontaneously.

'Now a few remarks on the patient's identification. There can naturally be no question of proof on my part, but I find it impossible

TSARINA MARIA FEODOROVNA
(Anastasia's grandmother)

TSARINA ALEXANDRA FEODOROVNA
(Anastasia's mother) soon after her marriage

TSAR NICHOLAS II

THE TSAR'S FAMILY on a visit to England 1909: *seated l. to r.*, Princess Mary (later Queen Mary), Tsar Nicholas II, King Edward VII, the Tsarina Alexandra, the Prince of Wales (later King George V), the Grand-Duchess Maria; *standing l. to r.*, Prince Edward (later King Edward VIII and Duke of Windsor), Queen Alexandra, the Princesses Mary and Victoria, and the Grand-Duchesses Olga and Tatiana; *seated on the ground*, the Tsarevich and Anastasia

THE RUSSIAN ROYAL FAMILY with the Rumanian royal family 1914: *back row*, Grand-Duchess Maria, King Carol of Rumania, Anastasia, Grand-Duchess Tatiana, Prince Carol, Crown Prince Ferdinand, the Queen of Rumania ('Carmen Sylva'), the Tsar and, sitting near him, the Grand-Duchess Olga; *middle row*, the Tsarina, Princess Ileana and Crown Princess Maria

ANASTASIA
in 1904

THE GRAND-DUCHESSES
Olga, Tatiana,
Maria, and Anastasia

*Below:* ANASTASIA in 1907, in 1908, and in 1914

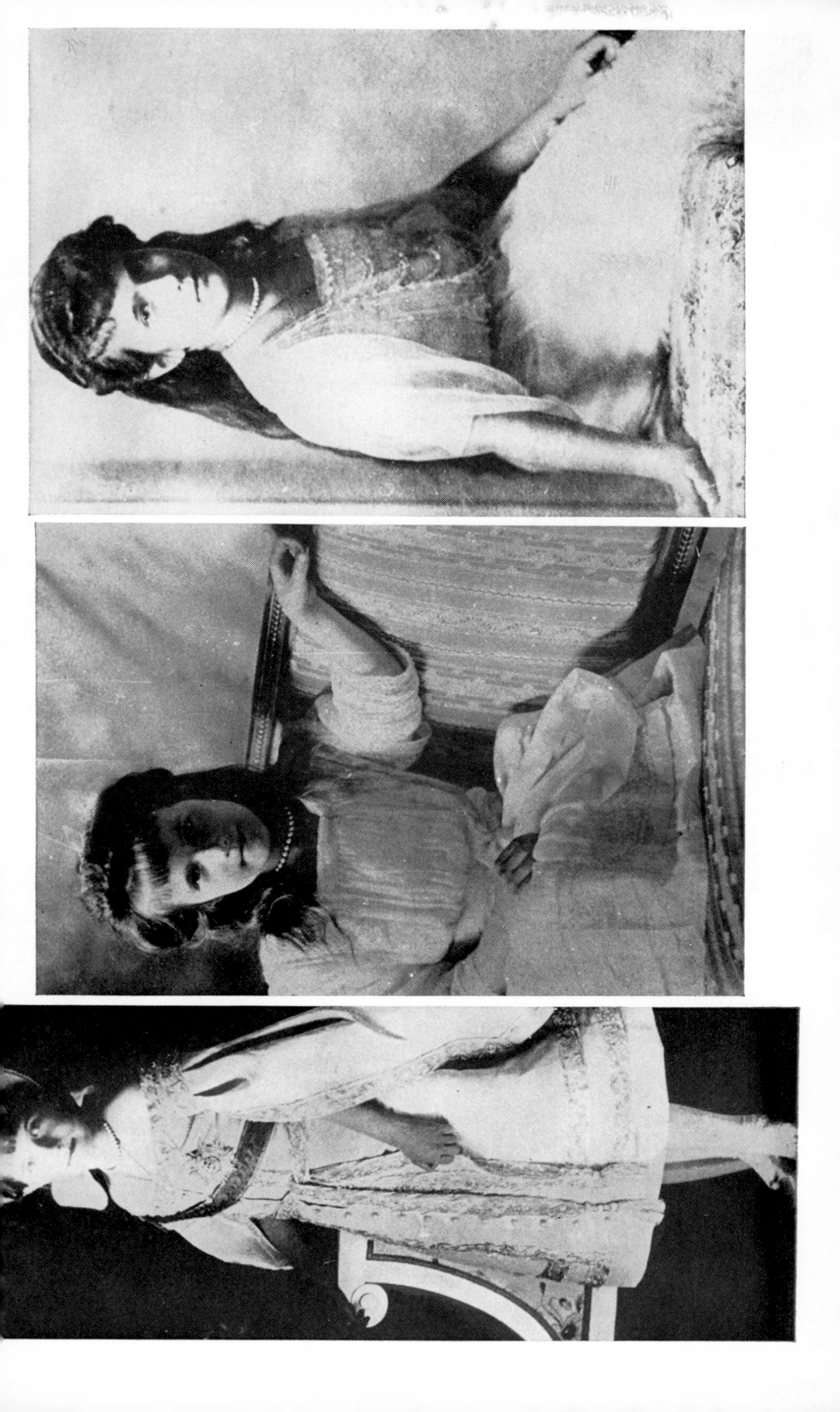

OLGA, THE TSAREVICH, ANASTASIA, TATIANA during the early internment at Tsarskoe Selo

ANASTASIA AND MARIA with Captain Felix Dassel (behind Anastasia) in front of the hospital at Tsarskoe Selo in 1916

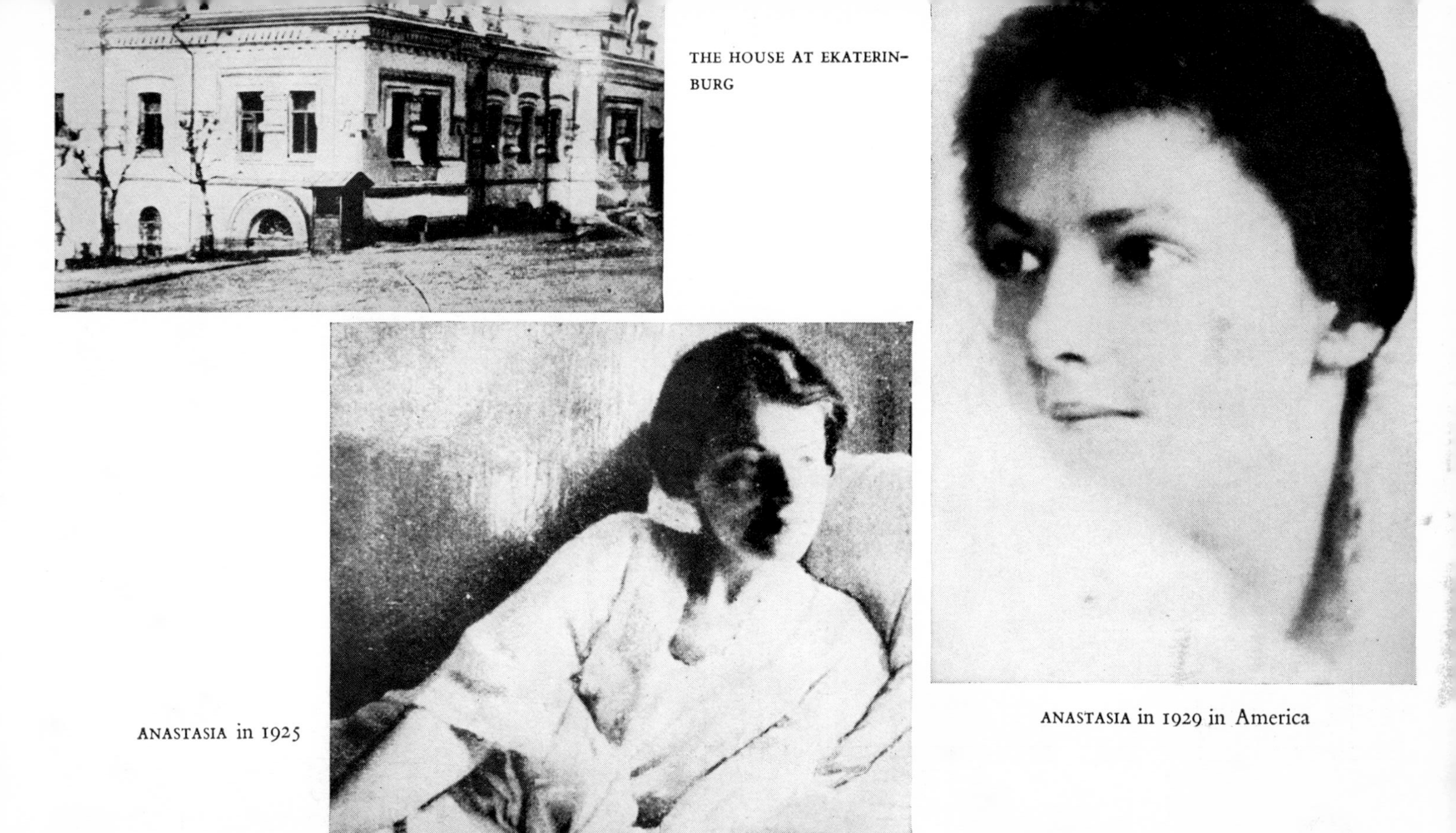

THE HOUSE AT EKATERIN-BURG

ANASTASIA in 1925

ANASTASIA in 1929 in America

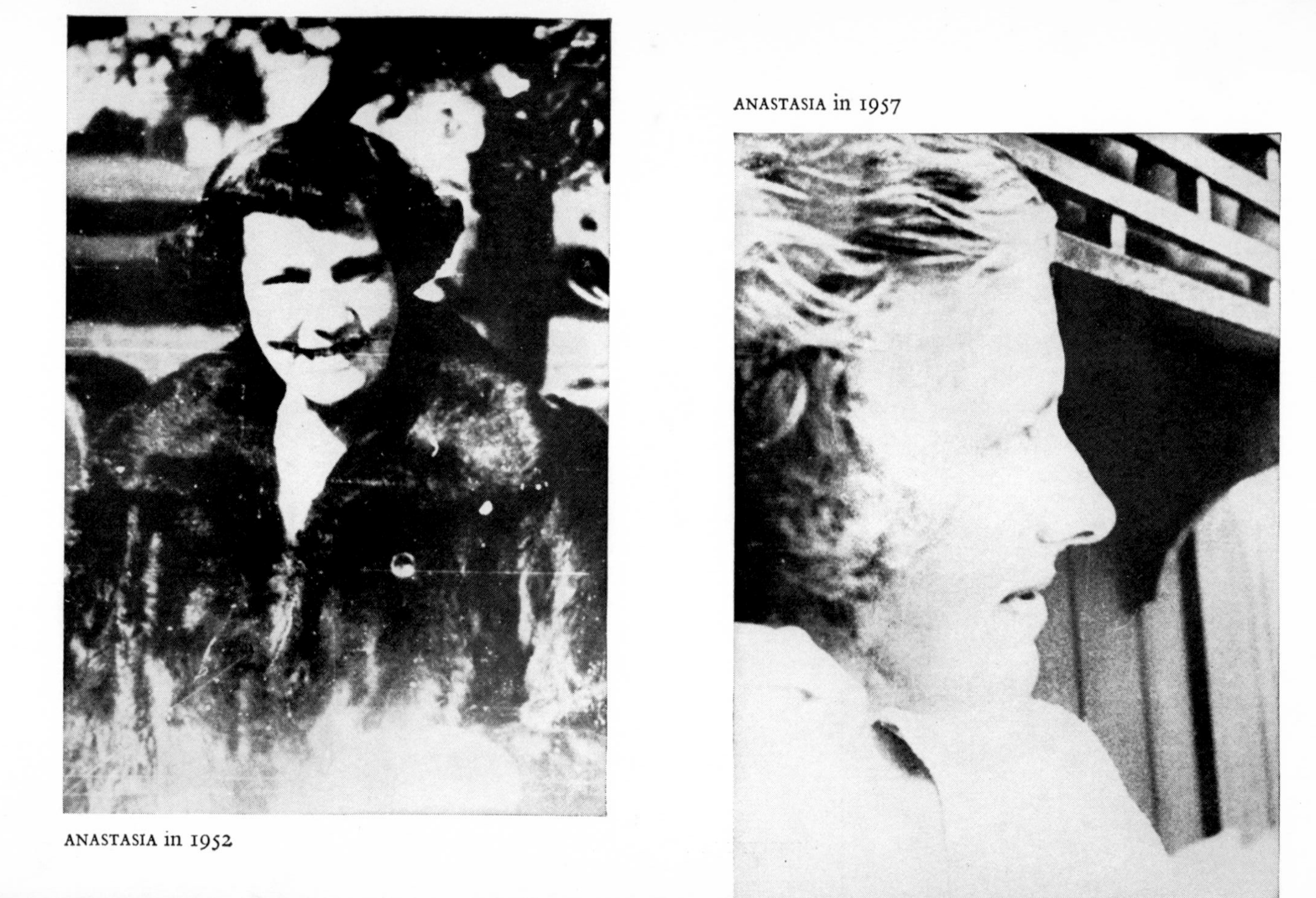

ANASTASIA in 1952

ANASTASIA in 1957

to believe that her memories rest on suggestion and that her knowledge of many small details can be caused by anything but personal experience. Moreover, it is psychologically scarcely conceivable that anybody who for some reason was playing the part of another person should behave like the patient and show so little initiative towards the furtherance of whatever plans she might have.'

Miss Smith had indeed hit on a sore point when referring to the Grand-Duke of Hesse's visit to Russia in 1916. Anastasia had no political motives for mentioning this visit; she merely regarded her knowledge of it as evidence of her identity, for which the Grand-Duke would thus be an important witness—since it had been kept a strict secret. He, on the other hand, and even more Count Hardenberg, seemed to see her as an unwelcome witness in a matter which had much better remain secret. They were perhaps influenced by the repercussions of a similar affair, which had come to light not so long before.

Soon after the end of the war it became known that secret negotiations for a separate peace with France had been initiated by the Empress Zita of Austria through her brother, Prince Sixtus of Bourbon-Palma, who (with the Austrian Emperor's consent) had been serving with a Red Cross Group attached to the Belgian army. This undisputed fact was seized on and discussed so widely in German nationalist papers and those hostile to the monarchy, that in the early 'twenties every German knew about it. The former Austrian Empress was called a traitor, and the principle of the monarchy was doubtless much harmed by the whole business. So if Anastasia were now acknowledged at Darmstadt, the German press might also consider the Grand-Duke's visit to Russia as proven, and Count Hardenberg may have been afraid parallels would be drawn with the Sixtus Affair. As soon as he heard of Anastasia's remark, he evidently decided to take all steps to prevent her being acknowledged.

The Grand-Duke's peace-feelers, of course, were a very different matter, being made at a time when Germany was militarily strong; so that the terms proposed would have probably been advantageous. Beyond a desire to stop further bloodshed, the Grand-Duke was chiefly concerned with the growing revolutionary storm in Russia, which might sweep from their throne his sister and her husband as well as other European sovereigns. The German Emperor may have been kept informed about the correspondence, but did not know about the Grand-Duke's journey to St Petersburg, if the evidence given to Gleb Botkin (son of the Tsar's personal physician) is to be believed. Botkin was living in America after the war, and in 1927, at the invitation of the North American Newspaper Alliance, he visited Germany, going to Seeon Castle in Bavaria, the Duke of Leuchtenberg's home, in order to identify Anastasia there. Botkin heard this account of the disputed journey from the Duke, and the Duke had it from Prince Rupert of Bavaria, nephew of Prince Leopold of Bavaria, who had been German Commander-in-Chief, Eastern Command.

The Grand-Duke of Hesse really went to Russia trying to make a separate peace for Hesse, Saxony and perhaps also Bavaria (Botkin cannot remember); so it was quite possible Anastasia should have seen him during the war. Prince Rupert never said anything about the journey in public, however: it might have harmed the monarchist aspirations he still cherished, and it would have been considered treasonable under the Weimar Republic, as also under the Emperor William, assuming the latter did not know about it.

Botkin also heard that Prince Rupert had received a letter from General Hoffmann, expressly stating that Anastasia was indeed the Grand-Duchess and was right about the Grand-Duke of Hesse's journey to Russia. Hoffmann, it may be recalled, had concluded the peace of Brest Litovsk with the Bolsheviks; he was chief of staff to Prince Leopold, Rupert's uncle. He also did not wish to publicise the matter, for fear of compromising the former German rulers, but threatened to publish his documents unless a Berlin evening paper stopped the campaign it had opened against Anastasia. A fortnight after this, however, (8th July, 1927) General Hoffmann died.

Even if the German Emperor was ignorant of this particular mission, officially inspired peace-feelers had certainly been put out before, and not only on the Hesse Grand-Duke's initiative. This is proved by an extract from *My Mission to Russia*, the memoirs of Sir George Buchanan, British Ambassador in St Petersburg (published in 1923):

'While the Emperor's internal policy, inspired as it was for the most part by the Empress and those in her immediate entourage, cannot be defended, the two following stories, told me by Sazonov (the foreign minister), will show how irreproachable was his attitude towards Germany.

'Early in December (1915) Count Fredericks, who had for years past been Minister of the Imperial Court, received a letter from his former friend, Count Eulenburg (the Grand Marshal of the Court at Berlin), suggesting that they ought both to direct their efforts to putting an end to the existing deplorable misunderstanding between their Sovereigns, and to bringing about a *rapprochement* that would enable their governments to negotiate peace on honourable terms. The Emperor, on being told of this letter, commanded Count Fredericks to read it to him, and the latter proceeded to do so in the original German. His Majesty at once stopped him, saying, "Read it in Russian. I do not understand German." When the Count had finished, the Emperor took the letter and underlining a passage in which Count Eulenburg had spoken of "their old friendship," wrote in the margin, "that friendship is dead and buried." He then sent for Sazonov, and told him to prepare a draft reply. When, on the following day, Sazonov brought him a draft in which Count Eulenburg was told that if the Emperor William wanted peace, he must address a similar proposal to all the Allies, His Majesty said that on reflection he had decided that the letter should be left unanswered, as any reply, however repellent, might be taken as evidence of his desire to enter into negotiations.

'A few weeks later further overtures were addressed to His Majesty through another channel. A Miss Vassilchikov, belonging to an old Russian family, had, when war broke out, been living in her villa on the Semmering, where she had remained ever since. She had recently gone to Darmstadt, on the invitation of the Grand-Duke of Hesse, and had been sent by him to Petrograd charged with the mission of inducing the Emperor to conclude peace. She was empowered to say that the Emperor William was prepared to grant Russia most advantageous terms; that England had already made overtures to Germany for a separate peace; and that a reconciliation between Russia and Germany was necessary for dynastic reasons. The Grand-Duke gave her a written statement in the above sense for her to give to Sazonov, as well as two open letters for the Emperor and Empress. On arrival at Petrograd she at once went to the Ministry and handed the Grand-Duke's statement and letters to Sazonov. The latter told her that she had acted disgracefully in undertaking such a mission, and the Emperor, to whom he made a report on the subject, was so angry that he gave orders to have her interned in a convent.'

The Tsarina's attitude to peace overtures is shown in two letters to her husband from Tsarskoe Selo, which also confirm that she was in correspondence with her brother, the Grand-Duke of Hesse, much earlier in the war. The first (9th March, 1915), referring to Miss Vassilchikov, says: '. . . I enclose a letter from Masha (from Austria), who has been asked to send it to you on matters of peace. Of course I never answer her letters now . . .' The second is dated 17th April, 1915:

'. . . I had a long letter from Ernie, I will show it you on your return. He says, if there is anyone who understands you and knows what you are going through, he is the man. He embraces you tenderly. He is longing for a way out of this dilemma, someone must start to build a bridge towards discussions.

'He has therefore had the idea of sending a delegate quite privately to Stockholm, to meet a man you also send (privately), so as to work towards the removal of many present difficulties. He had this idea because no real hatred for Russia exists in Germany. So he is sending someone who should be there on the 28th (that is two days ago, and I have only just heard of it), and he could only spare the man for a week. So I wrote an answer at once and sent it to his delegate, saying you were not back yet, and he had better not wait, and that although one was longing for peace, the time was not yet ripe for it.

'I wanted everything to be settled before your return, for I know you will find it unpleasant.

'W., of course, (the Emperor William) knows absolutely nothing of this.

'He (Ernie) says their position in France was like a mighty wall, and as his friends told him, in the North and the Carpathians, too. They believe they have 500,000 prisoners of ours.

'The whole letter is very nice and affectionate—I was extremely thankful to get it, although the business about the man waiting was complicated with your absence. E., too, will be disappointed . . .'

By the end of 1916 the Tsarina's desire for peace, particularly natural in a former German princess, was increased by seeing Russian armies in retreat and the German successes of the time. But although she set herself to improve the lot of German prisoners-of-war, she presumably felt obliged to reject the Grand-Duke's peace overtures; while the Tsar was doubtless too closely watched by the British and French ambassadors to have given active encouragement to such an approach. Yet as the Grand-Duke's visit never came to anything in the end, it is a little strange that ten years later he should have been worried about the publicity it might receive from the case of the disputed Grand-Duchess Anastasia. Moreover, the campaign he launched against her, so as to deny the visit's occurrence, showed such a sense of insecurity and was contradicted by so much outside evidence, that it cast considerable doubt on his reliability in other matters as well.

A year after Amy Smith's unsuccessful visit to Darmstadt, Mrs Rathlef wrote an article on Anastasia, which was published by a Berlin evening paper. She did not mention the Grand-Duke's journey to Russia, having been informed from Darmstadt that the whole business would be extremely embarrassing. But Hardenberg no doubt feared it would come out if Anastasia's identity were proved, and accordingly the so-called 'Darmstadt statement' was given to the press in March 1927, according to which Mrs Tchaikovski was a woman very susceptible to the influence of what she read and of public opinion, who had fallen victim to a *canard* of Anglo-French newspapers. Otherwise she could not have had the fantastic idea that she had seen the Grand-Duke of Hesse in the middle of the World War. Of course he could never have gone there, being a general on the Western Front. It would soon be realised what 'secret powers' were behind Mrs Tchaikovski, and what their nefarious aims were.

Mrs Rathlef replied in the same newspaper, pointing out the absurdity of the suggestion that Anastasia was in league with the Bolsheviks, when they had killed her whole family, had almost killed her, and had left her with an obsessive fear that they were pursuing her. It was equally stupid to pretend that a Grand-Duke trying to start peace negotiations, probably with a special mission, could not have found ways and means of travelling to Russia incognito, despite the war, by way of a neutral country like Sweden. Again, if Anastasia was supposed to have read about the peace-journey from the Anglo-French press, why were the papers in question not named and the appropriate issues given?

The storm over this particular question died down at the time, but in recent years several people have provided further evidence for the existence of the Grand-Duke's journey. One is Baroness Osten-Sacken, who in 1953 made a declaration on oath as to what she had heard from her cousin, Baron Buxhoeveden (the Tsar's master of ceremonies in the winter of 1916-17 when the Grand-Duke's journey took place). Other witnesses are the Crown Princess Cecilie, Count Dimitri Kotzebue (former counsellor to the Tsarist Legation in Oslo), Dr Karl Wagner, a professor at Heidelberg University, and Lahr Larski, former colonel in a Russian guards regiment who, on 19th April, 1949, wrote as follows to Prince Frederick Ernest of Saxe-Altenburg:

'. . . I was seriously wounded as early as January 1915, and consequently spent all 1915 and 1916 in a nursing home in Finland. One evening I met Colonel Mordvinov there, a high officer of the Tsar's. He was escorting a travelling "foreign nobleman" in transit, whom I at once recognised as the Grand-Duke Ernest Louis of Hesse-Darmstadt. The Empress' brother was familiar to me, because in 1905 or 1906 I and Bariatinsky happened to accompany Tatishchev, the adjutant-general attached to the German court, as improvised "deputation" bringing the Grand-Duke the tragic details of his only daughter's sudden death at Spala.

'When Mordvinov saw I had recognised the Grand-Duke, he asked me to make no sign of this and to keep quiet about it. He told me the Empress' brother was travelling incognito, under the name of a Prince Thurn-and-Taxis.

'I can add that so far as I recall there is a full statement by Mordvinov in the file which Baron Taube (professor of international law) handed over to the Grand-Duke of Hesse, at the request of the Grand-Duke Alexander, for safe-keeping in the Grand-Ducal archives at Darmstadt.'

Princess Cecilie declared on oath at Stuttgart on 2nd October, 1953:

'. . . I am aware that the younger generation at Hesse adopts the same intransigent attitude to the identity question as did the late Grand-Duke. I am told that this probably dates back to a statement made by Mrs Anastasia Tchaikovski in the middle—or perhaps even the beginning—of the 'twenties, anyhow very soon after she started telling who she was: the statement that her uncle, the Grand-Duke of Hesse, visited her parents in Russia in 1916. If the view is still held today that such a visit never took place, I can assert from personal knowledge—the source is my late father-in-law—that our circles knew about it even at the time. So in my opinion, by making such a statement (which I only heard of much later), Mrs A. T. was giving strong evidence that at least she had intimate knowledge of high politics and the most secret dealings of the Imperial family.'

The Grand-Duke of Hesse died in 1937, and a few weeks later almost all his immediate family were killed in a plane crash; the only survivor was his second son Prince Louis, who out of filial devotion is quite sure that the journey to Russia was never made—because his father never told him about it. But at the time of the journey Prince Louis was only seven.

Declaration by Baroness Pilchau, at Hamburg on 20th January, 1957:

'My brother, Count Dimitri Kotzebue-Pilar, knew the late Grand-Duke Ernest Louis of Hesse-Darmstadt well. In 1916 my brother was in Oslo as counsellor to the Imperial Russian legation there. The Grand-Duke sent an adjutant to my brother at Oslo, asking for assistance in travelling to Russia via Haparanda. The Grand-Duke's journey thus took place with my brother's help, and as he told me himself the above facts about the journey, I was surprised to learn from the press that the late Grand-Duke apparently denied with great persistence that he ever made such a journey.'

Statement by Professor Wagner at Heidelberg in April 1957:

'In 1916 I was visiting a former school-friend called Alexander Borodin at Tsarskoe Selo, when the Grand-Duke of Hesse-Darmstadt was there. All sorts of things were suspected about this secret mission. I am ready to repeat this statement on oath.'

Disappointed in her original hopes of the Hesse branch of the family, Mrs Rathlef soon received new impetus from the part living in Denmark; Copenhagen, indeed, had to some extent become the centre of the exiled Russian nobility, owing to their relationship with the Danish royal family. They also were accordingly much concerned about the rumours of Anastasia turning up in Germany, and Prince Valdemar of Denmark, brother of the Russian Empress Dowager (Anastasia's grandmother), sent a letter to Herluf Zahle, the Danish Ambassador in Berlin, asking him to investigate these rumours. He sent it by Alexis Volkov, formerly the Tsarina's groom-of-the-chamber, who was now sixty-six, and had gone through trials almost as hard as had his murdered mistress.

He had been with her on the day of the Revolution at Tsarskoe Selo, and accompanied the family on the bitter road to Tobolsk and Ekaterinburg. There he was parted from the Tsarina and thrown into prison with most of the rest of the Imperial suite. They were taken to Perm, lest they should fall into the hands of the advancing White Russian armies; and at Perm Volkov heard of the murder in the Ipatiev House. But the newspapers referred only to the Tsar's execution, saying nothing about what had happened to the rest of the family. Volkov was to have been shot on the 21st August, 1918, together with Countess Hendrikova and the companion Miss Schneider. There were eleven prisoners in all, escorted by twenty-two Red Guard, led by a marine; there were no Russians among the guard here either. The execution party set off in the middle of the night, travelling on and on over the arid steppe, till just before dawn they reached a wood. A terse order: 'Halt!—and Volkov, thinking 'now or never,' leapt across the ditch and dashed into the wood. Three bullets whistled behind him, the first dangerously close, but the last so far away that he knew he was safe. A volley of shots told him the fate of his fellow-prisoners, which he had escaped. After wandering for months, he at length reached Vladivostok, but could not leave the Far East and return to Europe until 1922. He was now in Copenhagen with the relatives of the former Empress Dowager.

Three years later, on 3rd July, 1925, the grey-haired old man met his mistress' youngest daughter, the Grand-Duchess Anastasia, at St Mary's Hospital, Berlin. Nothing had been said to her about this visit either. Volkov came with Herluf Zahle, and they first visited Berg, the hospital chaplain, who was specially concerned with the welfare of the Russian refugee patients. Anastasia was sitting in the garden with Mrs Rathlef. So as not to give her a shock, and to allow Volkov the chance of forming his own judgment, he was taken to the office window, from which Anastasia could be seen unobserved. When she passed it on her way back into the building, he remarked to a friend of Mrs Rathlef's that Mrs Tchaikovski had a resemblance to the Grand-Duchess, but he had been told she did not speak Russian, and he was surprised at this if she really was the Grand-Duchess.

Berg informed Volkov that this phenomenon was quite common with war-wounded soldiers, and that although recovery was bound to be very slow, Mrs Tchaikovski had recently shown a marked improvement, understanding certain Russian expressions and pronouncing others quite correctly; she also remembered some English words. 'And how does she come to speak such good German?' asked Volkov in surprise; to which Berg replied that in the last five years she had been among Germans all the while and had therefore been obliged to learn the language. Even so, he said, her pronunciation and sentence construction were not correct German, but betrayed the foreigner. Volkov seemed satisfied with these explanations.

Following this conversation, the meeting between Anastasia and her mother's former groom-of-the-chamber took place in Berg's study. When he saw her at close quarters, Volkov was disappointed, saying: 'The Grand-Duchess was much fuller in the face, she looked much healthier. The expression on her face now doesn't remind me of the Grand-Duchess.' He was also upset that she did not speak to him, but only talked (in German) to Berg, Zahle and Mrs Rathlef, so that his rôle was more or less confined to that of mute observer. It is strange he should not have realised after his own grave experiences that a woman's face would look different, that she would seem different altogether, when she had been seriously wounded and then had seven years of the deepest suffering and exhausting illness. The only thing that impressed him was the friendly gesture with which she invited him to sit down, a regal gesture such as he had witnessed so often at court. The patient also offered him her hand very cordially when he left, and he reverted to his first impression, declaring: 'I cannot say with certainty that Mrs Tchaikovski is *not* the Grand-Duchess.'

* * *

On days when I felt better, I could sit in the hospital garden and also walk about a bit. Usually Harriet Rathlef sat with me, and sometimes Mr Berg joined me. Then I would go back to my room. Once Berg brought along two gentlemen, one of whom was to play an important part in my life—someone I shall always be grateful to, even though he afterwards had to withdraw from me somewhat. He was Herluf Zahle, the Danish ambassador in

Berlin, a very tall good-looking man, who had been sent to me by Prince Valdemar, my grandmother's brother. The other man's name I only heard after his visit: he was Alexis Volkov, my mother's groom-in-the-chamber. As I also heard afterwards, he was intended to recognise me and report to my relations in Copenhagen his impressions of our meeting.

The meeting did not go as planned; but here I am thinking less of Volkov than of myself. The first time I saw the old man, I kept on wondering where I could have seen him before. But however hard I looked at him and however much I racked my brains, I could not remember, it completely escaped me. Once I thought I had a clue, but then it disappeared again. It's really awful how full of gaps my memory is.

Afterwards I was lying in bed, exhausted by the visit, and Mrs Rathlef was sitting near me, when I suddenly remembered. It came to me dimly, almost like in a cloud, a face I had seen a long time ago. I believed this man had some special post with my father. Mrs Rathlef then told me who the visitor was and where he had come from. She also told me he had been surprised that I talked only German and not Russian.

Two days later Mr Zahle again brought Volkov to see me. Now I knew who he was, I may have felt some reserve because of my relatives in Denmark, anyhow the conversation with him would not flow properly at first. But then Zahle intervened. He had brought some photographs of my family, which he proceeded to show me. When I saw them, I felt myself right back in the time of my happy childhood. Mama was on one of them, and I had to kiss the picture for joy at seeing her again. On another I immediately recognised Uncle Ernie, my aunt and their sons. How quickly I should get well again, I thought, if I were acknowledged by my relatives and surrounded with the same loving care as I used to be.

Soon after this I could not help losing my temper. I heard Volkov again expressing doubts to Mrs Rathlef about my not speaking Russian. I was offended that this man, who after all had only been one of Mama's servants, should allow himself such suspicions, and I told Mrs Rathlef not to give him any more explanations or try to convince him about me. But she calmed me down, whereupon Volkov asked me some questions about other servants whose work had brought them in touch with us children. I knew at once who he meant, and he was specially moved when I at once named the tall sailor Nagorny who had looked after my ailing brother Alexi like a children's nurse. He had last seen Nagorny in Siberia. Now there was a better contact between us, and we also parted very cordially.

The next day Volkov came to see me once more, this time only with Mrs Rathlef, because Zahle had had to go to Copenhagen. I felt rather exhausted. The conversations we had had in the last few days had awakened so many memories that I had become very agitated. Still, I wanted to oblige Volkov by seeing him, and went into the waiting-room at the arranged time, but had to lie on the sofa; Volkov sat down opposite me. First he asked me if I knew who Tatishchev was, and I told him Tatishchev had been my father's adjutant-general, who had afterwards accompanied him to Siberia. 'Right,' said Volkov, and proceeded to show me a picture of Grandmama. I looked at it for a long time, but felt surprised she was not wearing black as she always used to. I of course enquired after her health; she was nearly eighty. Then I asked Volkov to break the news gently to her when telling her my story; for the shock might be fatal. While I was still thinking of my grandmother, I suddenly remembered another sailor who had been with my brother besides Nagorny, he was called Derevenko. But I found it very hard to pronounce the name, the doctors once told me this was connected with the injuries to my brain. On the other hand I remembered clearly that this Derevenko had sons who had played with my brother. After a while I also recalled that there was a second man with the same name, the Dr Derevenko who had been my brother's special doctor. All this Volkov confirmed.

He then asked me if I remembered the Grand-Duchess Olga Alexandrovna. Of course I remembered her. We were always particularly fond of Papa's youngest sister, she was very close to Mama also. After this he wanted to know where I had kept my jewellery in the last period of my captivity, whereupon I told him how we had distributed them all over our dresses and underwear, sewing them into the hems. But now I was tired of being examined, and wanted to see if he too would pass a test. As he did not know German, I asked Mrs Rathlef to translate my questions into Russian for him. I asked if he remembered the room in our summer-house 'Alexandria,' where Mama, when we arrived each year, would take her diamond ring and scratch on the window-pane which year it was together with her and Papa's initials. Volkov remembered this clearly, and we both had to smile. Then he again asked *me* a question, whether I remembered St John's Convent. I told him that the convent was in Siberia and that was where the nuns had always come from to sing with Mama and us girls. Volkov was quite shattered at my knowing this.

As these memories and the conversation in two languages had been a great strain for me, and given me a headache, we parted. The tears were pouring down Volkov's cheeks, and he kissed my hand several times. When saying good-bye to me, he said, weeping: 'Everything will come all right.' Then he slowly left the room, turning back once more at the doorway.

When I was alone again and thought of him, I said to myself: Volkov is someone I should get to come and live with me. Then I should at least have a loyal person I could talk to about the past. On the other hand he was old and wouldn't want to spoil things with my relations, who were providing for the evening of his life. When Mrs Rathlef went out of the hospital with him, he said to her (as she afterwards repeated to me): 'Please try to put yourself in my place. If I now state that it *is* her, and then others say the opposite—how should I look!' If he had stood up for me more firmly, it would have helped me far more with my relatives than did the vague statements he made. Later, when he was told in Copenhagen that Baroness Buxhoeveden and Monsieur Gilliard had refused to acknowledge my identity, and informed that after this he could hardly dare assert that I was Anastasia, he became unsure of himself. Yet on his deathbed, so I am assured, Volkov said he could not die without declaring that he did really recognise me. I shall always remember him kindly for this despite everything.

* * *

Volkov's visits had an unfortunate effect on Anastasia. It was not the first time she had relapsed into a state of extreme weakness after the tragic past had been conjured up, and when this was aggravated by acute physical pain, she allowed full rein to her passionate temperament. At such times she could behave intolerably to her best friends.

On this occasion her whole condition was worsened by the tuberculous arm, which once more kept her constantly in bed. The swelling increased, her temperature went up to between 102 and 104, and she had terrible pain. After ten days the arm was swollen to a shapeless mass, and the doctors decided on an operation, opening it up very thoroughly to let the pus flow off. Anastasia was under anæsthetic over half an hour, but stirred in the middle, weeping, demanding her mother (as she had done before when in bed), and moaning that they had taken her away from her family. Such delirium is, of course, common enough with patients under anæsthetic, but the unusual phenomenon here was that she called for her mother *in English*, a language she had forgotten when fully conscious; it emerged from her subconscious mind while under the anæsthetic. This happened on another occasion, when she was in the Mommsen Nursing Home.

The operation did not fulfil the doctor's hopes. On the contrary, the patient's temperature went up to over 105, she lost weight, and continued to be in great pain, so that she had to be given morphia and other pain-killers. Mr Rudnev was called in, a well-known surgeon who happened to be in Berlin at the time; he was consulted over Anastasia's case by a Miss G. Spindler, another Russian, the lady who had made enquiries about Anastasia in Rumania: both she and Rudnev had formerly lived in Moscow. Rudnev recommended a further operation, and afterwards the patient had to be taken to a different hospital, better equipped for treating so difficult a case.

But Anastasia was not only in acute physical pain, her mental anxieties were so great that they came out in her delirium. She remembered that Zahle had gone to Copenhagen, and could hardly wait for his return. Copenhagen was now the centre of her feverish fantasies, she dreamed only of soon going to see her dear grandmother once more. At last the Ambassador was standing by her bed. She recognised him through the mist of fever, overcome with joy to see the 'Tall Man' again, as she jokingly called him. But then he at once faded to a vague figure, and the future grew dark: almost as if she guessed how her hopes from Copenhagen would fade as well. Yet she always retained her confidence in Zahle, recognising him from their first meeting as a man of integrity and goodwill.

A family council had evidently been held with Zahle at Copenhagen, for even before he returned to Berlin, Gilliard and his wife (*née* Tegleva) had gone to the Danish Embassy there, on receipt of an urgent letter from the Grand-Duchess Olga in Copenhagen. Mme

Gilliard was the former governess at Tsarskoe Selo; Anastasia had been looked after by her from birth, and called her Shura. The Grand-Duchess Olga wrote to her in these terms:

'Please go at once to Berlin with M. Gilliard to see the poor lady. Suppose she really *were* the Little Girl! Heaven alone knows if she is or not. It would be such a disgrace if she were living all alone in her misery, and if all that is true. . . . I implore you again to go as soon as possible; you can tell us what there is in the story better than anyone else in the world. The extraordinary thing is, she says that one of her aunts, she can't remember which, used to call her Shvipsik! May God grant you his aid! I embrace you with all my heart.

'PS. If it really is her, please send me a wire, and I will come to Berlin to meet you.'

On 27th July, the Gilliards arrived from Switzerland in Berlin. On the following afternoon they were briefly informed of the situation by Zahle, who had just returned from Denmark, and then driven straight to St Mary's Hospital. So as not to allow even the suspicion of previous influence, Zahle requested Mrs Rathlef not to ask Gilliard for his name in the first instance; he only told it her after the encounter. She showed him and his wife into the patient's room.

* * *

A few weeks after Volkov had been with me, I was visited by a lady and gentleman I did not know. Mrs Rathlef had brought them into my room. It was towards evening, and I was lying in bed. I still had a high temperature, and a few days before this the second operation had been performed on my elbow. Although the visit was anything but welcome, I shook hands with them, not having the slightest idea why they had come to see me. Frankly, I did not even care why, being much too apathetic and weak to bother about such things; nor did I ask Mrs Rathlef their names.

They both sat down by my bed, and I saw they were scrutinising me very intently. After a while the man began to address me in German, but he spoke it with a foreign accent. He asked rather mockingly whether I still ate as much chocolate as I used to. Was he trying to make fun of me because when I went past sweet-shops I often looked wistfully at the chocolates in the window, having no money to buy anything? I muttered something and then leaned back on the pillows again. Then he asked me another question, and I did not answer at all. Then they both left, I think, but soon afterwards Mrs Rathlef returned with the lady. They did something to my bed, as if they were going to move me to another bed, I remained completely passive.

It was not till after their second visit that Mrs Rathlef confessed to me—she herself had not known at first—that they were Monsieur Gilliard and Shura (I shall speak later of the way I learnt that they were married). Shura, who had known me from my childhood, wanted to recognise me by my feet, and told Mrs Rathlef: 'The feet look like the Grand-Duchess's. The bunion on the right foot is worse than that on the left.' Then they went away again. Neither of the Gilliards had been able to do much with me. Was that surprising in view of my condition?

On the following morning they returned once more, but it was the same as on the previous day. Gilliard again asked me some questions, but I felt much too weak to answer them, especially as I was still annoyed with him for the stupid question about the chocolates the day before.

He probably recognised the futility of his efforts, for I now saw them making signs to each other with their eyes. Anyhow, Gilliard suddenly pointed to his wife and asked me whether I did not recognise this lady, to which I replied in the negative. According to what he later asserted in his book, I answered after some hesitation that she was my father's youngest sister the Grand-Duchess Olga, having made this guess because of Mr Zahle's return from Copenhagen. This is simply not true, I shall talk later of how I met Aunt Olga. It seems more likely to me that I was continually rambling in delirium about Aunt Olga (as Mrs Rathlef assured me afterwards) and once even called out that she was standing outside the door laughing at me for having come down in the world like this. To calm me, Mrs Rathlef even opened the door so that I could see Aunt Olga was not standing outside.

Altogether Monsieur Gilliard made some extraordinary statements about these two visits. Of my appearance he asserts that I have a long nose with a rather prominent point to it and a big mouth with full fleshy lips, whereas the 'real Anastasia' had a straight nose turned up at the end and a smallish mouth with delicate lips; that the shape of my ears also does not tally with those of the 'real Anastasia,' nor does the expression in my eyes or the sound of my voice. The only identifying mark he has to allow is the pale blue of my eyes, which were always being commented on for their similarity to my father's. On the other hand, he is surprised, as was Volkov, that I did not speak Russian. Although he admits this might have been caused by the rifle blows on my head, he enquires, with the same sarcasm he used on me at our first conversation, whether this 'huge mouth' might also be caused by the rifle blows, which cost me seven teeth, and whether this is why my face has changed so much.

When I read these remarks, I was really disgusted. As, however, his book was not written until four years after our meeting, I can only think that he worked up these statements some time later. There was only one point which startled him at the time, and that is a point of which nobody can know except the people concerned: the nickname 'Shvipsik,' which Aunt Olga used to like calling me by. Aunt Olga, who had learnt about this from Mrs Rathlef through Zahle, mentioned the joke-name in her letter to Shura. Mrs Rathlef once brought me in hospital a bottle of sweet wine, and as I enjoyed it so much, I asked for a second glass. 'Don't drink so much,' said Mrs Rathlef, 'or you'll get tipsy'—in German, 'Sie bekommen einen Schwips.' I had to think for a moment where I had heard the word before; till I suddenly remembered Aunt Olga and the nickname 'Shvipsik' she was so fond of calling me by.

It was at this time that a conversation also took place between Mrs Rathlef and Shura about the injury to my hand. I have already related how as a child I once had the fingers of my left hand crushed, when I was getting into the carriage and the servant slammed the door too early. One finger was so badly injured that it had remained a bit stiff ever since. Well, Mrs Rathlef asked Shura whether she remembered such an accident, to which Shura replied that she couldn't say for certain which of us four girls it had happened to, though she did clearly remember its having happened. When I heard of this later, I was very disappointed, for I had always been specially fond of Shura.

It was the same with another bodily mark. As a child I had a brown mole on my shoulder, which was later cauterised as being a disfigurement. Shura did not remember this either. But quite some time afterwards the matter of the mole was confirmed by

Mr Sablin, a former naval officer who had served on my father's yacht, the *Standart*. He told Mr Rudnev's friend, Miss Spindler, that he had always teased me about it as a child, saying I was 'branded' and could never get lost, I would always be recognised by this brown mark on my shoulder; afterwards he saw that it had been removed.

* * *

Concerning the finger injury of which Mme Gilliard professed not to know, a lady who had formerly lived in Russia wrote the following letter to Mrs Rathlef:

'I was married in Russia, living first in Siberia and then in Petersburg until 1905. My uncle, Admiral Shilling, was chief secretary to the Grand-Duke Alexis Alexandrovich (Alexander III's unmarried brother), and lived in the Grand-Duke's palace on the Moika; my two cousins were ladies-in-waiting to the Empress; and I well remember how often there was talk of the Tsar's children, especially of Anastasia as the most lively and probably the naughtiest.

'One day, however, to everybody's dismay, we heard of the following accident and I do not understand how "Shura," the governess, can fail to remember it, seeing that it has engraved itself on the memory of someone comparatively far removed like myself.

'One of my cousins or my uncle related with great distress how having had a good romp the children were supposed to go out for a drive; but when they were getting into the carriage, the footman slammed the door, crushing Anastasia's finger. Even today when I write this I can still remember how I felt on being told about it. I suppose it was because it upset me so much that I have never forgotten it.

'I often asked afterwards how the hand was getting on, partly because as a doctor's wife I was interested in whether the finger could be saved, and also because I was worried about the poor child who had been so badly hurt. It was a long time before her hand was really better.'

The finger-crushing is also remembered by Dr Karl Wagner (the university professor mentioned above), who writes in his statement of April 1957:

'The accident happened to the Grand-Duchess Anastasia in 1903-4 when I was a schoolboy at Tsarskoe Selo in the Emperor Nicholas Grammar School (1899–1904). Owing to carelessness on the part of a court servant slamming a carriage door, the first joint of the middle finger of her left hand got crushed. Everyone was extremely sorry for her.'

Directly after the Gilliards' visit Anastasia ended her stay at St Mary's Hospital. Mr Rudnev's files contain the following notes:

'. . . On my first visit to St Mary's Hospital, where I was called in for consultation . . . I found the patient in an extreme depressive state. She refused to answer any sort of questions. I traced her complaint to a staphylococcic infection in her left arm, which had aggravated the chronic tuberculosis there. This illness caused a very high temperature, 102–104 degrees, a thorough weakening of the organism, and disturbance of the nervous system.

'To save the patient's life and if possible her arm (since it looked as if we might have to amputate), I decided to operate, and she was accordingly transferred to the Mommsen Nursing Home. . . . While under anæsthetic she was delirious and spoke English. Before the operation I talked Russian to her, and she answered all my questions although in German. For many weeks, both before and after the operation, she could not do without injections of morphia and trivalin. . . .'

* * *

After Gilliard and his wife had gone away again, I left St Mary's Hospital. The evening before, Mr Zahle, Mrs Rathlef and the Gilliards had discussed what should happen to me, since it seemed important that I should go to a better hospital. Mr Rudnev considered a new operation on my arm absolutely necessary, and he put his private patients in the Mommsen Nursing Home, so it was there I was taken.

I can still remember the journey across Berlin by ambulance. As I was in great pain, the least shaking was a torture for me. I felt every cobble-stone, every unevenness in the road surface, and could not stop groaning. Half fainting, I reached the nursing home. But when I was being carried down the corridor and heard some street musicians singing a song outside in the yard, I got new hope. It was a Russian song, the *Volga Boatmen*; it seemed to me a good omen.

As my condition was deteriorating all the time, the operation had to be performed immediately. The doctors had warned me earlier that they might have to amputate the arm. Rudnev abandoned this idea, but it was a very difficult operation and lasted a whole hour; he was hoping to have saved the arm. Within a short time the wound had to be opened twice more, since pus centres kept forming. At the last of these operations they even had to remove part of the bone, because it was already eaten away by pus. The whole elbow right to the lower part of the arm was one great wound. To reduce the pain I received injections every day of morphia and other drugs, although these also agitated me again. Apart from fruit, which I enjoyed, I couldn't eat anything —and this weakened me still more. The whole of August my life was hanging in the balance.

They took excellent care of me in the Mommsen Nursing Home. Besides Mr Rudnev, the house doctor, Dr Lothar Nobel, was constantly attending me. For months he gave up his spare time to sit by my bed and comfort me when I was near despair; though it was a long time before I gained confidence even in him. I kept on being frightened that I would be recognised and dragged before the public eye. Besides these anxieties I suffered all the time, especially at night, from a dread of being alone. As this made me very restless and it was feared I might again do myself some harm, Mrs Rathlef now moved completely to the nursing home. Later I did not like to feel so completely dependent on her, but at this time I was indeed happy to have her, and she again showed me much kindness.

To give me pleasure, she once presented me with a white Angora cat, which I called Kiki. That was an extremely good idea, for I found the little creature very charming and amusing, and with this companion I forgot my pain. I have always been very fond of animals. I used to have a small Pekinese. He had eyes round as a ball, and you could see his tongue quiver when he was pleased at something. His fur was soft as silk—I think it was brown. He was terribly fond of chocolate, just like me. Whenever I ate chocolate, he had to have some too. Altogether he used to want what I was eating. To tease him, I once gave him a slice of lemon from my tea-cup, and he ate it with delight just because I had given it him. He also drank tea when we had some.

Among my constant visitors at this time I think especially of Herluf Zahle, who came to see me almost every day with his charming wife Lilian. They both cared for me as if I had been their own child, and always brought joy into my sickroom. I also owe Zahle the material help I received now and later from Prince Valdemar of Denmark, with whom he interceded on my behalf, as I afterwards learnt. Right from the start of our acquaintance he had such confidence in me that he showed me the letter the Prince had sent him about Volkov. I can still remember the black edge to this letter, which gave me a terrible shock because I thought Grandmama must be dead; but it had some other reason.

The story of the 'swastika sign' belongs also to this period, a story which was told everywhere because it sheds such light on my strange memory. Once when Zahle was visiting me at St Mary's, I walked to the window and looked at his car, which stood outside. I asked him about the mascot, and then remembered the mascot on my mother's car, this same swastika sign, an old Indian symbol which was supposed to bring luck. Nobody who was asked could remember it, not even Volkov, and the matter was forgotten. But now Zahle came to the Mommsen Nursing Home bringing a book which had a picture of my mother's motor-car. With the magnifying-glass he had picked out the little swastika sign above the bonnet exactly as I had described it to him. The book had only just appeared, so I could not have had any previous knowledge of it, as my enemies asserted.

Another time he put my memory to a hard test. I had been talking of my childhood, as I was so fond of doing, and saying how we often stayed with our relatives at Pavlovsk, the Grand-Duke Constantine and his family—I have mentioned this already. Zahle asked me what we used to call our aunt in the family circle. I remembered that she was a princess of Altenburg and her name was Elisabeth, but didn't know what we used to call her. Zahle said I should think about it. Then he asked me who Aunt Ella was, and I could not at once answer this question either. It was evening, the night came, and I lay awake unable to stop thinking of the two questions Zahle had given me to answer. Next morning when he arrived, I suddenly remembered the name and told him that Aunt Ella was one of my mother's three sisters, the Grand-Duchess Elisabeth Feodorovna, wife of the Grand-Duke Sergius of Russia. The answer to the other question only came to me on some later occasion. The aunt in Pavlovsk, the Grand-Duchess Elizaveta Mavrikievna, we always used to call 'Aunt Mavra.' Incidentally, I had no idea then that Aunt Ella had also been a victim of the Bolsheviks in 1918. I was convinced she was still living in Russia, hiding in a convent, and I was definitely hoping to see her again some day.

* * *

'Aunt Ella' had been murdered in 1918 with the three sons of the Grand-Duke Constantine and of 'Aunt Mavra.' The latter, who was the Duke of Altenburg's sister, spent the last years of her life at her home in Altenburg Castle; and from 1925 onwards she received detailed news of Anastasia from Berg, who had always been unreservedly convinced of Anastasia's identity. During her last illness 'Aunt Mavra' sent an urgent message by the Duke's son-in-law, Prince Sigismund of Prussia, to his mother, Princess Irene, and to the Tsarina's other sister, Princess Victoria,[1] in England. She begged them to take seriously the case of Mrs Anastasia Tchaikovski and make thorough investigations. She said she was by no means sure the woman in question was *not* her great-niece; and when she was well again, she would go to Berlin herself to visit the woman. Unfortunately, she died a fortnight later (early 1927).

* * *

In September a slight improvement was seen in my condition. I got rid of the high fever which had been tormenting me for three months. Although I still had a temperature and my general mood was not of the best, I did feel better again. Kiki, my cat, helped to entertain me, and I also began to look at illustrated magazines again; only I did not like reading. Mrs Rathlef then began trying to make me walk again; after the long months in bed this proved a great strain. Once she told me I could already stand up straight as a soldier. Yes, I was a true soldier's daughter, my father had been the best and bravest of soldiers. I had always had to keep step with him too, a thing Mrs Rathlef could not understand. She started with the right foot, whereupon I taught her that one should always start with the left.

I was once presented with a postcard showing my whole family. I was naturally very much moved, and wondered for a long time

[1] Lady Victoria Milford Haven, widow of Prince Louis Mountbatten (Battenburg), the former British Admiral of the Fleet and first Marquess of Milford Haven.

where it must have been taken. I think it was in Odessa. Papa had become very cross with me because I would neither sit still myself nor let my brother sit still, so I spoilt the photograph. He appeared in the picture with a very grim face, just as he was when annoyed. I didn't look much better myself; it was the expression I wore when I was being naughty. Mama had her beautiful pearl necklace on, she liked pearls best of all; except for the broad pearl 'collar' belonging to the crown jewels, which she did not like: it covered the whole neck and was very uncomfortable, but sometimes even so she had to wear it for public occasions. My pearl necklace was the shortest on this picture. That was because we sisters were given some pearls every year on our name-day, so that the necklace got longer every year. It is the same necklace I had sewed into my skirt when we were in Siberia, the one Tchaikovski later sold in Rumania.

I remembered another picture Mama once took; I think it was on a picnic. We children were still quite small then and all wore sailor suits and sailor caps. We were all very fond of taking photographs, my sisters had flat cameras while I had a little box camera; I specially enjoyed making the prints. I was once shown by Mrs Rathlef another picture from this happy past. It was in an English magazine and dated from the time when Queen Alexandra of England died—she was the elder sister of the Empress-Dowager, the widow of Edward VII. All the members of the English royal family were there.

The other picture, the one that all of us were on, was taken on Papa's yacht, the *Standart*, and we all wore the big hats which were then fashionable. Mrs Rathlef was surprised at my immediately recognising the yacht, because the deck of any yacht looks much the same. But I had recognised the *Standart* by the long curved points of the awning stretching over the whole deck. I myself did not cut a very good figure on the picture. I stood stupidly there with my feet crossed and an idiotic expression on my face. Somehow I always seemed to come out looking stupid, while the others usually came out very well.

I am still sad today that I couldn't save my family photos; I used to have so many, and was specially fond of some of them. My parents too always carried their favourite pictures around with them. Mama had a medallion with a picture of my three sisters—my brother and I had not yet been born then; and Papa never parted from a picture of my mother. Now I carried around my whole treasury of pictures in two envelopes. There was a green one in which I kept the postcards I was given with the pictures of my family, and a yellow one with any others which interested me and which I cut out of the illustrated magazines now and then.

I recall one more picture, because I got a shock when I discovered it in one of these magazines. A man looking like my father sat in a royal carriage; it was not Papa, however, but the English King George V; he had the same profile, the same beard.[1] The first moment it did not even occur to me that he might not be my father. On this picture the English king was driving to the opening of Parliament.

During the time I spent in the Mommsen Nursing Home, a small incident occurred. However unimportant, it seems to me in retrospect like the presentiment of a visit I was later to receive. It was a warm September day. We hadn't gone far with my efforts at walking, so Mrs Rathlef pushed my bed to the open window to give me a little distraction. Children were playing below, and suddenly I pricked up my ears. One of the children several times called out a name I had long been racking my brains to find: the child had called 'Shura.' With the sound of this name my memory seemed at once to start functioning again. I knew in a flash who Shura was, Shura who had always been with us children, who had brought me up and always been so intimate with us. She had loved us so well I was sure she would have let herself be killed for me if that might have saved us. But where had she got to? I didn't even know if she was still alive. I had no idea then that she had actually been with me a few weeks before at St Mary's when I was in so high a fever. Nobody had told me, neither Zahle nor Mrs Rathlef. Only in my delirium I am supposed to have shouted for her and a girl called Lisa, to come and help me get dressed. Apparently I said I had to get away so as not to be shot. But at that time I could not remember her either when I was fully conscious. Now, through the child's shout, Shura had all at once come back into my memory.

[1] George V and Nicholas were first cousins, so the resemblance is not surprising.

Soon afterwards Zahle came to see me again. This was naturally an opportunity to talk of Shura too. First he showed me photographs Gilliard had sent him from Switzerland, but said nothing about Gilliard and his wife having been in Berlin before. Whatever the occasion might be, Zahle always wanted me to remember spontaneously any people or occurrences from the past. The picture he showed me then was of a group. He asked me if I recognised the people on it. I almost snatched the photograph from him, and although very excited I pointed at once to the centre, where I recognised my brother Alexi with his tutors. One of them must be the English tutor,[1] who always held his head a little on one side, and on the right stood M. Gilliard. Below sat two small boys who always played with my brother—the sons of Derevenko the marine;[2] then I recognised a governess, whose name was something like the Russian for cherry, 'Vishnevskaia,'[3] I think; and there too Shura was sitting. I asked Zahle if Shura was still alive, and when he told me she was, I became very excited, wanting to know where she lived. He said, in Switzerland, and she could not travel alone. I suggested Gilliard could surely fetch her if he did not live far from her. Zahle promised they both would come.

Although in the next weeks I waited in suspense for this visit, I had rather mixed feelings about it. Of course I looked forward to meeting these people I shared so many memories with, but then I would wonder what the point of such a meeting might be. Gilliard would ask me such a lot of questions, as others had done so often before; it would agitate and tire me, and there was so much I couldn't remember. But I did look forward to seeing Shura.

I can still remember the day Gilliard came to me with Zahle. It was a fine sunny day at the end of October. But I also remember that I did not at once recognise the short dark man as my brother's tutor, let alone as the visitor to St Mary's. Of course in the last weeks I had seen a great many people I did not know, who had been brought to me by Mrs Rathlef, so that I may not have been

[1] Mr. Gibbs.

[2] Confirmed by Gilliard.

[3] Actually Vishnezkaia.

thinking of Gilliard at all. But this first failure to recognise him must have had some other reason.

As usual I shook hands with the visitor. Then he asked me straight away if I knew who he was. I scrutinised his face and made great efforts to get some sort of association for it, but I did not succeed, I first had to size up this face. There was something about it I felt was odd—and I told my visitor this. We did not get into conversation. When he had gone and I was alone with Zahle and Mrs Rathlef, enlightenment came to me, and I said to Zahle it could only have been Monsieur Gilliard, my brother's tutor. Nervous and suspicious as I had become, I had not dared to say it to him direct. Perhaps there had also been some feature on this face which I did not like, so that I unconsciously guessed I was not dealing with a friend. Anyhow, it is quite wrong if Gilliard asserts in his book that I had been prepared for his visit and therefore professed to recognise him at once. I had to make sure first.

The next morning he appeared for the second time. After I had invited him to sit down, I looked closely at my visitor once more. Although he looked much younger and healthier than when I last saw him in Siberia, I had now recognised him completely. I also knew now what had led me astray the day before: Gilliard was clean-shaven. I asked him what he had done with his beard. Gilliard admitted that he used to wear a beard, but had it shaved off when he had to hide from the Bolsheviks. Then he fell silent.

I leant back on the pillows, having found the visits rather a strain, and waited for Gilliard to express his joy and remind me of things that had happened in the past. Nothing of the kind occurred, but instead he sat stiffly on his chair, with a sort of hostility emanating from him. Suddenly he said, as if in an interview: 'Please chat a little. Relate everything you know of the past.' I was very offended by his manner, and said in surprise that I did not know how to 'relate' and had no idea what I should 'chat to him' about. Then he showed his true face, and all at once I dimly recalled the mocking expression I had seen on that stranger's face at St Mary's. He said rather loudly that he could not help being astonished by my bad memory. Now I too became sharp with him, and asked if he thought *he* would remember so much from the past after being almost killed. He had no answer to that. We could not get into any real conversation, but as he was leaving, I asked him when Shura was coming to Berlin. Although she had in fact travelled with him, he gave an evasive answer, telling me he couldn't say for certain. Gilliard does not mention this conversation in his book.

At this time I learnt that he had already written another book about our family—as had my mother's friend Anna Vyrubova, to whom we were very attached. In neither case, I am sure, would my parents have approved. I find it unfitting that people who have enjoyed our confidence should reveal things to the public which only belong in the family.

The afternoon of the same day we heard a knock. I was lying in bed. Mrs Rathlef went to the door. A lady in a purple coat came in, followed by Zahle. The lady came straight over to my bed and held out her hand with a smile. I knew at once who my visitor was, and kissed her hand. I was so delighted, I forgot about everyone else there—it was Aunt Olga. I at once enquired how Grandmama was, especially about her heart. I was always anxious about her health and was now glad to hear that she was well. Aunt Olga asked after my health, and we talked of my illness. Then she admired my cat, Kiki, who rubbed his way across the room, sometimes jumping on the chairs or my bed. She talked to me only in Russian, though, and I answered in German, which was always rather a strain for me.

When Aunt Olga left the room for a moment after two hours, Zahle asked me who the lady was. I told him it was Papa's sister, my Aunt Olga, the one who had always called me Shvipsik. He expressed surprise that I had not addressed her by name straight away, but why should I have done? Later, I heard that they were wanting to test me by this meeting. After Gilliard's previous visit it was supposed that I should be expecting Shura and not Aunt Olga. That day Aunt Olga stayed till the evening. We parted very cordially; she bent over my bed, and I again kissed her hand. Then I asked Mrs Rathlef to accompany her to the nursing-home's front door, but I believe she did not do so, although such an attention should always be shown to a Grand-Duchess.

As may be guessed, the visit had excited me so much that I could not go to sleep and could hardly wait for the next day when

Aunt Olga was to come again. My head felt very hot, but I had no fever, it was just that I was bursting with joy, and kept on thinking that now at last everything would be all right and I need not be afraid any more. I began making plans to travel. Grandmama would be happy to give me a home, in Copenhagen there were bound to be good doctors who could continue my treatment. Kiki should come with me too a basket could be bought for him.

The next morning Aunt Olga was with me by nine, and I was overjoyed that she had come so early. She sat down by my bed and showed me pictures of her two small sons. In her first marriage Aunt Olga had married Duke Peter of Oldenburg, of the Russian line of the Oldenburgs. The marriage was dissolved with my father's consent, whereupon, shortly before the Revolution, she married the Duke's adjutant, Colonel Kulikovsky, by whom she had her sons. I looked at these children's photographs with a certain melancholy.

Aunt Olga went on talking about her sons, and I now asked her hundreds of small details connected with the children. I remembered that in a room of ours at home there had been tiny children's chairs; I also recalled a staircase which 'turned round,' that is, a spiral staircase. I asked her if that was right or if I was dreaming. She confirmed it and was very pleased.

Since we had begun talking about home, I began comparing how untroubled my life had been then and what cares I had today. Aunt Olga thereupon brought the conversation round to financial questions. She knew that through Zahle I was receiving an allowance which was collected for me in Denmark by Prince Valdemar, my grandmother's youngest brother; and she had heard another thing from Zahle, it now transpired: I had told him my father had deposited money with the Bank of England before the war, but that this could not be found, since it was not known in what name the deposit had been made.[1] She wanted to hear further details, so I told her of the conversation my father had in Ekaterinburg shortly before his death, with my mother and us sisters. The money was about twenty million roubles, to be divided between the four of us, so that we should each have received five million. It was deposited under a name I had now

[1] See translator's note page 262

forgotten, though I remembered the name as being of one syllable and German-sounding with an 'a' in it. The sum was to be paid out on the giving of this name.

I had no idea then what immense difficulties I was laying up for the future by giving this information: since till then no one in the family except my mother and sisters had known anything about it. When Aunt Olga returned to Copenhagen, she repeated to my relatives there everything I had told her, and the enquiries made in London confirmed, as Zahle later informed me, that I had been right about the fortune. That morning we talked of many other memories, I felt cheerful once more, and we laughed together. At noon Aunt Olga left me, having been invited to lunch with Zahle.

She returned in the afternoon, accompanied now by another lady, who I could see was obviously excited. This lady came straight over to my bed and asked me in Russian how I was. I shook hands with her, recognising her at once. Although I had been so much looking forward to her coming, I was now so excited I could do nothing but smile at her. Aunt Olga bent over me and asked encouragingly: 'Well, who is it?' 'Shura,' I said. Shura was with me in the room, I simply could not grasp it. Aunt Olga clapped her hands for joy at this recognition, and exclaimed with a radiant face that we should now talk Russian, as Shura did not know any German. I did not like this because I always spoke German now, and I said a few words in German to Shura, asking her to sit down.

I had to keep on looking at her, so incredible I found it that she was there. In my joy I did not know what to say. Without thinking, I got hold of a small bottle of eau-de-Cologne standing on my bedside table, and poured some on to her hand so that she could moisten her brow with it. I meant to show her my love by this, for I was terribly fond of scent and had always enjoyed sprinkling Shura with it in the old days; as a child I used to say in jest that she ought to smell like a bouquet of flowers. Shura laughed with tears in her eyes, she too was much moved by our reunion. How much we had both gone through since we last saw each other! Then I asked her when she had come to Berlin. 'Three days ago,' she said, and I was cross that she had not come to see me till now. It was a good thing I did not know that she had once been to see me, in St Mary's; I should certainly have been offended at that.

Then Shura said, I suppose to divert my attention: 'Did you know that I was married?' Shura married—I was amazed. But Shura had always belonged to us children, how could she have married! Then she said I should guess whom she had married. I shook my head—how was I to guess that? She said she was married to M. Gilliard. I was even more dumbfounded at this, in fact I was really shocked, and exclaimed: 'Good Heavens!' Afterwards I was sorry about this, I hadn't meant to hurt Shura's feelings. But as Aunt Olga and Mrs Rathlef laughed, I realised no offence had been taken at my exclamation; to excuse myself, I said it was just that I hadn't been able to grasp it. After the recent conversations I did not feel very fond of Pierre Gilliard—and my outburst cannot have increased his liking for me.

Later in the afternoon Colonel Kulikovsky also came—Aunt Olga's husband, who had accompanied her to Berlin, and so did Gilliard. The whole room was now full of people. In this room, where I had suffered so many torments, there was now all at once an atmosphere of happy excitement. Mrs Rathlef, as she afterwards told me, had run off in joy to tell Mr Rudnev about it. He too was quite flabbergasted at the transformation which had taken place. He told her even Gilliard had asked him whether he thought I would completely recover, and had referred to me as Imperial Highness and Grand-Duchess. On that day they all felt that every doubt about my identity had disappeared and that the recognition was an acknowledged reality. I should now at last come into the environment where I belonged, and would no longer need to go continually from one person to another, accepting charity from strangers—and also injuries.

In the evening, when all the visitors had gone and I was alone again with Mrs Rathlef, we talked once more of what had happened in the day. I thought Shura looked very thin and unwell, and told Mrs Rathlef she should buy more cream next day so that Shura should get something fortifying to drink. Then she told me that Gilliard in his turn had said to her in quite shattered tones that I looked terrible, it was dreadful to see the change in me, and he would do everything to help me out of this situation. If he were not tied to Lausanne, where he was teaching, he would have stayed here to help clear up my case. He would go everywhere and talk to all the people who had seen and known me while I was at Berlin—for my fate was the most awful thing he had ever heard. If I had known that evening just how much trust there was in Gilliard's promises of help, I should scarcely have been so happy. Could this man really do such a thing, or did he only write the account of this visit in his book long afterwards, when he had already turned away from me?

The next days, which I spent with Aunt Olga, Shura and Gilliard, simply flew by. As always when there were a lot of people around me and I was excited, I had violent headaches. I did take part in the conversation, but could only talk a little, and found it particularly unpleasant when I was asked direct questions, as Gilliard was always doing. My dislike of this has lasted to the present day, and even more, my dislike of things being touched on which I should rather not be reminded of; people should be able to appreciate this.

In those days Aunt Olga seemed to me rather depressed, although I could not guess why. Gilliard kept urging me to tell him about Tobolsk. But I did not wish to be reminded of Tobolsk. Hadn't he enough delicacy to spare a sick person the pain of talking about so dreadful a time, which was followed so soon by the death of her family? Shura, too, said something once which made me angry. They were talking about my hair, saying it had a natural wave and was very beautiful. She seemed to be hinting that although I always used to have this beautiful wave, she now felt it had got darker. Well, whose hair does not get darker with the years?

When we said good-bye, Aunt Olga kissed me tenderly on both cheeks. I was unhappy, of course, that she had to leave me again, so she said: 'Don't be sad, I shall write to you, and Mrs Rathlef will also write to me often. Just you get well, that's the main thing.' The Gilliards went away too the day after. Shura was extremely upset and found it hard to part from me. Gilliard promised to come back when I was better and felt more like answering his questions. He asked Mrs Rathlef to keep him constantly informed, so that he could answer from Lausanne any questions he might be asked. This terribly involved business, he said, must now be cleared up once and for all.

* * *

Gilliard's account of the visit is a very different story. According to him, Mrs Tchaikovski gave no spontaneous sign of affectionate recognition towards the Grand-Duchess and his wife, nor had they been able to detect the slightest resemblance to Anastasia. The patient understood Russian, though with some difficulty, but could not speak it. None of the photographs shown her awakened any special memories in her mind. The only point the visitors were really struck by was the confidence with which she identified the Imperial family on the pictures, the Tsar, the Tsarina, the Tsarevich and the Grand-Duchesses; and Gilliard found a way of explaining this, saying that a fortunate chance had thrown some light on the whole extraordinary business. Colonel Kulikovsky learnt from a man called Baumgarten, who used to be in his regiment, that between 1922 and 1925 Mrs Tchaikovski had moved in Berlin's Russian circles. So Gilliard at once went with Kulikovsky to see Schwabe, whose wife he also met; and now he heard all the emigré gossip of the last few years. 'This visit,' he wrote, 'was a real revelation for us, who did not know Mrs Tchaikovski's past.'

The sort of things 'revealed' to him were the following: the story of what had happened at the Kleists; the statement that Anastasia had her teeth extracted in Dalldorf, but they had certainly not been smashed by rifle blows; that Mrs Tchaikovski gained all her knowledge about the Imperial family from Mrs Tolstoi, who was living at Tsarskoe Selo before the Revolution. Mrs Schwabe even had an explanation for the nickname 'Shvipsik.' A former Russian officer called Bulygin was at Berlin in 1922; the Grand-Duchess Olga had sent him to Siberia in 1918 to search for the Imperial family. 'Shvips' was the password, writes Gilliard, and when Mrs Tchaikovski was at the Schwabes', Bulygin had spelt it out letter by letter to see if it aroused in her mind any memory of the old nickname the Grand-Duchess Olga used to call her niece. Moreover, Mrs Tchaikovski had a Polish accent, crossed herself like a Roman Catholic and once called out 'Jesus Maria.'

That evening the Zahles gave a small supper at the Danish Embassy for Olga, her husband and the Gilliards. Gilliard related the adverse comment on Anastasia which he had heard at the Schwabes, and became so excited on the subject that Zahle had to ask him to calm down, pointing out that by drawing over-hasty conclusions without checking the facts, he was in danger of unfairly influencing everybody else present. Kulikovsky, however, was obviously on Gilliard's side already, for he insisted that Mrs Schwabe should give her account to Olga direct.

Despite Zahle's warning, Gilliard had made up his mind when he went back to Switzerland. 'The personal enquiries were completely negative,' he wrote. 'We felt quite sure we were in the presence of a stranger, especially as she was incapable of answering a single question on the Imperial family's intimate life. . . . In that case, who on earth is she? Is this a pathological case, is she under hypnotic influence, or is she a lunatic?' As for Mrs Rathlef, he dismissed her as merely giving Mrs Tchaikovski instructions, under the pretext of helping revive the patient's memory.

Hypnosis? Count Hardenberg had already suggested this to Miss Amy Smith when refusing to let her see the Grand-Duke of Hesse. The Gilliards seem to have found things easier at Darmstadt, where they spent two days on their way home; for they were allowed to see the Grand-Duke in person and give him their impressions. Gilliard, in fact, learnt more than he dared hope. The Grand-Duke told him that he had sent for the plaster-casts of Mrs Tchaikovski's ears and feet, and that these differed fundamentally from the shape of his niece Anastasia's. He particularly remembered Anastasia's ears, since the upper part of them had a slight deformity, which was quite common in the Hessian family: he had often teased his sister, the Tsarina, about it, telling her that Anastasia had the same ears as his uncle, Prince Henry of Hesse.

Legal experts all over the world were soon to argue about these ears and feet, which had become all the more precious now that their owner was suddenly revealed as the heiress to a large fortune, of which nobody had previously heard. For after Anastasia's unsuspecting remark, it was simple enough for the Grand-Duchess to guess the 'one-syllable German-sounding name with an "a" in it' as being that of the former Imperial finance minister, Bark; of whom she knew that the Tsar had sent him on a private mission to England just before the war. Mrs Schwabe, with her talk of a Polish accent, had also brought in a fine red herring; and Anastasia's enemies, now all joined up, began to feel confident of their victory.

For the moment, however, she was still surrounded by friends, at the Mommsen Nursing Home, and here in contrast is their picture of the visit from Olga and the Gilliards. Mrs Rathlef writes: '. . . Several times the Grand-Duchess remarked that the patient was much more like her niece Tatiana, an opinion shared by the Gilliards. She even admitted that she would believe it at once if told this patient was Tatiana. Before her departure she confided to the Danish Ambassador:

"With my reason I cannot grasp that it might be Anastasia, although my heart tells me it *is* she. And as I have grown up in a religion which teaches me to follow my heart rather than my reason, I cannot forsake this unhappy child . . ."

'Mme Gilliard turned away from the bed (on leaving Anastasia), overcome with grief, embraced me weeping and sobbed: "I loved her so much, so much. Why is it that I must love the girl here just as much? If you knew how I felt now! Can you tell me why I love her so dearly, the poor patient here?" . . . These words betray a genuine distress and great perplexity. Gilliard hurried her away, evidently displeased with his wife's agitation.

'Before leaving Berlin, the Gilliards told Mr and Mrs Zahle: "We are departing without being able to say that it is *not* the Grand-Duchess Anastasia Nikolaievna . . ."

'If, instead of confining their visit to a mere four days, amounting to a few hours altogether, the Grand-Duchess Olga Alexandrovna and the Gilliards had taken time to go and see her every day, had waited and been patient perhaps for several months—as we have waited and been patient—then she might have spoken to them freely and told them just as much as she has done to the doctors, Mr Zahle and myself . . .'

In a second statement of 15th March, 1926, Mrs Rathlef dealt with Gilliard's charges, of which she had only just learnt: '. . . I myself have now been with the patient for over nine months, seven of them day and night. I know she would never retain anything she was told unless she had experienced it herself; and this applies particularly to names. It is quite inconceivable that if the Schwabes had "spelt out" a name to her a year or eighteen months ago, she would have retained that name for more than three days. She forgets from day to day all external happenings; and even quite important things, though she may suddenly remember them, will go right out of her mind again. I have never heard her say "Jesus Maria," even in her worst delirium; though she sometimes wakes at night in an agony of fear, dreaming that men with rifles are threatening her and her family. Once when I was fast asleep she woke me up in the middle of the night, exclaiming: "I've just seen my sister Olga in the bath"—and another time: "I'm sitting on a roof with my brother, I'm holding him by his belt so that he shan't fall, but he gets nearer and nearer the edge." After such dreams she is soaked in perspiration, extremely scared, and has to be comforted like a small child. I have never caught her telling the smallest lie, and indeed have seldom seen a person so devoted to the truth. Whenever she does not know something exactly, she will tell you she can't really answer, because she is unwilling to say anything untrue . . .'

Mrs Rathlef's other comments on Anastasia's character and behaviour at this period are also illuminating: '. . . In her development she is only sixteen or seventeen years old, though she combines this with the bitterness of an old woman. When she is feeling all right, she is very cheerful and full of amusing ideas. . . . If she has anything sweet to eat, she will eat it all up at once; she is incapable of saving it up. She is full of pity for beggars. She wants to own every dog she sees, and can play ball with her cat like a little girl. She has little knowledge of people, and is usually very suspicious but sometimes blindly trusting. She is frightened of strangers and above all that someone might recognise her. She is generous and amiable, but terribly headstrong and can persist for days in some piece of obstinacy; although these tantrums are painful for her, she cannot find it in her to yield.

'Politics is one of the only things that interests her. She is excited by anything about Russia. Then again, she is interested in the European courts and knows all the mutual relationships. Another interest is for fashions; she is very anxious to be well dressed and is delighted as a child by any new handkerchief she may get. But then the reaction comes: she is depressed, tired of life, blames God and the world for letting her be parted from her parents, sisters and brother. She also blames Russian society for lacking the courage to save a single family which in good times they had cheered. Then she cries a lot, has no appetite and feels unable to leave her bed—until I succeed in taking her mind off on to something else . . .

'. . . From the beginning I felt the patient was by no means feeble-minded, but quite an intelligent person, although her horizon was narrow and her range of interests very limited. After being continually ill for eight years, with such an illness and such experiences, after knowing nothing but hospitals and doctors all that time, she has certainly remained to some extent in a state of naive childishness. Her interest and inner life was always concentrated exclusively on the time of her childhood, and she would return to it in every conversation whenever there was the slightest opportunity. To judge from her present character, she must in happier times, when she was well, have been very vivacious and cheerful by temperament. Despite all her pain and suffering, she has often shown a kind of impishness and gaiety, even enjoying teasing the people with her; but for the most part, alas, she had been too ill to exhibit many signs of gaiety and high spirits.'

Mr Rudnev, in his medical records for the end of March 1926, also refers to Anastasia's visitors, and has this comment on Gilliard's charge that her appearance was very different: 'After her operations the patient was extremely emaciated, weighing less than six stone, and had no fatty tissue whatever. Her temperature was round the 100 mark, and she had the most acute pain in her arm, so that she often had to be given up to eight injections of morphia in twenty-four hours: in such circumstances her features might very well have undergone a considerable change. Moreover, the Grand-Duchess Olga treated the patient throughout as she would have done her niece, and the Gilliards also spoke of the patient as if she were the Grand-Duchess Anastasia.

'I should like to state the following,' Rudnev goes on, 'concerning my observations of Mrs Tchaikovski's physical and psychological condition, and also certain facts pointing towards her resemblance to the youngest daughter of His Majesty Tsar Nicholas II.

'. . . While making a thorough examination of the patient, I found a scar on her breastbone, the result of a former tuberculosis, of which I was already informed by Dr Neupert, medical superintendent of the West-End Hospital. On the skull, between the right temple and the back of the head, I found bone-scars which could not anatomically have been caused by tuberculosis, but had the character of scars originating from a blow with a heavy object which had injured the osseine. The X-ray shows that the bone was in fact damaged and that a hæmatoma took place.

'The patient is very anæmic, and so emaciated she is little more than a skeleton; there are slight murmurs in the lower half of the left lung caused by a former pleurisy. On the left knee there are puncture marks from an attempt to heal an inflammation of the knee. On the right foot I noted a severe deformity, apparently congenital, in that the big toe bends right over to the middle, forming a bunion. From the doctors who used to treat the Grand-Duchess Anastasia I had previously heard about the shape of her right foot and the abnormality there.

'By changing the patient's dressings every day, I gradually succeeded in winning her confidence, and am therefore in a position to comment on her psychological condition. She could speak clearly and sensibly of everything concerned with her physical state, but when it came to the future she insisted it was all hopeless and she was only waiting for death; also she could not believe she would ever be well enough to do anything with her hand again. These thoughts depressed her to such an extent she lost all interest in her environment and saw only hostility in everyone around her. For a long while I was prevented by this suspiciousness from questioning her about her past and her grim experiences. Six or seven weeks after the operation, however, she began to take more nourishment, and her general condition showed some improvement—including her memory, which has been seriously affected; and then she could give me further information about her childhood—facts, moreover, which could only be known to the immediate family of the Tsar Nicholas II.

'I myself happen to have seen the Grand-Duchess Anastasia with her sister Tatiana at the castle in Moscow[1] the day war was declared. I was walking past the castle with Dr S. T. Feodorov, by the side of the Troitsk Gate in the Kremlin, when a paper pellet was thrown at us from one of the castle windows. I asked Feodorov who could have done this, so he suggested we crossed to the railings on the other side. From there we saw the Grand-Duchesses Anastasia and Tatiana, dressed in white, though they quickly withdrew from the window when they saw us.

'Remembering this incident . . . I asked the patient: "Tell me what you did at the castle window the day His Majesty declared war." She thought for a bit, then burst out laughing and said: "Oh dear, how awful. My sister and I misbehaved and pelted the passers-by with paper pellets." I cannot believe there was anything resembling telepathy or the like in this answer.

'Nor did my conversations with the patient ever give grounds for considering some form of hypnosis or supposing she had the ability to read others' thoughts and feelings; there were no signs of her being clairvoyant. On the contrary she betrayed a severe depressive condition, and a lack of memory even in relation to things which had only just happened to her. She is still affected today by this forgetfulness. She finds it extremely hard to concentrate, nor can she yet tackle any brainwork. I believe, however, that with time these defects will disappear, and can state that the process has already started in recent months, now that she has overcome her fears of strangers and the new environment . . .'

Dr Lothar Nobel, registrar at the Mommsen Nursing Home, also has notes for this period: 'Mrs Tchaikovski has now been in this nursing home for almost eight months, during which time I have visited her every day. I have thus been able to observe her psychological condition without her knowledge, and report as follows:

'Since her temperature has come down it is possible to exchange a few words with the patient. She has an obviously foreign accent, probably Russian, and though she chooses her words carefully, her speech is not stilted. She is basically friendly, polite and agreeable, but shows a distinct shyness and nervous reticence, especially when she detects an allusion to her past in questions or conversations: she shuts up at every question of this kind, excusing herself on the grounds of overstrain and the pain in her arm. She is completely lucid over time

[1] According to another account the incident occured in the Winter Palace at St. Petersburg.

and place, nor is there any abnormality in her movements, bearing, opinions or attitudes. Her mood is variable: she is sometimes in reasonably good spirits, at others very depressed . . .

'When she does answer questions about her past, her answers come slowly and hesitantly. She screws up her face to think very hard, and finds it a great effort to remember the names of people and places. However, she has at length completely lost her nervousness and suspicion with me, and once she has been led on to the subject, will relate many details of her own accord. It is best to guide her by indirect questions, for when she is asked direct ones, her face still assumes that tormented, searching expression, and she will answer: "I can't stand any more, it's too much of a strain. I've forgotten everything, and I'm no more use in the world because my memory has gone." Or alternatively she will complain about how she tries her hardest to forget the terrible things she has been through, and then someone keeps coming to stir it all up again, making her feel sad and despairing.

'Sometimes when feeling better she talks spontaneously of people she knows well; gives details of her former life at Tsarskoe Selo, of childish pranks; summer trips to the Crimea and voyages in the Finnish Islands on the *Standart*, her father's yacht; of an occasion when the yacht was damaged; of her pet dog and her brother's illness. She even describes the hours of the shooting, her escape through Russia on a farm-cart, the treatment of her head injuries with cold compresses, her stay in Rumania, her journey to Germany, her despair and attempted suicide; her stay in the various hospitals; and finally gives details of her time in Dalldorf which, as far as one can check up, completely correspond with the reality.

'For instance, she says she was photographed in Dalldorf, and tells of a patient who later died of tuberculosis—the dates she gives are right—how this patient left some food and another patient fell upon it, to Mrs Tchaikovski's great dismay; and how this second patient also died afterwards. But she denies having read books and asked for papers and magazines. The way she relates all this is completely natural and free from any histrionic gestures. Sometimes she even forgets things she has told me herself, and when I mention them again is amazed at my knowing about them.

'Her recollections of her past life are like islands in a sea of forgotten or repressed facts, but during the period of my observation the land "coming above the surface" has markedly increased, doubtless helped by the improvement in her general condition and the healing of the wound on her left elbow. . . . Her recollection of events after she left Dalldorf is accurate and comes readily, as does the description of her illness, her stay with families and in hospitals, the names of her nurses and other details in her present existence . . .'

* * *

The winter of 1925–26 passed without anything special happening for a while. At Christmas I could not help thinking a lot about home, although Easter with us is still more beautiful than Christmas. But even so I felt sad when hymns were sung in the nursing home. The last time we all sang together was when the nuns used to come to us from the Ivanov Convent; that was in Tobolsk—Tatiana sang the best of all, I never sang as well as that. But then visitors came to the nursing home, especially Mrs Zahle, who was continually bringing me presents. I had now got so many handkerchiefs that I picked out one for Shura and sent it to her—having first given it a good sprinkling with scent.

Since leaving Berlin, Aunt Olga had often written to me. For Christmas she wrote me a letter, again in very affectionate terms, and sent it with a jumper she had knitted herself. I was delighted, of course, and felt almost convinced that my recognition was only a matter of time, and that I should soon be travelling to Copenhagen. Mrs Rathlef answered the letter in my name, but it received no reply, and since then I never had any more direct contact with Aunt Olga. I could not explain to myself the sudden change, but in the second half of January I was all at once told some dreadful news. A Danish newspaper said that Aunt Olga had gone to Berlin to settle my affair and contained a categorical denial—'with support from the most authoritative source'—that either she or any other people had found any similarity between the 'unknown woman' and me. I was thunderstruck. Could it really be true that Aunt Olga was disowning me so quickly, had so soon fallen under other influences?

I found it equally inexplicable—at least till I had seen through their motives—that early in the New Year Gilliard and Shura should have broken off their correspondence with Mrs Rathlef, which she had been carrying on in my interest. Till the end of January their letters were extremely friendly, they both asked after my health and sent very kind regards. Gilliard kept on explaining how much energy and care were needed to complete the task satisfactorily, and urging Mrs Rathlef not to inform any outsiders of the things she was writing to him about me, lest the clearing up of my case should be jeopardised. To other people, however, he declared that he had never taken the whole matter seriously; and indeed that emerges from his letters to Mrs Rathlef.

And now it became clear what was going on. As Gilliard writes in his book, the Schwabes were once more behind things. Schwabe had drawn his attention to the fact that a pamphlet about me was soon to appear, with which Mr Rudnev was closely connected, so something had to be done to counter-balance all the efforts made for me by such an authority. Gilliard also admitted that he had only continued his correspondence with Mrs Rathlef 'to gain time till he had new evidence against me in his hands.' Now that Schwabe had made contact with Colonel Kulikovsky, Aunt Olga's husband, and Gilliard with Darmstadt, I found only too much justification for my suspicions that my relatives in Copenhagen and at the Hessian court were now in league against me, and had a special interest in this 'new evidence.'

* * *

Extracts from the Grand-Duchess Olga's letters to Anastasia between October and December 1925:

(*Undated*): 'I send you all my love and think of you the whole time—it is so sad to leave you, knowing you are sick, suffering and alone. But don't worry, for you are no longer alone, and we shall not forsake you. Kind regards to Mrs Rathlef. Eat enough and take lots of cream.'

*31st October:* 'My thoughts are with you. I think of the time when we were together and you stuffed me with chocolate, tea and cocoa. How is your health? You must be very good, eating plenty and doing what Mrs Rathlef says. . . . I hope you will soon feel quite well again. I'm looking forward to your next letter. Olga.'

*4th November:* 'I'm sending my little patient my own silk stole, which is very warm. I hope you will wrap this stole round your shoulders and arms, and that it will keep you warm in the winter cold. I bought it in Japan before the war. Did you receive the postcard? I'm waiting for news of you. I am always thinking of you, and send my very best wishes to the three occupants of No. 18 (Anastasia, Mrs Rathlef, Kiki). How is little white Kiki? Best wishes to Mr Rudnev. All my love. Olga.'

*25th December:* 'Very many thanks for the book. I am longing to see you. It was extremely kind of you to think of my boys. . . . I was so pleased to hear that your health had permitted you to go to church. I have already packed one of my sweaters for you, one I have worn myself and like very much, but can't wear now because of being in mourning for my aunt. . . . We are going to celebrate our Russian Christmas while everyone round us is celebrating a Danish Christmas. Best wishes. Kind regards to Mrs Rathlef. How is Kiki? Olga.

The Danish newspaper Anastasia refers to was the *National-Tidende*, which on 16th January, 1926, carried the following statement, under the headline: 'Spurious Daughter of Tsar—Mrs Tchaikovski':

'We are able to state, with support from the most authoritative source, that there are no common identifying marks between the Grand-Duchess Anastasia daughter of Tsar Nicholas II, and the lady in Berlin known under the name Tchaikovski, who claims to be the Grand-Duchess. All the rumours currently circulating in the German press are entirely without foundation.

'Although this journal has previously published Mrs Tchaikovski's story and pointed out its improbability, the story still keeps on appearing in the German press, and a book is being prepared in Berlin to prove Mrs Tchaikovski's imperial descent.

'By way of a categorical denial, in order to settle the matter once and for all, we can disclose that the Grand-Duchess Olga went to Berlin and saw Mrs Tchaikovski, but neither she, nor anyone else who knew Tsar Nicholas' youngest daughter, was able to find the slightest resemblance between the Grand-Duchess Anastasia and the person who calls herself Mrs Tchaikovski.

'At first Mrs Tchaikovski professed to be the Grand-Duchess Tatiana and only later the younger sister Anastasia. The Grand-Duchess Olga last saw her niece when the latter was already fifteen; it is impossible that she can have altered to such an extent that all her former characteristics have disappeared. Mrs Tchaikovski speaks only German, with a Bavarian accent, but the Grand-Duchesses Tatiana and Anastasia did not know this language.

'Mrs Tchaikovski leaves the impression of a poor highly-strung invalid who believes in her story and is confirmed in the belief by the people around her. We hope she can be freed from this *idée fixe* in the Berlin clinic where she is now being treated.'

The Grand-Duchess Olga's own views are expressed in a letter to Princess Irene of Prussia dated 22nd December, 1926 (presumably in error for 1925):

'I was more moved than I can say by your kind letter, which was completely unexpected to me. I have often thought of you since I had to go to Berlin last autumn to see the poor girl said to be our dear little niece. Well, there is no resemblance at all, and it is obviously not Anastasia. I know that you also visited her, I was told of your visit by Grünberg, the old police inspector.

'It has been claimed that she recognised me, but I will tell you how it all went. She had been prepared for my visit. She herself confessed to me that she was told: "On Tuesday you will have a great treat. Somebody is coming from Denmark." After that she could guess at once and expect her "aunt." She was unable to give an answer to a single one of the small intimate questions I asked her.

'It was pitiful to watch this poor creature trying to prove she was Anastasia. She showed her feet, a finger with a scar and other marks which she said were bound to be recognised at once. But it was Maria who had a crushed finger, and someone who believed it was Anastasia must have told her this.

'For four years this poor creature's head was stuffed with all these stories, she was shown a mass of photos, etc., and then one fine day she hoped to spring her memories on the world.

'Monsieur Gilliard and his wife, my husband, and also old Volkov (who used to be Alix's groom-of-the-chamber), have all seen her and talked to her, and none of them believes she is our Anastasia. It has been claimed, however, that we all recognised her and were then given instructions by Mama to deny that she was Anastasia. That is a complete lie. I believe this whole story is an attempt at blackmail, but I am also convinced that a lot of people really believe in it—only they are the people who never knew Anastasia.

'During the four days we were in Berlin Monsieur Gilliard and my husband visited all the Russians she had once lived with, learning thereby a great deal that is significant. They were told, for instance, that she heard about the nickname "Shvipsik" from an officer I had met in the Crimea who afterwards came to Berlin. He took an interest in the patient and asked her if she knew this nickname and who used to call her by it; of course she could not answer. But afterwards she suddenly said: "My Aunt Olga called me Shvipsik." Everyone was astounded, and enquiries were made to see whether it was true.

'As you see, a natural cause can be found for all these things, if one takes the trouble to look for it. But with the present case most people have only one wish: to complicate the story or legend still further.

'One more thing: she claimed that there was a swastika sign on her mother's car, but Monsieur Gilliard managed to find out that in June

1923 a Russian officer gave her a photograph on which the swastika on the car was clearly visible to the naked eye . . .'

Despite her denial in this letter, Olga's attitude may have been influenced by the known or presumed wishes of her mother, the former Empress Dowager. For a long time Maria Feodorovna had refused to believe that her son and his family had perished, since this would mean the end of the Tsardom: for her they must all be alive and nothing had happened to them. But if the patient in the Berlin nursing home turned out to be the Tsar's youngest daughter, the picture she had so carefully built up would be torn to shreds; if that woman *were* Anastasia, she would be a living proof that the rest of the family were dead. The Empress Dowager certainly wavered, however, after Olga's visit to Berlin, and in any case later developments suggest that her wishes were only one of the causes for Olga's change of front.

* * *

There's a lot more I have to tell about the end of my stay in Berlin. Since my closest relatives, as well as Gilliard, had publicly revealed their hostility, and my grandmother maintained her negative attitude, the Berlin emigrés—and now the Parisian ones as well—made a dead set at me and poured out a flood of calumnies about me. And just then, on top of all this, my health took a turn for the worse.

I was still in the Mommsen Nursing Home, and although on the whole I felt better, a new centre of pus had formed on my arm at the end of February. Dr Nobel informed Mr Rudnev, who came to see me at once and told me the best thing would be to open the place up. After all the operations I had been through I was once more in utter despair, and could not stop the tears coming. Mr Rudnev soothed me, however, so that I agreed to the new operation. But I was badly shaken when he put on his white overall coat there and then in my room; I hadn't anticipated that it was to be performed immediately. He put the coat on so clumsily, though, feeling for the sleeve several times without success, that in the end I had to laugh at him, and the fear of being cut open vanished in a flash. The operation was successful, and from then on my health gradually improved.

After I had recovered sufficiently, with God's help, to be able to get up, I felt the need to go to church; even though Mr

Rudnev, probably thinking of all the mental shocks I had had, suggested that a visit to church might be too much of a strain for me. But I wanted to become a human being again. During my grave illness it was very hard for me to keep the right faith in God, and after all the terrible things I had been through, I began to doubt Him and blame Him so much that I could not receive the Holy Sacrament—for one cannot do this unless one is in harmony with God. Nevertheless, every evening after my bed had been made up for the night, I had Mrs Rathlef push my image of the Blessed Virgin under my bad arm, as we had been taught to do when we were ill by Father Gregory. Once, though, I was really cross with her, when she carelessly put it in head downwards—for that is a sin. On another occasion I had to smack Kiki, my cat, when he dared play with the image of St Nicholas hanging at the top end of my bed. Mama would never have allowed such a thing.

Despite Rudnev's warning, one of the first times I could go out, I went to the Russian church (which is in Nachodstrasse), accompanied by Mrs Rathlef and Miss Spindler. On the way Miss Spindler had to buy me six candles, which I then placed before the image of the Redeemer, one each for my parents, my three sisters and my brother. But I must admit that being in church excited me so much that I felt near to fainting—especially as it was very hot in the church. Mrs Rathlef brought me a chair, and Miss Spindler and Mr Urvanzov[1] sat down near me as a precaution. I kept thinking of the last Mass which a priest held in the Ipatiev House at Ekaterinburg a few days before the death of my family, and of the copper crosses Mama distributed at the beginning of the war; I was scarcely able to cross myself.

Although my appearance in the church was known to nobody except Mr Urvanzov and Colonel Markov,[2] it was soon asserted in Mrs Schwabe's circle that instead of crossing myself in the orthodox manner from right to left, I had done it like a Roman Catholic, and that Mrs Rathlef bent over me to point out this mistake. Gilliard also took over this fairy-tale in his book, in which he made another statement purporting to show that I could not be the 'real Anastasia.' During my Aunt Olga's visit, at which

[1] A writer, president of a committee formed to investigate Anastasia's case.
[2] Leader of the Russian Monarchists.

he and his wife were also present, I was shown a little picture of St Nicholas, which in the past I had always carried about in a medallion; and yet, says Gilliard, I made no comment but gave it back without a word. This statement is just as malicious as the other, for why should I have said anything special about the saint's picture, when it was so familiar to me and hung over my bed. Incidentally, this picture can be seen on a photograph taken in my room long before the visit.

Another story my fellow-countrymen dared spread about me is the following: a refugee in Berlin once obtained permission from Mr Rudnev to see me, and during the conversation I showed her a picture Gilliard had sent me from Switzerland; it was the last photo taken of me at Tobolsk. Mrs Rathlef, who also looked at it, remarked that I still wore my hair exactly the same way as I used to. I could not help laughing about this, and said it was indeed funny that although I had forgotten so much, I did still know what my hair-style was like before. A few months later there was a report in a Paris paper, which among other false statements said emigrés had watched me secretly doing my hair and all the time comparing my hair-style with that on the picture sent me by Gilliard.

A further incident connected with Gilliard was the visit made to Rudnev and Mrs Rathlef by Mr Savich, the former president of the Petersburg High Court. He introduced himself to Rudnev on the pretext that as a lawyer he was better qualified than anyone to arrange the evidence that would lead to my identification; he said he was firmly convinced I was the Grand-Duchess Anastasia, and would do anything to help me. As Rudnev did not doubt his sincerity, Mrs Rathlef gave him some of this evidence, but instead of returning it in three days, as promised, he only did so after five weeks, and one group photograph which had been included was now missing. Soon after this Savich gave a talk in Berlin and Paris on the subject, 'The Spurious Anastasia,' containing the most extraordinary falsehoods—I was supposed to be the wife of a Latvian criminal who was a member of the Moscow Cheka. At the end of his talk he convicted himself of lying, by saying that this did not correspond with the latest information. But the next day all the papers had a report of the talk without this final comment; and Colonel Markov gave a similar talk.

I was told that Savich had no success with his tendentious lecture and that all the sceptics who had attended it left the room with a new readiness to believe in my identity. I particularly remember Savich, because he later collaborated with Gilliard in writing the book against me and because he also got in touch with the Grand-Duke Cyril at Coburg, from which I had long guessed that he was on my enemies' side. Schwabe too, of course, was in contact with Cyril and his entourage. Earlier, when he was still for me, I had once given him my opinion in no uncertain terms about these Coburgs, saying I could never forgive what Cyril did to my father at the time of the Revolution.

I have another memory connected with the Coburgs. Mrs Rathlef read me a newspaper report that Crown Prince Carol of Rumania, son of Queen Maria, had abdicated. I remember that there was once talk at home of Carol marrying my sister Tatiana, while it was contemplated to give Olga to Prince Adalbert of Prussia, the German Emperor's son. I have sometimes mentally reproached my parents for the fact that my two eldest sisters were not married early; for then they would probably have been spared their terrible fate, and I should now have a home. Olga might have been happy with Prince Adalbert; I have already related that he once stayed with us before the war—when, it's true, I found him pretty conceited. Tatiana, however, would scarcely have been satisfied with Carol. On the whole, though, one cannot be sure he wasn't right to abdicate from the Rumanian throne; I also would not have liked being bossed by his mother, one of these Coburgs.

* * *

Two letters referring to Anastasia's visit to church point to her complete honesty in this matter. One is from L. N. Urvanzov in Prague, dated 18th June, 1926, to Mrs Rathlef:

'Here are the answers to your questions:

1. I am still firmly of the belief that Mrs Tchaikovski is really the Grand-Duchess Anastasia Nikolaievna.

2. Nothing she does affords the slightest evidence against this.

3. She crossed herself in church in the Russian Orthodox manner without any reminder or suggestions from anyone else.

4. When I was standing in the entrance hall of the church talking to her, she several times answered me in clear correct Russian.

5. Colonel N. E. Markov, whom I invited to join our committee, has not once visited her, although the committee recommended him to do so and she agreed to see him.

6. Colonel Markov withdrew from the committee on personal grounds, because he was afraid of taking further part in this work.

7. On the photographs of her as a child the Grand-Duchess had a fringe, but she now does her hair so that it is all combed back over her head (as she did in Siberia).

8. Mrs Tchaikovski presented me with a photograph and wanted to write her name on it. As she is very clumsy at writing and was afraid of leaving out a letter, she took a sheet of grey paper in my presence and wrote her name on it several times before signing the photograph; then she wrote her name independently and without any help.

9. I saw and can testify that you sympathise with her as a human being, not as a Grand-Duchess; that you are not expecting any reward for it either, but only trying to establish her name in order to reach the truth.

10. I consider Dr Rudnev a most able, warm-hearted and responsible man, who is no respecter of persons and is leaving no stone unturned to discover the truth as well as to cure Mrs Tchaikovski.

'I must add that my mind is much occupied and disturbed by this business, and I am distressed that no progress is being made on it.'

The second letter is from Miss Spindler in Berlin, dated 27th July, 1926, and addressed to General A. Spiridovich in Paris. The General was chief of the former imperial bodyguard, and Miss Spindler (writing at Rudnev's suggestion) warns him to treat with great caution the reports of Savich and Markov. She points out that Markov was behind Anastasia in the church, and therefore could not have seen the way she crossed herself, as it was possible for L. N. Urvanzov to do.

'At the Grand-Duchess' request,' she goes on, 'I placed six candles in front of the Sacred Image of the Redeemer. (It was about the third day after she got up for the first time following four months of serious illness.) When I returned from the altar, I saw her cross herself in the Russian Orthodox manner, as she also did later, till the moment when she had to be taken out into the fresh air because she was feeling faint—whereupon she was taken home.

'I must add that apart from Markov and Urvanzov nobody knew of the visit to church, and the "painful impression made on the congregation" could not have occurred, as Colonel Markov claims in his talk, because she behaved in no way differently from the rest of the congregation. This talk was based wholly on unchecked rumours and stories, like all the sensational news in the papers.

'N. E. Markov asserted even before the visit to church that, according to a certain Schwabe, the Grand-Duchess crossed herself in the Roman Catholic instead of the Orthodox manner and once with a deep sigh exclaimed: "Jesus Maria." I have come to know the Grand-Duchess very thoroughly and can testify that she has never departed by a hair's breadth from the true Orthodox faith and that she knows this faith better than many others do . . .'

* * *

Among my visitors at the Mommsen Nursing Home there were also people who were well disposed to me. Besides the Zahles, for instance, there was the former Ambassador, Serge Botkin (cousin of the Dr Botkin, my father's personal physician, who was murdered with my family). He was now head of an organisation for the care of Russian refugees in Berlin, and always took my side against the attacks of the other emigrés. I am specially grateful to him for having got in touch with my uncle, the Grand-Duke Andrew, on my behalf—I afterwards met Uncle Andrew in Paris, when he recognised me for the person I am.

I also formed a firm friendship with Botkin's closest colleague, Baron Osten-Sacken, who often came to see me during these last few months I was in Berlin. I talked a lot with him about the past, as well as unburdening myself about my troubles in getting acknowledged. I could talk to him as to an old friend—for Osten-Sacken used to be stationed at Petersburg; he had served at Peterhof where I was born. In 1915 he once went to the front with one of Mama's hospital trains, and she had a court lady present him with an icon from her. So we had many associations in common, and after he had presented me with this icon, which Mama had once held in her hand, I felt complete confidence in him. Whenever he came to see me, he always brought flowers, which I am so fond of, and sometimes also chocolates or chocolate cigarettes (since I did not smoke at that time); he himself liked smoking. Later we also went out for walks together.

But the word 'smoking' reminds me of a small incident which occurred at his first visit and which left me very agitated for the whole night after his visit, until the explanation for it appeared. Having first asked me for permission to smoke, he took out a cigarette-holder shaped like a small pipe. When I saw it, this holder in red and gold at once seemed familiar to me, because it was exactly like the one Papa had always used when smoking. I simply could not understand where Osten-Sacken had got it from, thinking it must surely have been destroyed at the time of the murder and the burning of my parents' bodies afterwards. But although I was very excited, I did not give any sign of it. When he had gone, however, I told Mrs Rathlef, and asked her to ring him at once the next morning to find out where the holder had come from—though only if he did not know who I was. The whole night I was unable to sleep, and could not stop crying in terror that it might be Papa's holder. Then came the explanation.

Osten-Sacken was given it in 1917 at Petersburg by a friend who had bought it at the famous store called Alexander's. It was the model which Alexander had when making Papa's pipe-shaped holder. Some time later, when Osten-Sacken next came to see me, I told him the reason for my excitement, which he quite appreciated. I asked him to make enquiries about it at once with Gilliard or Aunt Olga, though without exciting Grandmama. There must surely be a lot of people altogether who knew of this holder and had seen my father with it. Finally a coloured sketch of it was made and sent to various people in Paris who had been in the Tsar's immediate entourage. They too confirmed that he had always used such a holder.

Another time we talked of amateur theatricals, which used to be a common pastime among our society at home. Osten-Sacken said they had always been a torture to him as a child, and even the thought of them made him ill days before; whereas I never minded acting at all. He asked me where I had last acted, at which I had to think for a bit. Then I remembered that it was at the beginning of our internment at Tobolsk. I could not help laughing at the recollection of a particular occasion on the stage, when I was unlucky enough almost to lose my costume. I found it terrible then, all the audience laughed like anything, and I was teased about it for weeks afterwards.

I also talked to Osten-Sacken about more serious matters, particularly politics and the relationships between Europe's royal houses, in which I am specially interested. Although I knew he had a boundless love for Russia, and I wanted to avoid anything which might have hurt him, I could not help giving vent to my hatred of present-day Russia. The cruel treatment by those Russian-speaking beasts in Siberia, who tortured us to death, was still too close a memory, and had utterly changed my former love for my homeland. That is also the reason why I no longer like speaking Russian. But I did not conceal from him my views on the degeneracy of Russian society, which had always served selfish interests instead of the country's. The officers drank more than they served, and all those who were nearest the throne indulged in intrigues and finally broke their oath to the Tsar. Papa was always too good-natured. But the Russian people too, who put up with such terrible things—like the murder at Ekaterinburg and all their murders—they won no better fate than to be enslaved. Osten-Sacken said one must think of other causes leading to the Revolution, specially the spiritual leaders.

The thing I always found worst of all was that no one came forward to save our family, and it could just be destroyed without any hindrance. This is why I refuse under any circumstances to return to Russia. Sometimes I think my struggle is really futile, when I have been deserted even by my closest relatives and people once very near to me, like Gilliard and Shura. Who can have worked on them so that after having spoken to me they could turn against me? Altogether I cannot understand why everyone and everything has conspired against me, and why so much that might have been settled quite simply, has been deliberately complicated. For example, why didn't Uncle Ernie come to see me? I had them plead with him so hard to come. Was he afraid? After all, I knew him well from pre-war days and saw him again in 1916 on his brief visit to our home. I don't understand his refusing to admit that he visited Russia, which would have helped me so much. Although Osten-Sacken realised all this, like a good friend, he advised me not to throw in the sponge too soon but carry on my struggle to the end.

* * *

In a letter to Botkin of 23rd February, 1926, Osten-Sacken confirms Anastasia's description of his conversations with her, especially the great interest she took in political and dynastic questions. 'I have noticed,' he adds, 'that she never tells an untruth. Her exactitude, devotion to the truth and honesty sometimes verge on the comical, but they certainly say a great deal for her character. . . .'

Mrs Rathlef also recalls how she once began to read to her patient from Tolstoy's 'Folk-Tales,' at which the latter said she did not want to hear anything by Tolstoy: she could not stand him, because he had been one of the many causes of the Revolution by having incited the peasants with his doctrines. It is characteristic that Anastasia should ignore his literary importance in deference to her family's political outlook.

She was extraordinarily interested in Lytton Strachey's *Queen Victoria*, which was being much talked about at the time, and listened enthralled to readings from it, although by no means in agreement with the book's satirical content: in fact, she criticised the author's tastelessness as an Englishman in speaking of his former queen in so sarcastic a vein. Her belief in the divine right of kings and tsars was here breaking through, and in all religious matters Anastasia is very clearly Alexandra's daughter, with piety and mysticism winning the upper hand under Rasputin's influence. That influence can be traced, of course, in many other aspects of her character.

When Mrs Rathlef read the papers to her, she always showed an interest in the political news, making accurate comments now and then on pre-war politics, especially as they reminded her of particular things. For instance, there was news of a League of Nations conference in session, and a reference was made to Briand. 'Who is Briand?' she asked. 'I've never heard anything about him. It used to be Poincaré—I know him, he once stayed with us.' She remembered the French statesman bringing all four of the Tsar's daughters presents, with which they were highly delighted; it was shortly before the outbreak of war. She was also well informed about Bismarck and spoke of him with great respect; altogether she was attracted by strong characters. When a trade agreement had been concluded between Germany and Russia, she said: 'Europe's whole tragedy has only come about because no alliance was formed between Germany and Russia.'

She became very excited by any news about Soviet Russia, and her whole hatred for the Bolsheviks found vehement expression. She was absolutely convinced that Germany was responsible for the triumph of Bolshevism in her country, declaring: 'They sent the Bolshevik leaders into Russia, trying to harm us—and they certainly succeeded.' Her views on Russia's future were equally firm: 'Russia's liberation will never come about through the emigrés. The Russian emigrés, with a few exceptions, can have no importance for Russia's future. I believe only in the peasants. The liberation will only come about through the peasants.'

* * *

When I felt better, I began to go out a little. Sometimes Osten-Sacken accompanied me, sometimes Urvanzov, and Mrs Rathlef was almost always with us. Once I expressed a longing to eat *Borsch* again, a proper Russian cabbage-soup; so she and I went to one of the various Russian restaurants in Berlin where such specialities could be found. The *Borsch* tasted splendid, and we were waited on by Russian refugees, who were also very friendly. I nodded to them on entering—they were standing round everywhere, because there were so few diners. When we had sat down, Mrs Rathlef told me I shouldn't have nodded like this, which surprised me greatly. I had not thought about it at all, but had been taught as a child never to fail to give such a greeting.

But then, while we were eating, I got my own back on her. She told me she had seen at the cinema the latest picture of Queen Alexandra of England, driving through the streets of London with her lady-in-waiting—who was sitting by the Queen stiff and expressionless. I explained to Mrs Rathlef that it was the duty of a lady-in-waiting to sit like this, and chaffed her about its being lucky she wasn't a lady-in-waiting, and could still nod to everyone as I had just done on entering the restaurant—which made us both laugh. Although Queen Alexandra, widow of King Edward VII, was the sister of my grandmother in Copenhagen, I have no special memories of her. She had always been very hard of hearing, and finally lived in almost complete retirement. I only know that she could not wear low-cut dresses because an operation had left big scars on her neck.

We spoke of other sovereigns as well. Osten-Sacken had just presented me with an album of the Romanovs, which Mrs Rathlef had also looked at. The album contained no pictures of Catherine the First, and quite right too, for this Catherine was a dark chapter in our family history—only in the past could an upstart like that have come to the throne. The Romanovs, of course, really died out altogether, and our family only had Romanov blood on the female side. Only in Russia too could a petty

German princess like Catherine the Second dare depose the rightful Emperor and reign herself. Mrs Rathlef was amazed at my knowledge, thinking we had never talked of such things at home. I informed her, however, that we had to know our family's history very thoroughly, and I remembered it all very well.

On many other occasions too we talked about court ceremonial. As I am so fond of uniforms, I repeatedly asked Zahle to visit me just once in his diplomatic uniform, putting on all his orders—but he never did. One day, however, Mrs Rathlef and I went to the cinema and saw a film with a lot of uniforms in: it was 'The Waltz Dream.' I enjoyed it very much, but it had many mistakes on questions of ceremonial. How, for instance, could a prince consort fail to have been instructed in the correct form of ceremonial at a wedding, so that he was even about to kiss his bride full on the lips? The court chamberlain was quite right to prevent that. Also the bride in this film had far too many ladies carrying her train. A bride is never given as many as that, an emperor's daughter has even fewer; besides, the train was far too long. Mrs Rathlef said my criticism was a bit severe, seeing that after all it was only a comedy. Then, to chaff me, she said it surely never happened in real life that princesses were so naughty to their ladies-in-waiting. I understood the allusion, and had to admit that alas it often did happen. But on the whole the film was very pleasing with all the uniforms and the ladies' jewellery.

Altogether I am very fond of jewellery, and always admired Mama when she put hers on. We children also had jewellery, though not so valuable. Remembering a particular piece of jewellery, I once asked Mrs Rathlef to get me a green bracelet—it might be quite cheap but had to have green stones. She was surprised at this and asked why the green was so essential. I explained to her that when we were at home the four of us girls had always worn bracelets of green malachite, a stone common in the Russian mountains. It was a simple stone, but I loved that bracelet and wanted to be reminded of it. In one of our castles the window-seats and pillars were also of this stone, and I had, too, a little jewel-case of malachite. But I had another bracelet as well that I was specially fond of—it was half of gold and the other half set with coloured stones. There weren't as many stones, though, as I had, on the escape to Rumania, sewed into my clothes. About that, by the way, the most varied rumours have been spread, and even Zahle once asked me whether it was true that each of us sisters had precious stones on her weighing two pounds. Of course that would have been too heavy and too conspicuous. No, there weren't two pounds weight in stones, but there were certainly a great many of them, especially emeralds and diamonds.

I once went with Urvanzov too to a Russian restaurant. He had told me Russian songs were sung there, and as I like these songs so much, we went there. But the restaurant was mainly frequented by emigrés, and to avoid being seen by them, I made it a condition that he should order a private box. I sat there in the background, nor did I greet the waiters this time—following the instructions of my 'lady-in-waiting,' Mrs Rathlef. The singers were six gentlemen and two ladies in Russian national costume—former Russian officers with their wives, making a living in this way. They sang with fine natural voices, and I was much moved. When they launched into the song *The Black Hussars* I got quite excited, for this song happened to be a favourite of mine, and I also remembered how my eldest sister had once been the head of a Hussar regiment. Afterwards there was dancing. How I would have liked to dance once more!—but here, of course, it was impossible. I was always very fond of dancing, and could never have enough of it.

By the end of March 1926 my health had improved sufficiently for me to be discharged from the nursing home. Rudnev informed Zahle that he felt I ought to take a general cure after my grave illness, somewhere where the climate was healthy, so that I should fully recover my strength mentally as well as physically. As I have repeatedly pointed out here, there was really no hope of this, but even so I was ready to comply with my benefactors' wishes and go to Lugano, which was where they decided I should now stay. Zahle had hinted that the resources put at my disposal through him were limited, and that one could live more cheaply at Lugano than in another nursing home. I afterwards heard that 22,000 marks were paid out for the eight months I spent in the Mommsen Nursing Home, and although I have never had a good grasp of the value of money—because in the old days I used not to have anything to do with it—I still found this amount very high despite my operations; but of course there were two of us.

We travelled to Switzerland in April, but I can't say my expectations were as high as might have been supposed. Our stay there seemed inauspicious right from the first; for we arrived in dull weather, hardly any of the landscape was visible, I was very exhausted by the journey, and instead of going to a comfortable hotel (as I had expected) we stayed in the first place at an Italian boarding-house which was indescribably dirty and did not even have a garden. After a few days we moved, Mrs Rathlef having found at Paradiso a small hotel called Tivoli where it was a bit better, although there was no running water. But of course we had to economise—I kept hearing that from my companion all the time I was in Switzerland. The room with full board cost rather more than eleven Swiss francs per head, and then there were the extras. I told her to write to Berlin asking if it wouldn't be better for us to move to France or Italy, where it was cheaper; and this she did.

But I had other reasons as well for not feeling too happy here. I had heard that my name appeared every fortnight on the list of visitors to the resort, so Shura and Gilliard would find out I was here, because Lausanne was in the same country. And if Shura did *not* come, that would upset me still more, now that the contact with Aunt Olga had also been broken off. Another thing was that I felt watched. While out walking I often met a man who was definitely a Russian; he stared at me very hard, and no doubt he also knew who I was from the list of visitors. I was so scared he might do something to me or kidnap me; it would not be the first time the Bolsheviks had done such a thing, even in Switzerland. If only Osten-Sacken had been there, I should at least have had male protection. Mrs Rathlef agreed about this and wrote several times to Botkin that Osten-Sacken should be asked to come.

Altogether, I probably felt more hunted at this time than was justified, but my nerves were still in a very bad state. Once we made a steamer excursion on the lake. As with all novelties, I at first found this extremely pleasant, but then I suddenly saw near me a man who spoke French and was just like Gilliard. This gave me an awful shock. Although I would have liked Shura to be with us, I had no wish to see her husband again after his behaviour in Berlin. Mrs Rathlef thought the French-speaking gentleman looked more intelligent than Gilliard, but then she had underestimated his intelligence before, or at least his ability to fit in wherever he went. Mr Gibbs, our English tutor, was quite different, a frank, straightforward person. Anyhow, this incident left me exceedingly agitated.

At first we used sometimes to go out for drives. I was too weak for long walks, besides which the bunion on my right foot was somewhat inflamed, and I had difficulties in walking. These outings were very nice, of course, but things were a bit different at home in Russia. I can still remember driving out as a girl with my sisters. There were four seats in the carriage, which was open and had a low door you slammed. I usually wore white. We drove along the wide sand-tracks across the expanse of plains, not so enclosed as here among the mountains. Altogether I find Lugano rather depressing with this fenced-in feeling and its narrow lanes. When we drove through the streets in Petersburg or Moscow, they were much wider and longer. In the towns our drives always had an official character, we were escorted by officers and drove past at great speed. When we got back home, we nearly always had headaches from nodding to the crowds all the time.

The longer I was in Lugano, the more my anxiety and nervousness increased, without my really knowing why. Perhaps it originated in my depression at being deserted by those from whom I had least expected it, and so I had a premonition that storms were gathering around my person through their doing. Perhaps I was also affected by the anxiety of Mrs Rathlef, who corresponded tirelessly with my last remaining friends, like Botkin, Zahle and Osten-Sacken, about my identity being acknowledged and my future financial support. Her letters to Gilliard all remained unanswered, though Shura did write once more; but there was nothing of any importance in her letter, and it could not calm me. Once there was a letter from Mrs Tolstoi, who was obviously still devoted to me. Then we heard of an exchange of letters between Gilliard and Zahle, who had come to Switzerland on my affairs; but instead of going to see Gilliard, he eventually sent a stiff note refusing to go, because Gilliard would not listen to sense. For the same reason, no doubt, Botkin, who once stayed in Paris, did not look up Gilliard on the way—although I had actually hoped he would do so. And to crown my worries, Osten-Sacken wrote to me: 'No money, our enemies triumph.' That was the situation.

In order to distract me, Mrs Rathlef arranged a systematic routine. I must have some 'mental occupation,' as she put it. But she went about it too strictly, so that I began to resist her. As she did not speak English herself, she had discovered an old English teacher, a woman, with whom I was to read, speak and also write English for an hour every day. In fact this experiment was successful, my knowledge of the language gradually returned, and eventually I even enjoyed my English lessons. Then I was to do an hour's embroidery every morning and evening. I was always quite clever at such work, and I found it fun too, so that I was as impatient as a little girl to get on with it. I also took up my drawing again, though with less success. Twice a day before meals I went for a little walk, so far as my foot allowed me, and on warm days I lay out on the balcony.

Then all my anxiety burst forth again. I was haunted night and day by the question of getting my identity acknowledged, and our financial worries were now so great that Mrs Rathlef had to refuse almost all my wishes. We quarrelled with each other a lot. In the end she left me for several hours almost every day, and said she would leave me altogether unless I became more sensible. I began to be suspicious of her, and treated her just as badly as she treated me. I think now that I was perhaps unfair to her, for she had really done a great deal for me. At the time, however, I felt she was laying down the law in everything she did, and that is a thing I have never been able to bear. Meanwhile, without her knowledge, I had written in my distress to Mrs Gisell, with whom she had come to see me a year before, asking her to inform Zahle of the position. And so at last, in the middle of June, Osten-Sacken arrived in Lugano, sent by Zahle, and Mrs Rathlef left me.

* * *

It is sad and strange that Anastasia should have broken on such slender grounds with someone who had served her so devotedly. There has always been a streak of unreasoning antagonism in her character, perhaps inherited from her grandmother—she once admitted having some of her grandmother's worse traits; and when she felt deserted by close relatives and former intimates, it aggravated her resentment so that she assumed her very best friend to be really against her. A few years before, she had used Inspector Grünberg as scapegoat after Princess Irene refused to recognise her; now, with Shura's defection, the new scapegoat was Mrs Rathlef—whose letters of this period show a despair fully equal to Anastasia's own:

30th May, 1926 (to Serge Botkin): 'I should be grateful if you would keep me informed about how things stand at the moment and what points still await clarification. I hope this business will be settled by autumn. In June it will be a year that I have devoted my whole energy, time and intelligence to this poor lady, a task which really her relatives should be doing—for it is just when they are in doubt of how to react, that they ought to care for her and get to know her so as to reach a conclusion. Instead of that I, a stranger, am obliged to carry through this far from easy task.

'It would be easier if my patient had some appreciation of how complicated everything is, and would realise that those around her—I and the others—have the best intentions towards her. I know from conviction and observation that her memory is not as bad as it seems. There is a terrible lot of obstinacy and refusal to face things. May God grant that it is all settled soon. For this responsibility, which now rests on my shoulders alone, is heavy to bear. Nor do I think that her bad moods, and for that matter her constantly changing moods, combined with the resistance which makes all my work so difficult, will change in a different environment. For three days she has not been speaking to me, and won't leave her room; also she's again eating too little. I hope to hear from you soon.'

Lugano, Monday: 'Have just received a shattering letter from Osten-Sacken. He writes that everything is hopeless, there is no money, and the enemies triumph. Gilliard doesn't answer me either. What is to become of the poor child? It wrings my heart. Better she should have died than be thrown on the streets again. I don't think I could get over the breakdown of her case. I am so devoted to my little patient, whom I wrested from death. My heart bleeds when I talk of it. . . . Please tell me what is to happen now. . . . Is she to go back to dusty Berlin? My studio is too small and primitive, I can't restore her to health there. And don't forget that she is ill, needs air and good food.

'My God, what is to happen? Really people are mad to take such a sin on themselves. Would it not be possible for Mrs Tolstoi to have her? She loves her, she has written again—I mean, if the worst comes to the worst. . . .'

*4th June:* '. . . She is giving me a terrible lot of trouble. She has again become so obstinate and bad-tempered that I have no alternative but to leave her. I believe she is very unhappy, and her whole despair descends on me as on a lightning-conductor. She can be so charming, but at times like this she is a little devil, spiteful and shockingly unfair. . . .'

Lugano (undated): 'You have heard from Baron Osten-Sacken how dreadfully hard it is to deal with the patient, how she keeps running off, won't let her arm be dressed, has locked away all the dressings and ointments I need, and refuses to eat. Every morning I try to persuade her to have her arm dressed, and to sit in the sun on the balcony for the few minutes she should. Either I get no answer at all, or else she shouts at me to leave her in peace. . . . You know my position in this matter and all I have done for her, how I have tried with all my strength to help her win her rights, how I nursed her when she was at death's door. . . . She knows all that, yet somehow she does not feel one is trying to help her. On the contrary, her moods and rudeness go so far that I must really ask you to do something to let me retire from this work. . . .'

Osten-Sacken's impressions are given in a letter to Zahle from Berlin, dated 29th June, 1926:

'. . . Having returned to Berlin today, I beg to report to your Excellency as follows. Following your instructions I left Berlin on the 18th, arriving at Lugano the following day, to find Mrs T. in a quite extraordinary state of agitation—I have never seen her like it before. . . . In the evening we went out for a walk, I asked her what exactly the matter was. At first she refused to talk about the whole thing, saying it was all so dreadful, so revolting, that she couldn't and wouldn't talk of it. But when I told her I wanted some explanation, that I hadn't been sent for my own amusement but that you had asked me to try to get things back to normal, she yielded, though with great reluctance, and answered my questions. As soon as Mrs R. was mentioned, which naturally happened all the time, she showed an irritability and bad temper out of all proportion. . . . She said she had lost her faith in everybody, and more in the same vein. I realised during the conversation that she has become suspicious of us all as well, so I proceeded with the utmost care and gradually managed to awaken some trust in her. . . . Without venturing on any judgment as between the two ladies, I would think that they have simply got on each other's nerves and so no longer get on together. . . . An immediate separation was required, obviously; but it was hard to persuade the patient that Berlin, where she wanted to go, was not the right place for her. However, I succeeded eventually in that too. . . .

'After I received your telegram with instructions to go to Oberstdorf, I met with great resistance, as I have already mentioned, and had to contend with fits of temper against Mrs R., suspicion of us all, and tears. We had over three hours arguing about it and I faced accusations that we all wanted to shut her up in an asylum, we were all against her, we talked and wrote only wicked and cruel things about her, she would have no more to do with anything or anyone, and so on—till eventually I managed to get her admitting of her own accord that she believed me, saw I was right, and only asked me to tell her frankly where I was taking her. When I had explained to her what Oberstdorf was and said there was not the slightest question of an asylum, she agreed to go there. From that moment on the spell was broken. Mrs R. left the next morning, and the patient was a different person, chatty, energetic, even gay. I deliberately left her on her own quite often, both indoors and to go for walks. I left her also to pack her things herself; she gave her whole mind to this and did it all perfectly competently.'

* * *

At the end of June, after Osten-Sacken had been about ten days with me at Lugano, I left with him for Oberstdorf in the Bavarian Allgäu, where Zahle had got me into the Stillachhaus Nursing Home. At first I had strong misgivings and vigorously resisted Osten-Sacken, seeing that I did not know what sort of a 'nursing home' it was, and was terrified of being put in an asylum again. Once during our quarrels Mrs Rathlef had hinted at such a thing, but of course in quarrels people say a lot they don't mean, and my own behaviour had certainly not been angelic either. Still, I think my anxiety was understandable: a sane person who has once been shut up for over two years in an asylum, will naturally be frightened to death of going through such an appalling experience a second time.

I did not need to have this anxiety at the Stillachhaus, it was a real nursing home and very well run. I had complete freedom as long as I obeyed the normal rules and the doctors' orders; nor was I made to mix with the other occupants of the home. I was given a very nice room on the first floor with a balcony where the birds came flying in, and where I had a fine view on to the wide valley of Oberstdorf, with wooded mountains in the background. Although at first I was still rather depressed and apathetic, I did not feel nearly so fenced in here as at Lugano. Right from the beginning I went for walks with Osten-Sacken, and enjoyed the fields and meadows with cows grazing and sometimes valleys to be seen instead of only endless mountains. I am no city child, and have always been very fond of nature, flowers and animals.

I had to stay in bed a lot, eat plenty, go for walks and take sunbaths; special attention was paid to my arm. If I did not have meals in my room, I would go down to the dining-room, where at my request a table had been reserved for me at the very back of the room, so that I should not be noticed and needn't speak to anyone—for all I wanted then was to be alone. But with time I got used to people again. The doctors, Dr Saathoff and Dr Eitel, were very pleasant, so was the matron, Miss Wasserschleben; and as I wanted to continue my English, I soon found an old lady with whom I could once more take lessons; she was over eighty and very amiable. Otherwise I did not mix with anyone, and when Osten-Sacken left for Berlin, I was thrown completely on my own resources. The mountain sun and good nursing soon produced their effect on my health, so that after a while my wound healed and I felt a great deal better. This was lucky, for after two months I received a visit, quite unexpectedly, from a Russian friend—a visit which was to prove very important for me.

* * *

On 29th June, 1926, just after Anastasia had been admitted to the Stillachhaus Nursing Home, Osten-Sacken wrote as follows to Zahle:

'. . . The wound on the left hand is open, but the doctor thinks it will definitely heal in three or four weeks with regular treatment by sun-baths. To increase their mobility, the patient needs to exercise the fingers of this hand and also the arm and shoulder, whereby a comparatively normal use of hand and arm should certainly be achieved. After studying the X-rays I showed him, Dr Eitel expressed his opinion that the patient's condition is caused more by psychological factors than by external causes of a physical nature, despite the damage to the skull which can be observed. He is therefore far more worried about her mental state, her inhibitions and obsessive fears, by which she is completely dominated; he is also surprised at her forgetting of languages, but added that such cases are medically familiar. While talking to her, he asked if she had seen Duchess Vera (daughter of the Grand-Duke Constantine of Russia), whereupon she promptly replied: "I have never been in Württemberg." When he asked about Darmstadt, she said she had been there three times; he was astonished at the answer to his first question, indicating absolute knowledge. He told her that he had spoken to Vera, which she found quite natural. But she has not really come out of her shell yet.

'I was extremely interested by the doctor's views on her personality and the whole business. On the brief period of his observation, he felt she undoubtedly came from the highest circles; she had an unusually profound and generous temperament—"a Russian temperament," to use his own words; showed no signs at all of shrewdness or pretence; was equally certainly a person who had gone through an appalling number of dreadful experiences, an altogether sick and unhappy person you could not help being extremely sorry for and would do your very best to help in every way out of sheer humanity. . . . He laughed loudly at somebody's suggestion that the patient spoke a Swabian, even an Allemanic dialect. He is a Swabian himself and went to an Allemanic school; and he finds not the slightest trace of these accents.

'He is deeply impressed by her bearing, nature and amiability; her manner is typically "aristocratic," as he puts it, a manner which could only be native to her; going purely on his feelings, he is absolutely convinced of her origins, and is filled with boundless pity for her, which, as he says, simply impels him to do everything he can to help her. He very much hopes she will settle down, and that after a while she will be able to receive visitors, to give her this feeling of appeasement which he says is so necessary.

'Throughout these last days the patient has been specially concerned about two questions, to which she is always harking back. One is her bad arm, which she is in despair about yet longs to have healed; the other is her great desire that enquiries be somehow taken up again in Rumania as quickly and energetically as possible—for she swears the solution to the riddle is to be found there, and that the people she says rescued her and were so good to her could certainly be found by proper investigations and would still help her today. She keeps on returning to this with much intensity, which, frankly, set me thinking, and in spite of all doubts has to be taken as an argument in her favour. . . .'

Two months later Anastasia was a good deal better, though by no means well; the visitor she refers to, who came to see her at this time, was Tatiana Melnik, married daughter of the murdered Dr Eugen

Botkin and niece of Serge Botkin. Mme Melnik lived near Paris, where the popular papers had several times spread stories of one of the Tsar's daughters reappearing; but these stories never proved true, so at first she paid no special attention to the latest rumours about Anastasia. Then her uncle told her there must be something in it this time, and she decided to make sure for herself. He put her in touch with Osten-Sacken, whom she met in Munich on 25th August. She was with her aunt, Mlle Degebory, and had been in Italy convalescing after a serious operation. To make a real recognition possible, if the Oberstdorf patient should in fact be Anastasia, the visit was kept a complete secret; when they reached Oberstdorf two days later and went to the nursing home, only Osten-Sacken was announced.

* * *

One day at the end of August I was informed in the nursing home that Baron Osten-Sacken had arrived and would like to speak to me. I was extremely surprised that he should not have written beforehand to say he was coming, and felt not a little agitated. Was he bringing bad news, which he would rather discuss with me in person—or did he even mean to take me away from Oberstdorf, just as I had settled down there so well?

It was afternoon, and I hurried downstairs. Osten-Sacken was standing in the hall. I felt much disturbed when I saw that two ladies had come with him. Seeing the surprise from my face, he at once explained that the two ladies were friends of his whom he had accompanied here; that the younger of the two needed a period of convalescence after an operation and wanted to stay in the nursing home. He therefore asked me to take the ladies under my wing, as they were complete strangers. I shook my head, feeling no wish at all to take up with people I did not know—all I wanted was my peace, so that I could continue my recovery. But when he persisted in his request, I asked him who the ladies were. He was unwilling to give me their names straight away, saying I might afterwards find that out myself; all he could tell me was that their family had been very close to my father. I replied that there had been many people of whom this could be said, but declared myself ready to make the ladies' acquaintance on the following day. Although I had only seen her for a brief moment, I felt as if I had some time met the younger one before.

I spent the whole night wondering who it could possibly be, but once more my dreadful memory for people let me down.

The next day I met Osten-Sacken for lunch. I told him he and his ladies should come and have tea with me on the balcony. After lunch, when we had been standing round in the hall for a bit, the two of them came up to us and shook hands with me. But it was only a fleeting encounter, at which Osten-Sacken told them of my invitation. I myself was far too excited to be able to talk to them. Although I felt even more convinced that I knew the younger lady, I still found it quite impossible to decide who she was. And it was just the same in the afternoon when she was upstairs with me. I was racking my brains so hard I scarcely spoke a word; and we did not get into conversation till she showed me a photograph album she had brought. This contained a great many pictures from the old days, in which I was naturally very interested, and it affected me powerfully to see them. The lady was extremely kind, seemed to be a very warm-hearted person, and she also claimed to know *me*. But at the moment it was too much for me to think where I had met her. It was not till she had left me that a connection dawned.

Osten-Sacken came to my room in the evening to take me down to dinner. But I was far too excited and I had a severe headache as well. But as I wanted to know at last who the younger lady was, I asked him whether she had not perhaps been sent by Mr Botkin; whereupon he replied that Mr Botkin lived in Berlin, while the ladies lived in Paris. I told him he had himself declared that the father of the younger lady had been with my father. When he assented to this, I took him at his word and said he had promised to tell me the names if I did not guess them. Now he admitted that it was Tatiana Melnik, our Dr Botkin's daughter. I had thought it was, and was happy to have it confirmed. I thanked Osten-Sacken for having brought her to me.

For the first time a feeling of joy came back into my heart, such as I had not experienced for ages. I at once felt complete confidence in Tatiana Melnik, and began to become terribly fond of her. Several times a day she came to see me in my room, we sat on the sofa, looked at pictures together and talked of past days. I could not listen enough to all she told me, and when I felt tired, I leaned my head on her shoulder. She talked to me about her children, who were also living in Paris, and showed me photos of them. Then we spoke of her eldest brother and I said how my father had called us children together one evening to inform us of this brother's heroic death in the war. As to Gleb, she told me that he was now a journalist in America. Sometimes I also visited her in her room, and the first time I was there I saw on her table a photograph of her father with her two brothers. The picture moved me greatly: Dr Botkin murdered, his eldest son fallen on the battlefield!—this fine Russian family too had suffered a harsh fate. On one of these visits to her room I also discovered the souvenir medallion I have already spoken of—the one her husband had received in one of our hospitals at Tsarskoe Selo.

Of course there were many memories from the distant past which made me feel rather sad, and when I was telling Tatiana Melnik about my experiences in the previous few years, I made no secret of the fact that I should find death a merciful relief. But she kept on finding ways of cheering me up with some amusing story or other; and then we even laughed a great deal.

When her time at Oberstdorf came to an end, I naturally found it very hard to let my newly won friend go. For days before she went I was depressed and upset. I did not fail, of course, to accompany the two ladies to the station, when they were setting off for a further stay in Italy. Then we said good-bye, a quite heart-rending good-bye, for now I should be left behind all on my own again. For a long time I waved to them from the platform, until the train turned a corner. But the next year I was to see Tatiana Melnik once more. This good friend was never again to disappear from my life.

* * *

Extract from Osten-Sacken's letter to Zahle, 9th September, 1926: '. . . After the first conversations with the patient about Ekaterinburg, etc., Mme Melnik said there could be no doubt it was the Grand Duchess Anastasia Nikolaievna. After she had studied and observed the patient sufficiently, I put strictly formulated questions to her. . . . I: "Who in your opinion is the female patient occupying Room 22?" Mme Melnik: "She is the Grand-Duchess Anastasia Nikolaievna, I recognised her, she is the same person I used to know; the lower of her face, her mouth, is altered, nothing else." I: "So in fact you recognise the patient who calls herself Mrs T. as Anastasia, the Tsar's daughter?" Mme Melnik: "Yes, I recognise her, I am not basing my answer on abstract reasoning." I: "Then I am entitled to state that you have recognised the Grand-Duchess Anastasia?" Mme Melnik: "Yes." I: "Are you willing and able, if required, to swear that you recognised the patient Mrs T. as Anastasia Nikolaievna?" Mme Melnik: "Yes, I am ready to confirm it on oath."

'. . . I must stress again that Mme Melnik's devotion to truth, honesty and disinterestedness are beyond all question. Her extreme attachment to the imperial family, tne sacredness of their memory, and her strong sense of responsibility, are indubitable, and offer every guarantee that she would never speak or act over-hastily in such a matter.

'Dr Eitel, the physician treating the patient, the matron and the sister . . . are all absolutely convinced that she is the Grand-Duchess Anastasia, having arrived at this conclusion from their personal observations, and they are only surprised that anyone at all can still doubt this.

'The patient is extremely happy in the nursing home, and the rest is doing her a lot of good. Her arm is better; and in Dr Eitel's opinion, although she must still be considered as seriously ill, having acute tuberculosis, she is by no means incurable; but to become capable of facing normal life, she may need to stay another year in the nursing home with treatment and complete rest, avoiding all excitements such as interrogations and unwelcome visitors.

'To recapitulate, I can only repeat most definitely that the success of the two Russian ladies' visit has exceeded all expectations. . . .'

Extracts are given below from the declaration on oath which Tatiana Melnik made in 1929:

'I am twenty-one. I first saw the Grand-Duchess Anastasia Nikolaievna in 1908, when my late father, Dr Eugen Botkin, was appointed personal physician to His Majesty the Tsar of Russia. For ten years, from 1908 to 1918, I often saw, spoke to and played with the Grand-Duchess Anastasia. In 1917 I followed her, the rest of the imperial family and my father, when they were banished to Siberia; and I stayed with them until forcibly separated by the Bolsheviks, about three months before the tragic deaths in July 1918 of Their Majesties, four of their five children—namely Olga, Maria, Tatiana and Alexi—and my father. . . .

'On or about 25th August, 1926, I met Baron Osten-Sacken at Munich and went with him to Oberstdorf, to see whether the "unknown patient" in the nursing home there was really the said Grand-Duchess Anastasia, as was asserted by herself and others. . . .

'Living with my family at Rives, in France, I had heard little about the case of this "patient," and had not taken any serious interest in the conflicting rumours until I heard from an independent source that her case was not nearly so insignificant as many people had suggested to me. I decided at once to do everything in my power to clear the matter up. . . .

'Her Highness was not informed of my arrival, but only knew that Baron Osten-Sacken had come. . . .

'When I saw her face at close quarters, particularly her eyes, so blue and full of light, I at once recognised the Grand-Duchess Anastasia Nikolaievna. And while we were walking along side by side, on our first walk at Oberstdorf, which lasted hardly ten minutes, I noticed more and more resemblance to the girl she had been before all the tragedies and bitter experiences. The height, figure, and colour of hair are exactly those of the girl Anastasia. In her face I discovered features I had known before; but the mouth has changed and coarsened remarkably, and because the face is so thin, her nose looks bigger than it used to. The eyes, eyebrows and ears, however, are completely similar. Those unforgettable eyes, and the expression in them, have remained exactly the same as they were in childhood days.

'Three hours later we went up to her room for tea, which was taken on the balcony. She went out there in great excitement, could not utter a word, but made a sign to us to sit down, and began to pour out tea, although her hands were trembling violently. The conversation turned on some local festival, and she brought out postcards showing the scenery. Then I said: "I also have photographs," and laid in her lap a big grey album, the cover of which had a small photograph of the hospital under the patronage of the Grand-Duchesses Maria and Anastasia. She noticed this at once and opened the album. But when she saw her own picture and that of the other Grand-Duchesses, she at once slammed it to again, saying: "I must look at this by myself." Then she went inside, and Baron Osten-Sacken advised me to follow her. She was sitting on the divan with the album in front of her, regarding intently the picture of the Grand-Duchess Tatiana and saying something I could not catch about Tatiana's face. It was obvious that she was utterly shattered, her eyes were full of tears. . . . She asked in bad German, pointing at the album: "You used to know her?"

' "Yes," I said.

' "And me also?"

' "Yes."

' "When did you last see me?"

' "In 1918."

'She shook her head as if she could not remember. "You don't recognise me?" I asked her.

' "No, no sleep, just think." I took this to mean that she thought so much she could not sleep. I told her I had recognised her, that I had come not to question her but only to be with her: and that I had photographs of her family.

' "Oh, where?"

' "Here in my room." She asked if she might see the pictures. Doubt would be impossible for anyone who saw her, as I did then, bent over these photographs, trembling, with the moaning cry: "My mother, my mother!" . . . I presented her with a picture of the holy seraphim of Tsarov (which I had been given by the Tsarina); she kissed it reverently and wept. Then I gave her a book-mark made by the Tsarina. She took it at once and asked: "Did my mother make this herself?" When I nodded, she kissed it fondly. For a long time we sat there looking at these objects.

' "Where are the dead?" she asked several times. "Have you nothing left from there?"

' "Nothing except you, Malenkaia." (Russian for "my little girl.")

' "Malenkaia," she repeated. "That's what my father called me."

'In connection with the photographs of my brother, I said that my eldest brother had been killed in the Great War. "Yes, I know," Anastasia answered at once, "Papa told us about it." I know from my father that the Tsar did tell us children about the rather unusual circumstances of my eldest brother's death.

'After dinner I went up to see her in her room. She was reclining on the balcony in the dark; but when I arrived, she put the light on and came into the room. Through her tears her eyes were shining with joy; she came over to me, laid her head affectionately on my shoulder, and stayed like this for ages. Then she sat down, still without saying anything, and gazed somewhere into the distance, as if she could see something beyond the bounds of her room. I felt she was capable of sitting like this the whole night, and decided to put her to bed.

' "I'll undress you, as my father used to undress you when you were ill." "Yes, measles," she answered, and I realised that she had become completely aware of who I was. For it was when the Tsar's children had measles, and only once then, that my father stayed up with the Princesses by himself and looked after them like a nursing sister. This fact has never been published, and apart from my father I was the only person to know of it.'

Further of Mme Melnik's impressions are also recorded in a letter she wrote to the Duke of Leuchtenburg:

'Her attitude to life is child-like, and altogether you cannot deal with her as with a responsible adult, but must lead and guide her like a child. . . . Conversation with her is difficult. She is solely interested in political questions, memories of the imperial family, and life in the still surviving courts. Apart from that she still enjoys listening to funny stories, which you must relate with as much humour as possible. Once you start on a serious subject, unless it is one of the three mentioned above, she stops listening and assumes a worried stare. . . .

'She plays patience, and although she says she played it a lot during the last weeks in Siberia, she cannot properly distinguish an eight from a ten. Once she bought something at the chemist's which cost 1.50 marks; she gave the chemist two marks and went away without taking the change. When this was pointed out to her, she went very red, and said afterwards: "The first time I went shopping, I flatly refused to pick up my change, not realising that money could be changed. When it was explained to me that this was quite normal, I was ashamed to go back into the shop, because they would think me stupid for not knowing such ordinary things."

'These weaknesses are obviously caused by some defect in her memory and her eyesight. She says that after her illness she forgot how to tell the time by a watch, so that she had to learn it again laboriously and even now has to practise this several times a day. She admits that she forgets almost everything if she does not have continual practice. She always has to force herself to get dressed, wash, and sew, lest she forget how to do these things. Recently she has had no practice in writing, so she simply cannot do it any more; whereas she did write sometimes when she was at Lugano.

'I tried to study her handwriting from the exercise books in which she did dictations at Lugano; but it is very hard, because her writing is just like a ten-year-old child's. Only the letter A is very like her former writing, and there she writes not *a* (as she began doing when a little older) but the A she used when about ten. . . .'

In July 1953 Agnes Wasserschleben, the former matron at the Stillachhaus Nursing Home, made the following declaration on oath:

'. . . Very slowly Mrs Tchaikovski began to recover and regain strength, with which went a change in her whole personality. But she did not like being in the mountains, which depressed her, and told me of her homeland, her gardens, and the journeys she had made with her family; such talk usually left her feeling very sad, and she kept on repeating how ready she was to die and how indescribably hard it was to be the only one left surviving after *such* experiences.

'Her confidence grew in me and all of us around her. As we did not plague her with questions, she told many stories of her childhood quite spontaneously. She spoke of her life at home, the simplicity there and the inexorably strict routine, by which her mother set the greatest store. She described the whole family, spoke with special fondness of her sister Olga, and kept on praising her sister Maria's affectionate character, which was a tremendous prop to her parents, especially during their hardest times. She became very vivacious in these conversations and could give most telling descriptions of people and their conditions, though it was always in such faulty German that much of what she found difficult to express in words could only be understood through her animated mimicry. Understandably enough, she lived wholly in the past and could not understand her present fate. To her extreme distress she had also lost touch with her religion, and kept asking for her grandmother in Copenhagen, imploring me to take her there. She was afraid the Empress-Dowager would die without her ever having seen the old lady again; she said that even if she were not received at Copenhagen, she might at least have the chance to see her grandmother in the distance going to church. She often expressed a wish to go into a nunnery, so that at last people might leave her in peace there, and she repeatedly asked me to take her to one.

'Gradually she also began to speak of her child. She kept begging for enquiries to be made in Bucharest, from which she was sure her own case would be cleared up and the child found. No doubt a longing had slowly grown up within her for this infant which, although conceived without love, did after all belong to her. She was very deeply hurt that her relatives wanted nothing to do with her. She told me how she had behaved stupidly at the meeting with her Aunt Irene, but said she was then in a poor condition physically, and soon afterwards became very ill. She felt insulted that they should have introduced Princess Irene to her under a false name and not told her anything about the visit beforehand; yet at the first words the Princess spoke, she realised it was someone she had known in her childhood. Once when I happened to mention the name "Hemmelmark," she became quite excited and asked where I had heard it from, because it was her uncle's estate. Then again, one day, when I had her to tea in my room, I was given another small piece of evidence for our patient's identity: she saw an ash-tray on the table with the initials of the Grand-Duke Ernest Louis of Hesse, and exclaimed as if electrified, "That's the monogram of my uncle in Hesse," and wanted to know how I had come in possession of the ash-tray. . . .'

Mme Melnik knew the Grand-Duchess Olga; four years before, indeed, she had sent a copy of her memoirs to the Grand-Duchess, who wrote to thank her for the 'most authentic and touching book. Such wonderful photographs of all my dear ones! And when I read about Anastasia, I remembered her so vividly. She was a little scamp, but so nice. I believe you will one day see them all again. Many thanks for the immense pleasure you have given me.'

Now Tatiana Melnik wrote to Olga from Oberstdorf, on 30th August, 1926:

'. . . At first glance I was struck by the face's resemblance to the Grand-Duchess Tatiana's; the whole manner and movements seemed that of the two eldest Grand-Duchesses. But on that evening I only saw her fleetingly, and did not meet her and talk to her till the next day.

'Her voice and look were enough for me to recognise her as the Grand-Duchess Anastasia Nikolaievna. There cannot be another being so much like her. I know that Your Imperial Highness saw the so-called "unknown patient," i.e. the Grand-Duchess Anastasia, in such a dreadful physical and mental condition that you were unable to recognise her; and I am convinced that if you were now to see her again, you would recognise her just as I have done. I have been living in the same building with her for a week now, and every day I discover more and more of her former features. The first evening she also recognised me from a distance as a familiar face, but could not remember who I was. The next day when we met again, she had remembered this too. . . .

'But how to help her, Imperial Highness? The past cannot be brought back. We cannot give her back her parents, her family, her position. But how is her morale to be restored, how is she to be given a new family, and the strength to live? She longs for death and asks despairingly: "Why was I left alive?" What can she be told she is living for? God's ways are mysterious. . . . She is young. She has the same wonderful soul as she always did; she has suffered so much, surely there should now be better days coming for her; but how can we help her? . . .'

The Grand-Duchess's answer, dated 13th September, reached Tatiana Melnik at St Remo, to which she had travelled from Oberstdorf with her aunt:

'Dear Tatiana Eugenievna, I have received your letter and hasten to reply. We took the matter very seriously, as is shown by the visits to the patient made by old Volkov, twice by Monsieur Gilliard and his wife (Anastasia's one-time governess), as well as by myself and my husband.

'However hard we all tried to recognise this patient as my niece Tatiana or Anastasia, we all came away quite convinced of the reverse.

'With every good wish, Olga.'

Tatiana Melnik had also written (on 3rd September) to Gilliard at Lausanne:

'Dear Monsieur Gilliard, Many years have gone by since I last had a letter from you, but time goes on as well as events. . . . A new event has occurred, the most tragic and incredible: Her Imperial Highness the Grand-Duchess Anastasia Nikolaievna is alive. We who all loved her, had so far only one consolation, to believe she was in another and a better world. Yet suddenly this poor martyred child, witness of the butchery of her whole family, is here amongst us. This summer I had read in the papers about the alleged Grand-Duchess Anastasia, but I wanted to test for myself the rumours circulating about the "unknown patient." And then it happened: when I arrived in the home where she is at present, I recognised her from the first conversation as Anastasia. I had already learnt from the press that you visited her when she was still very ill and obviously not recognisable. I am certain that you and your wife would now recognise her as I have done. . . .

'I have today written to the Grand-Duchess Olga Alexandrovna saying how I recognised her niece Anastasia, but I do not know if my words were expressive enough. You, dear Monsieur Gilliard, and your wife, who were always so devoted to the imperial family, even after their deaths . . . you will appreciate better than anyone how important it is that the Grand-Duchess Anastasia's psychological balance should be restored by the acknowledgment of her closest relatives. The joy of being once more in touch with her family would give her that new will to live which she needs so very badly . . . I should therefore be most grateful to you if you would let me know what you think about this. . . .'

What Gilliard claims to have thought is expressed in his book:

'I know Mme Melnik well enough to have no doubts of her seriousness, but knowing also her excitable temperament, I realise that she is liable to have shown a great lack of caution where Mrs Tchaikovski was concerned. She too, doubtless from earnest conviction, was in some haste to aid the patient's "weak memory" and "re-educate her brain." Of course Mme Melnik had heard from her father a mass of details about the life of the imperial family, so naturally the effect of her presence on Mrs Tchaikovski was noticeable soon after her arrival

—as is described in the words of one of Mrs Tchaikovski's fanatical adherents, "Mme Melnik works wonders. . . ." '

Undaunted by negative responses from these two people who knew and had recently seen Anastasia, Tatiana Melnik turned to other Russian relatives who might help. The Grand-Duke Andrew, the Tsar's first cousin (brother of Cyril), was living not so very far away, at Cap d'Ail in the French Maritime Alps; and although his mother had been on bad terms with the Tsarina, he was a much respected man. Accordingly Tatiana Melnik decided to give him a verbal account of her impressions of the Oberstdorf patient.

The Grand-Duke showed great interest, though at first he had no intention of taking sides in the matter. He wrote off to Serge Botkin as the head of the Berlin organisation for aid to Russian refugees, saying that up till then he had heard only what was said in the papers. Botkin replied on 19th October, 1926, with a full report:

'Your Imperial Highness, I had the honour to receive your letter, and will try to elucidate to the best of my ability the difficult question of the "unknown patient." I enclose a brief resumé for Your Highness to appreciate how she first appeared and in what circumstances she spent in Berlin the first years after her appearance. During this period she roused great interest among our fellow-countrymen, but unfortunately fell into the hands of people who, merely by being involved in the matter, undermined the confidence in her trustworthiness, thereby losing much valuable time. It must certainly be admitted that all one heard about the patient in those early days was so incredible that it rather suggested the stories of the great adventurers who commonly come to the fore in chaotic times.

'It was not till the summer of 1925, last year in fact, that the matter took a different turn. Prince Valdemar of Denmark, whose interest had been aroused by the rumours reaching him, asked the Danish Ambassador in Berlin, Mr Herluf Zahle, to investigate the case.

'Having gone into it thoroughly, Mr Zahle came to the conclusion that the patient's identity with the Grand-Duchess was altogether possible, and even probable. This conclusion was based on the following considerations:

1. Physical resemblances and the coincidence of special identifying marks.
2. Psychological attitude.
3. A whole succession of memories, indicating beyond doubt an intimate knowledge of the imperial family's home life.
4. Neither under anæsthetic nor in delirium did the patient show

knowledge of any circumstances or people outside the narrow circle of the imperial family.

'It was not till June last year that serious efforts were launched to prove her identity, and her companion made conscientious notes of all her conversations, as advised by the Danish ambassador. They include many recollections of her former life. Even apparently unimportant details in the patient's descriptions showed an amazing accuracy when they were checked; and it is inconceivable, especially with an amnesia attested by the doctors, that she could have based these descriptions on facts either read or heard about.

'Your Highness is better acquainted than I am with the latest developments, through the verbal report given you by my niece, Mme T. E. Melnik. I have not seen my niece since her visit to the patient and only know of her impressions from letters. Despite her relative youth she is a very sensible and reliable person, with an immense devotion to the imperial family, so that I cannot doubt her statements, which in fact confirm the evidence already available. . . .'

* * *

Soon after Tatiana Melnik had left me, I had a distraction of another kind. I needed extensive dental treatment and twice went to Munich for it, where I visited a court dentist called Lentrodt, who had his practice on Maximilian Square. I remember that Lentrodt was not only a very good dentist, but also a charming gentleman; and since my companion, our nursing home matron, had not said who I was, I felt free and unobserved. The treatment, it is true, was not very pleasant, and I repeatedly had severe pain. As I have already related, I had been obliged to have various teeth out, since the rifle blows at Ekaterinburg damaged my upper jaw. During the treatment Lentrodt discovered a peculiarity in my lower jaw which no dentist could fail to notice and which struck him so much that he now made plaster casts of upper and lower jaw. The two corner teeth in the lower jaw were badly stunted and hardly visible; he described this as a sign of degeneration which I must have had since my earliest childhood.

This matter looked as if it could be very quickly cleared up, since our former Russian dentist, Kostritzki, had settled in Paris and was sure to remember it. Enlightenment on this would also have been very important because Gilliard, who was bent on checking all my physical identifying marks by hook or by crook, claimed that neither my teeth nor the lower part of my mouth had been exposed to blows from a rifle butt. Gilliard had even, as he admits himself, had a sketch of my teeth drawn by Mrs Rathlef, without telling her the purpose, which he now showed around everywhere. But Kostritzki played a no less dubious rôle.

The following year, when I was staying with the Duke of Leuchtenberg at Seeon Castle and the campaign against me was in full blast, the Duke asked Kostritzki if he would come to Seeon and examine me, as he had repeatedly said there were special marks to be recognised in my teeth; but Kostritzki declined. The Duke then went to Paris himself, taking the plaster-casts, for which he had meanwhile asked Mr Lentrodt, so as to show them to Kostritzki; the latter, however, although he had agreed to see the Duke, now refused. At this the Duke sent Countess Mussin-Pushkin to him with the plaster-casts, but Kostritzki would not say whether they came from my teeth, and only declared that he would not have left teeth in such a condition. He did not mention at all the peculiarity with the corner teeth. Kostritzki equally avoided Lentrodt, who had travelled to Paris on my behalf at his own expense; he thought Kostritzki would have been bound to recognise his former patient instantly from the cast. What was one to think of this behaviour? Had Kostritzki too been gathered into my enemies' net?

My first stay in Munich lasted three days, I believe, and the second about a week. It was now November, but despite the dental treatment, I had time to see the town and district, with Miss Wasserschleben acting as guide. Once we visited the Residence, being shown over it by a former court footman, who wore a tie-pin bearing the signature of the last King of Bavaria. I was most interested in all the rooms and halls, and asked to be told what they had formerly been used for. A great deal was very different from our palace at home. In one hall I discovered a large green vase, the style of which I recognised immediately; I learnt that it had been presented by a Russian emperor.

There were other things too to remind one of Russia. On the way to the dentist we sometimes passed a Russian shop, from which I could not tear myself away. How I would have loved to buy something if I had had any money—a samovar, for instance. A little flat with a samovar has always been a dream of mine. And then we once passed a cinema, where there was a film showing about Russia, called *The Tsar's Courier*. I was terribly keen to see it, having an indescribable nostalgia for the old Russia. Miss Wasserschleben at first advised against going, lest I should be upset by the memories it aroused, but in the end we did go, and I am glad we did, for it was a good film, though it had some faults.

* * *

Miss Wasserschleben has given a vivid account of the visit to this film: '. . . I shall never forget the next hour. For the first time the patient forgot her surroundings, and followed the action with a vivacity which shattered me. She instructed me on the various nationalities living in Russia, exclaiming when they appeared: "Those are Kirghiz, these are Cherkassians"; and on seeing a difficult escape through the snow, called out: "I went through snow like that too." She made loud and unrestrained criticisms when a Russian wedding ceremony was not performed in the way she knew, and also criticised the film for some mistakes in the court formalities; but she was so struck by the good presentation that she kept gripping my arm with animated expressions of alternate pleasure and annoyance. I was on tenterhooks throughout, lest Mrs T. should attract attention to herself—as indeed she did; for after the film she was stared at curiously on the street, and I had a hard task shielding her from these stares, which might have led to people following her.'

According to another account, Anastasia *was* deliberately watched then, apparently for the first time, by a private detective called Knopf, who disguised himself inside the cinema by wearing blue spectacles. He was an agent for the Darmstadt court, and was to figure again in Anastasia's life.

At this time, the winter of 1926-7, Anastasia's well-wishers faced a big problem. If they went ahead with attempts to get her identity established, any set-back might worsen her health, which was still very much in the balance, and the excitement entailed by further confrontations might drive her back into stubborn silence, as it had done on earlier occasions. She herself was ready to meet such of her relatives as were willing to visit her, but the Oberstdorf doctors doubted whether she was yet up to it.

Apart from her uncle, the Grand-Duke Andrew, there seemed a

chance that her aunt, the Grand-Duchess Xenia, might help. She lived at Windsor, was a sister of the Tsar and the Grand-Duchess Olga, and the wife of the Grand-Duke Alexander, former admiral in the Russian navy, by whom she had six sons and a daughter: the daughter was married to Prince Felix Yusupov, one of Rasputin's murderers. But it transpired that Xenia (being ambitious for her sons as potential 'heirs to the throne') was bitterly against Anastasia, and Gleb Botkin (brother of Tatiana Melnik) reported having personally seen a telegram of hers to her sister Olga saying: 'On no account acknowledge Anastasia.'

So the best hope was the Grand-Duke Andrew, with whom Tatiana Melnik and Zahle were already in touch. Although his brother Cyril was also against Anastasia, the Grand-Duke went carefully into everything known about the 'unknown patient', apparently reaching positive conclusions, for he soon sent her a symbolic gift of money, at least indicating his goodwill.

Meanwhile the enemies at Darmstadt were not inactive. The Grand-Duke of Hesse summoned Gilliard to assist in a thorough examination of the case, during which Mrs Zanotti, the lady-in-waiting, asserted (on what authority it is not clear) that the plaster-casts of Mrs Tchaikovski's feet, now in the Grand-Duke's possession, showed no resemblance to the Grand-Duchess Anastasia's feet; and other evidence brought forward to identify her was declared to be equally negative. Then Count Hardenberg visited Zahle in Berlin, accompanied by Gilliard, explaining that the Grand-Duke felt it was best if all investigations were concentrated in one place. The matter of the plaster-casts was brought up, but as Zahle wrote to Serge Botkin in Paris, 'I asked Gilliard, in the Count's presence, whether he did not remember his wife having clearly told me and my wife that Mrs Tchaikovski's bare feet, at which she looked on my suggestion, were very similar to those of Anastasia Nikolaievna. Gilliard could not but admit this, and so in my opinion the whole business with the plaster-casts falls to the ground.'

At the end of January Zahle made a personal visit to Darmstadt for discussions with the Grand-Duke, who produced a tendentious summary of the discussions (seen but not signed by Zahle), implying that he had changed his mind about Anastasia; whereas the real reasons why Zahle withdrew from active support for Anastasia are shown in his letters (below) to Botkin and the Grand-Duke Andrew.

'All efforts made,' declares the Darmstadt report, 'to recognise Mrs Tchaikovski as the Grand-Duchess Anastasia have unfortunately proved vain. Some of the Grand-Duchess's closest relatives went to see Mrs Tchaikovski as soon as they heard rumours about the matter, but were unable to recognise her as the Grand-Duchess. Her identity has also been unequivocally denied by people in closest touch with the imperial family who have visited her, such as Baroness Buxhoeveden, Monsieur Gilliard and his wife. Certain unalterable physical identifying marks possessed by the Grand-Duchess Anastasia are not found on Mrs T., so that all further discussion of their identity is really superfluous, not to mention the fact that Mrs T.'s mentality, as reflected in Mrs von Rathlef's records, does not bear the slightest resemblance to the mentality of the Grand-Duchess Anastasia. His Imperial Highness the Grand-Duke added: "In these records there are assertions which are directly inaccurate and false: names given to relatives within the family circle, like *Aunt Nini*, which were in fact never used; other statements which clearly originate in accounts or descriptions Mrs T. has read; and others which no less obviously come from the constant association which she demonstrably had with Berlin's Russian emigrés. It can also be proved that these emigrés, believing she was the Tsar's daughter, sent her books and photographs from which she gained intimate knowledge on many details. . . . It is outside my scope and interest to initiate enquiries on who Mrs Tchaikovski really is.' (In view of subsequent developments this sentence is extremely ironical.)

'There was then a detailed discussion of various further points apparently confirming the identity of Mrs T. with the Grand-Duchess Anastasia. After studying the photographic evidence available His Excellency Ambassador Zahle satisfied himself that there were fundamental differences between the two. He also recognised that there were various inexplicable and incomprehensible inaccuracies to be found in the statements of Mrs T. and also in the information given by Mrs Rathlef and others.

'Finally His Imperial Highness the Grand-Duke expressed his heartiest thanks to His Excellency Ambassador Zahle for having handled the affair of Mrs T. so carefully on the instructions of His Imperial Highness Prince Valdemar; and said that in view of the lively exchange of ideas they had had during His Excellency's stay at Darmstadt he could only regret that they had not met before. In any case he would follow further developments in the matter with great interest, even though there was no longer any question of its being his niece.'

Immediately after his visit to Darmstadt (5th February, 1927) Zahle wrote to Botkin as follows: '. . . I hope you will understand my position. I am really left completely in the air. The mission I was given eighteen months ago by the Danish branch of the Russian imperial family has virtually been withdrawn now that the Grand-Duchess

Olga has pronounced so clearly against the identity of Mrs T. On the other hand she and the Empress Dowager have authorised the Grand-Duke Andrew to act for them in the matter, and all I am doing is to assist in handing things over. The letters I get almost every day from Dr Eitel are pretty alarming. It is impossible for my wife or me to travel out to see her, for if we had to explain that the Danish royal family was no longer supporting me, a collapse and absolute depression would be the natural result. I must of course write to you quite frankly, without concealing the painful facts. If it appears that neither the Grand-Duke Andrew nor the Duke of Leuchtenberg is willing to be actively involved, I really have no idea what will happen. . . .'

Zahle also wrote to the Grand-Duke Andrew on February 15th: '. . . My position has become extraordinary difficult, after the Grand-Duchess Olga has expressed to others (though not to me) her conviction that Mrs Tchaikovski is not identical with Anastasia Nikolaievna. As Your Highness will know, I was entrusted by Prince Valdemar of Denmark with the mission to clear up this mysterious affair, a task which up to the present it has been impossible to complete. Frankly, I am rather in the air at the moment, having no longer any authority to concern myself with the matter, either from the royal or the imperial family in Copenhagen; and still less from my government, which of course has nothing to do with all the work I have put in to maintain the present position—work I have carried out as a private individual without any pretence of official backing. From these facts Your Highness will easily appreciate that while obliged on the one hand to hold back, I am on the other hand anxious to maintain the *status quo* as long as I can. But I cannot conceal from Your Highness that the expenses which this objective has cost for a whole year have not been covered by the Danish court. I would not venture to express any definite opinion on the question of Mrs T.'s identity, but as at present I am the only person she seems to have confidence in, I am absolutely ready to use this confidence in order to guide her as common sense requires. I am exceedingly glad that Duke George of Leuchtenberg, showing a truly rare kindness, has decided to offer hospitality to the lady concerned, at least for the time being. In this way her life may be saved, an essential condition if the investigations Your Highness is undertaking are to have a chance of success. . . .'

* * *

The year 1927 had a bad beginning for me. The papers had started taking an interest in my person, after Mrs Rathlef had written articles about me in a Berlin evening paper. These articles may have been well-meant, and they recorded truthfully everything she had learnt from me or about me; but it was still painful to be brought into the light of publicity in such a manner. I was furious. Up till then my life in the nursing home had been lived in complete peace, without being noticed by people, but now all eyes seemed suddenly to be on me, and it was like running the gauntlet whenever I went into the dining-room or through the hall. This was so intolerable that I soon stopped going downstairs and took my meals in my room; I refused to be exposed to the gapers any longer—on whose faces you could see that they were taking sides either for or against me. For the papers already carried the first hostile voices attacking me at the instigation of Darmstadt. All that naturally caused the most horrible gossiping and stories.

Before long the police also began to take an interest in me. One day a local policeman arrived at the nursing home demanding my passport. He came right to my door, but the chambermaid refused to let him in. I had shown my passport on arrival and did not see why I should give it up now; but the policeman came a second time, at which Dr Eitel advised me to comply with the wishes of the police. I afterwards got it back at his insistence, but you can imagine how much whispering went on in the home about this, since the papers had already presented me as an impostor. I then learnt that a friend of Gilliard's, obviously on instructions from Darmstadt, had approached the Bavarian police with a request that my passport should be confiscated. Understandably, I was thoroughly upset, which was not exactly beneficial to my health, and saw the likelihood that I should not be able to stay at Oberstdorf much longer.

A few days after this incident with the police, I was thrown into new agitation. Out of the blue I received a letter from Zahle in Berlin, telling me that I should have to leave the nursing home, but that the Duke and Duchess of Leuchtenberg had offered to give me a home at Seeon. Even before this I had heard that Copenhagen had forbidden Zahle to go on looking after me, and that the Grand-Duke Andrew had undertaken all 'further investigation' of my case.

Distressing as it was to lose my good protector, Zahle, like this, the prospect was certainly heartening that a member of the imperial family was now to look after me, although I did not yet know what attitude he would take towards me, since we had never met at all.

But what attitude should *I* take to the Leuchtenbergs? I knew neither Duke George nor Duchess Olga. I only knew that he was Nicholas I's great-grandson and the nephew of Aunt Stana's first husband—I spoke of her at the beginning of these reminiscences. Zahle described the Duke to me as a very pleasant person, and the Duke himself wrote to me in the friendliest terms asking me to regard myself as his guest, and saying that he would even put me in a special wing of his castle so that I should feel completely independent. All that sounded very encouraging. But as I have an almost morbid dislike of any change of this kind and am always afraid of new faces, I wrote to Zahle declining. He was very upset, especially as he had no more resources to cover my stay at the nursing home. I received a second letter from him and his wife, who now offered to introduce me personally to the Duke and Duchess. Seeing that I no longer felt happy in the nursing home after the various incidents, I finally yielded and declared myself ready to move to Seeon.

* * *

Mrs Rathlef's articles in the widely read *Berliner Nachtausgabe* were supported by evidence based on her latest personal observations and on the most recent medical reports; so of course the other side also tried to produce such evidence. Their case rested on four points (as exposed in the 'Darmstadt Statement' to the press): denying that the Grand-Duke of Hesse visited Russia during the war; suggestions that Mrs Tchaikovski was in league with the Bolsheviks; her linguistic abilities differing from Anastasia's; and new evidence on the difference in physical identifying marks between Mrs Tchaikovski and Anastasia.

As to the last point, it was claimed that certain deformities on Anastasia's feet, known to various relatives and surviving servants of the Russian court, were not to be found on Mrs Tchaikovski's feet; that there was no foundation for statements that her appearance had been fundamentally altered by blows on the skull from rifle butts; and that negative results had been obtained from comparisons of Mrs Tchaikovski's ears with Anastasia's, which had been made at the Grand-Duke of Hesse's request by Professor Bischoff, a Swiss criminologist from Lausanne. But Shura (Mme Guilliard) had confirmed the deformation on the feet of 'Mrs Tchaikovski,' and X-rays showed that the bones above her teeth had been injured by violent blows; so there was nothing left but Professor Bischoff's comparison of the ears.

For the purpose of the comparison, the Professor had been given photographs in the possession of Gilliard (who also lived at Lausanne), one of these being part of a group photograph of the Tsar's children with shorn heads taken in 1917 after their measles. Even when shown the photograph just after it had been taken, friends of the family could hardly tell which of the Tsar's daughters was which: and it now transpired that Gilliard, to prove the lack of identity between Anastasia and 'Mrs Tchaikovski,' had given Bischoff Olga's picture identified as Anastasia's.

The first to notice this was the Duke of Leuchtenberg, who at once raised objections, asserting that it was Olga. Shortly afterwards the fact was confirmed without qualification by Prince Felix Yusupov (although hostile to Anastasia) in a statement to Zahle. Both Mrs Hesse, widow of the Tsar's adjutant-general, and a Mrs Barbara Kochubey, to whom the Duke showed the photograph, agreed with this verdict that it was not Anastasia but Olga; so, at a later date, did Gleb Botkin and the Tsarina's very close friend, Mrs Lili Dehn. Finally, a friend of Volkov's in Estonia declared that in his judgment it could anyhow only be Olga or Maria, who had rather round faces, and certainly not Tatiana or Anastasia, both of whom had elongated faces.

The Grand-Duke Andrew also wrote to the Duke of Leuchtenberg that he did not consider such comparisons as Professor Bischoff had made to be valid unless people of the same age were being compared, and that in fact the only reliable evidence of this kind for identity or the reverse would be from finger-prints. Skull measurements on living people were of very dubious value because the slightest bias in the instruments produced very different results, and such measurements were therefore of use only as an additional criterion; it was also questionable to base them on photographs, especially retouched photographs. But where Bischoff had been most remiss, the Grand-Duke Andrew concluded, was in not deeming it necessary to visit Mrs Tchaikovski himself. In these circumstances how could such a so-called expert opinion be given any weight?

* * *

At the beginning of March I moved from Oberstdorf to Seeon. Despite everything I had been through in the last weeks, I left the nursing home with a heavy heart, for I had been well off here and did not need to come in contact with people I didn't want to. The parting was made easier, however, by the fact that Lilian Zahle and Tatiana Melnik came to fetch me. In Munich we then met the Duke of Leuchtenberg, who took us to his castle at Seeon. Zahle had been quite right: the Duke was indeed a pleasant person—although the Duchess, a Princess Repnin, seemed to me rather a 'character.' I was sometimes doubtful, especially at first, whether she even believed in my identity, and that goes for her two daughters as well, though less for her two sons. But I admit I was somewhat suspicious that the Leuchtenbergs of all people should have brought me to their home, when I did not know them at all. Nevertheless, my reception by the Duke and Duchess was extremely hospitable and understanding, and I found no lack of care and consideration there.

I was given a room on the first floor, it was modest but well-furnished, and had a fine view on to the garden and lake. The castle itself was large and old, and looked rather dilapidated. It had originally been the seat of a Count Palatine, then a monastery. At the beginning of the last century it was taken over by Eugène Beauharnais' daughter, the Empress of Brazil, who left it to her nephew, the present Duke's father. Duke George probably did not have enough money to maintain it better; for this reason the Duchess let off some of the rooms to paying guests. I liked the castle's bulb-shaped towers, the flat landscape, the expanse of water, the moor and the birches, which always reminded me of Russia.

During the first weeks after my arrival, I stayed most of the time in my room or went for short walks with Tatiana in the garden. Once Miss Wasserschleben came to see me for two days. I saw my hosts only now and then, they often had visitors, and after the articles which had appeared about me in the papers I did not want to show myself to anyone. I was as angry as I was depressed by these articles, and Tatiana had a hard task trying to restore my morale. She took it very seriously, for she wanted to avoid my deciding to cut myself off completely from the outside world. The Duchess always sent fresh flowers to my room, she knew I was very fond of flowers. For Tatiana this was a pretext for trying to persuade me to go down to tea and thank the

Duchess. But she did not succeed. It reminded me of the way people tried to make my mother do something she did not wish to do. I told Tatiana this, and chaffed her that I too had a regular lady-in-waiting now.

After some while, when I had got used to the new conditions, it was unavoidable that I should meet other people in the castle. Yet it was often bound up with painful memories, since many of the guests were Russians. Once the Duke's brother came on a visit, Prince Nicholas. Although I had no alternative but to converse with him, our meeting was rather brief and formal. Tatiana asked me afterwards why I had been so stiff with him. As this Prince Nicholas had been one of my father's adjutants, she thought I had probably met him at Mogilev, the imperial headquarters during the war. But I must have seen the Prince at Tsarskoe Selo, and this brought a pang to my heart.

Another time I met in the garden General Hesse's widow, who lived at Seeon in an old mill-house and often visited the castle. I had already seen her once or twice, but at first could not recognise her, because she used to have a very different hair-style. As, however, her husband had once been palace commander, she knew what I looked like as a child. Even so, she was not, I believe, quite convinced of my identity. Anyhow, she used the opportunity of meeting me alone, to question me, as so many before her had done. Being angry about this, I scarcely answered her. Suddenly she asked me: 'Who is Conrad?' I knew very well who Conrad was, he used to give piano lessons to us sisters; and as at Mama's wish he had also given lessons to General Hesse's daughter, the General's widow knew all about this piano teacher, which very few other people did. The question seemed to her particularly suitable for testing me. I could not help laughing when reminded of Mr Conrad, and involuntarily mimed the hand-movements of someone playing the piano. She was astounded at this, and I now remembered who she was, so that I asked after her children, with whom we had played; from this time on she must have believed in me.

The meeting with Colonel Mordvinov was also planned as a test of my identity. The Duke had asked him to come to Seeon because he had once been in my father's immediate entourage. I was in one of the sitting-rooms with Tatiana, who was playing the piano, when the Duke came in and introduced a gentleman to me as a friend of his, though without mentioning his name. I knew at once that I had seen the visitor before some time, but could not remember his name, as so often happens with me. When they had both gone out again, I rushed over to Tatiana at the piano and asked her the gentleman's name. She told me it was Mordvinov, though without any explanation who Mordvinov was, and after half an hour I remembered that he had been one of Papa's adjutants.

Colonel Mordvinov was also consulted on another question which I alone knew about. Baroness von Meller-Zakomelski, the Duke's daughter, had shown me a finely-bound classic, the Grand-Duke Nikolai Michailovich's *Russian Portraits*. On one of the pages three portraits were reproduced, including a miniature of the Palatine Archduchess Alexandra Pavlovna, a daughter of Tsar Paul I. I knew this picture very well, the original must have been hanging somewhere in our house. The Duke then searched in a register, where it showed that the picture had been in my mother's possession; and Colonel Mordvinov, when consulted, thought it probably hung in the Winter Palace at Petersburg.

Mordvinov, however, whom I had only met briefly that one time in the music-room, maintained considerable reserve on the question of acknowledging me. Like so many people, he did not follow my father into banishment, although he was adjutant and employed particularly on confidential missions. I learnt afterwards that he was the man who accompanied Uncle Ernie to Russia via Finland in 1916. I can only suppose it was not very pleasant for him to be suddenly faced with one of his sovereign's daughters, whom he had regarded as dead. Like Gilliard, Isa Buxhoeveden and many other of my enemies, he probably had a guilty conscience, and he may also have been affected by 'Hessian influences.'

I had been just four weeks at Seeon, when an episode occurred which I at first did not grasp at all, but which later turned out to be a quite extraordinary intrigue launched against me by the 'Darmstadt circle.' Tatiana Melnik had left just before, and in her place Miss Wasserschleben was invited to Seeon to look after me, because I trusted her implicitly. Then the trouble came one of the first days in April. To my great surprise the Duke, who had only just gone to Paris, returned after two days. I could not understand what had made him come back in such haste, I merely guessed something must have happened to do with me.

The day after his return I had to stay in bed, as I was not feeling well. Then the Duke entered my room with a lady who was completely unknown to me. I wondered who on earth he had brought, as he had told me someone I knew was coming. But I did not know this lady here, and the Duke did not introduce her to me. Without saying anything, I looked hard at the stranger, so as at least to read something from her face; for of course she might really be someone I knew and I simply didn't remember her. But I could not find the slightest familiarity in this face. I only felt she was somehow sinister and unpleasant, so that I asked her to be good enough to leave me. She did not go, however, but remained standing just where she was. Meanwhile I waited for her to say something, instead of which she just stared at me blankly. After all I had experienced before, I guessed that there was something dirty going on, only I did not know what it could be. I looked at the Duke, repeated to him that I did not know the woman, and again asked her to go away. At this she did leave my room, presumably without achieving whatever she had come for. She had only been in the room a few minutes.

The next visitors, who obviously had some connection with her, were two gentlemen. They were also brought into my room by the Duke, and they were not introduced to me either. One of them brought me greetings from a family called Shanzkovski; all I could do was look at him in perplexity. Then the two talked of something else which I did not grasp. I could only let them stand there without talking to them, whereupon they also withdrew in evident embarrassment. But even now the Duke gave me no explanation about the strange visitors, though he promised to do so later. He just asked me to receive the two gentlemen again and this time without him. Despite my pronounced dislike of the whole business, I complied with his wish, but the second meeting did not seem to satisfy my visitors either. One of the two began to talk once more about a certain Francisca Shanzkovski, and as before I could only reply that I did not know anyone of that name. Then they went again. This visit also had lasted scarcely more than two minutes.

After a while the Duke returned alone. It can be imagined that I was extraordinarily worked up about the strange procedure and now at last wanted an explanation. The Duke altogether appreciated this and apologised for his behaviour, but said he had been acting wholly in my interest. He then told me that soon after Mrs Rathlef's articles had been published by the *Berliner Nachtausgabe*, the same paper had claimed I was by no means the Grand-Duchess Anastasia but really a Polish peasant-woman called Francisca Shanzkovski reported to the police as missing.

It was just when he was in Paris that these 'exposures' reached a sort of climax, and as Zahle wrote to him there that the *Nachtausgabe* wanted a confrontation between me and a witness who was supposed to have recognised me from pictures as that Pole, the Duke returned at once to Seeon. Painful as he found it, he had no alternative, he said, but to make this confrontation possible in the interests of truth. The witness who hoped to recognise me as Francisca Shanzkovski was the person who had visited me first: her name was Doris Wingender, and she was a free-lance contributor to the paper. The gentleman who had brought me the greetings from the Shanzkovski family was a private detective called Knopf, while the third visitor was Dr Lucke, one of the paper's editors.

I must admit that despite these explanations I was very disappointed in the Duke, all the more when I learnt that he had put the three visitors up in his house and given them hospitality; couldn't he have had them stay at the local inn? And was it really justifiable to present them to me as if I knew them? I was furiously angry. Fortunately, when they had all left me, Miss Wasserschleben came to see me, and I poured out to her my distress at this business, of which she had also been a witness, since the three stayed in the house. Now I was sick of Seeon, where I had just begun to settle down and thought I had found a quiet refuge. I asked if she did not know another nursing home where I could stay cheaply and live peacefully and not always be exposed to such confrontations. She tried to talk me out of this and to soothe my feelings as far as possible. It was lucky I did not yet know what lay behind the whole business.

* * *

If Anastasia was to be proved an impostor, as Count Hardenberg believed was essential in the interests of his master, the best way to do it would be by identifying her as somebody else, a woman of about the same age, from somewhere in the east, who had been reported missing about the same time as Anastasia was pulled out of the Landwehr Canal. Knopf, the private detective, equipped from Darmstadt with the 'Anastasia evidence,' found in the Berlin police records that a Polish peasant woman, Francisca Shanzkovski, had been reported missing in 1920 by a certain Doris Wingender, Francisca's landlady's daughter. This seemed very satisfactory for Knopf, but it would be still better if Francisca had turned up again for three days in August 1922, and then disappeared for the second time, the same three days when the unknown patient from Dalldorf Asylum, given a home by the Kleists, disappeared from the Kleists' apartment.

In fact, Anastasia was staying with Klara Peuthert for that period, but the paper did not try to trace her, while the Kleists and the Schwabes may well have been involved in the plot. Mrs Schwabe at least had been the first to suggest that Anastasia spoke Polish and was probably a Polish peasant. This was when she (Mrs Schwabe) was visited in 1925 by Gilliard and Kulikovsky.

At any rate Doris Wingender (now Mrs Rittmann) supplied Knopf with just the further 'evidence' required; she claimed to remember that her mother's lodger, Francisca Shanzkovski, had indeed turned up again for those three days in August 1922, only to disappear once more and be reported to the police as missing a second time; without result as on the first occasion. In 1927, however, recalling details from 1920 and 1922 with surprising precision, Doris Wingender (Rittmann) told Knopf: 'The unknown woman fished out of the Landwehr Canal was wearing the same clothing as Francisca Shanzkovski when she disappeared in 1920, and at her second disappearance in 1922 she took a dress borrowed from me!' This admirable witness, on seeing a photograph of Anastasia in one of Mrs Rathlef's articles in the *Nachtausgabe*, recognised her as Francisca Shanzkovski both by the resemblance and by the dress. The Scherl Publishing House, owners of the *Nachtausgabe*, offered Doris Wingender the sum of 1,500 marks if she could prove that 'the alleged Anastasia, called Tchaikovski, is really Francisca Shanzkovski, born at Borowielasz on 16th December, 1896.' It may be regarded as strange that the Berlin police, who since February 1920 had made strenuous efforts to identify the Dalldorf patient, did not in any way connect her with Francisca Shanzkovski—if the latter *was* twice reported to them as missing. A very cogent reason for their not doing so was that they believed Francisca to be dead.

Knopf had already visited her family in Poland, and a friend of theirs, one George Witt, afterwards went to Berlin to make further enquiries as to the truth of his story. The Berlin police informed Witt that to the best of their knowledge Francisca had been murdered in August 1921 by the mass-murderer Grossmann. Witt also saw Mr Rudnev of the Mommsen Nursing Home, from whom he learnt that their former patient was generally considered to be the Grand-Duchess Anastasia. Any doubts about Francisca's death were evidently suggested first by Knopf, not by the Berlin police, who up till 1927 regarded the 'unknown patient from Dalldorf' as in all probability being Anastasia. This is clear from their statements and records (especially Dr Grünberg's) quoted earlier.

In February 1927, while Mrs Rathlef's articles were still appearing in the *Nachtausgabe*, Hardenberg and Gilliard appeared at the paper's offices, offering Knopf's 'evidence' for a series exposing the 'Rathlef' Anastasia. The editors accepted the offer and arranged for Anastasia's confrontation by first Doris Wingender, then Knopf and the young staff-writer Lucke. While at Seeon, Lucke admitted to the Duchess of Leuchtenberg that Hardenberg had paid out 20,000 or 25,000 marks to get his case proved. (This emerges from a letter her lawyer sent that October to the *Tägliche Rundschau;* she was unable to remember which of the sums was mentioned.) Although the money was paid to Knopf, the paper's publishers may have had some further inducement from him if the knowledge of his being under high patronage was not enough.

Hardenberg had already called the Darmstadt police into action, and the letters passing between them—on his side extravagant praise for their zeal and on theirs obsequiousness towards the marshal of the Grand-Duke of Hesse's household—show clearly that they had pre-judged the case from the start of their investigations. They were shown photographs of the Grand-Duchess Anastasia and of 'the unknown woman' (some probably in Gilliard's possession), and by an examination of these they claimed to prove that the ears of the two women were quite different. An inspector in the criminal records department came to this conclusion by comparing the elevations and depressions in the ears, and Darmstadt's police superintendent proudly informed Hardenberg that ears, although less often noticed than other features, were a very good means of indentification, since you hardly ever found two people's ears being alike in every respect. In May, however, despite the satisfaction they and Hardenberg felt at such a conclusion, they were obliged to admit to the Berlin police (on enquiry from the latter) that they had not established the identity of 'the unknown' and did not know whether her particulars tallied with those of Francisca Shanzkovski.

While the *Nachtausgabe* refused to accept the failure of the 'confrontations,' there were other papers, such as the *Tägliche Rundschau* (mentioned above), which showed sounder judgment; and the argument continued through the summer of 1927. The Duke of Leuchtenberg, the only eye-witness at the meeting between Anastasia and Doris Wingender, declared that neither of the two had shown in her behaviour the slightest sign of ever having met the other before. Moreover, the Duke asked, if Anastasia had really been a Polish peasant, as was made out, how could she possibly have learnt up all her knowledge of Russia and court life there? Her whole way of thinking, her judgment of people and things, was typical of a member of the Tsar's family.

Miss Wasserschleben, of course, was firmly convinced that the former patient at the Stillachhaus Nursing Home was Anastasia—her whole behaviour and personality betrayed her origins and the world she was used to—and Dr Saathof, the nursing-home's medical superintendent, considered it quite impossible that she was a deliberate impostor. Almost always, he said, she had behaved exactly the reverse from what might be expected of an impostor, even at important moments and those when she was acting completely impulsively or instinctively. Thus she had never made any efforts to win over people on whose opinion and goodwill her position might depend, and in fact, for all her usual modesty and charm, she had followed her impulses quite indiscriminately without bothering about their consequences. Dr Saathof also rejected without qualification the suggestion that she was of low birth, saying that despite the vast gaps in her memory her bearing was so distinguished one would have taken her for the scion of a good family even without knowing anything about her origins.

General Hoffmann, former chief of staff to the Commander in Chief Eastern Command, was so sure Anastasia was the Tsar's daughter that when asked if he had seen her, he replied: 'I don't need to see her; I know'—he must have based this very decided opinion on knowledge gained during the war. In the 'Anastasia file' at Berlin Police Headquarters there is a letter from him formally demanding that all doubts as to her identity be abandoned. Until his death in July 1927 Hoffmann took a leading part in the various efforts to establish her identity, and he was one of the people who encouraged the Duke of Leuchtenberg to take her into his family circle.

In the autumn, shortly before Anastasia left Seeon, Mrs Rathlef, in agreement with the Duke, tried to end the Shanzkovski business for good and all by arranging for another confrontation, this time with Felix, Francisca's brother. He was with Anastasia about half an hour, but owing to his Low German dialect she understood scarcely anything he said. Although supposed to regard her as his sister, he never called her Francisca or addressed her by the familiar 'Du.' Afterwards he was asked to sign a statement on oath that she was his sister, and was assured he and his family would not be asked to support her. Refusing to 'sign a false statement and land myself in prison,' he said there was merely a likeness between this lady and his sister, but the likeness was only full-face, not profile, and there were many differences between the two. His sister's feet had been quite normal, her ears were not pierced, and she had never worn ear-rings. The formal declaration he made included the statement: 'There is no doubt at all that the lady did not know me or who I was.' He also said that he and his sister were devoted to each other; so after being declared missing in 1920, she would never have turned up again at the Wingenders in 1922 without letting him know she was alive and safe.

This should have settled the matter, but eleven years later, Anastasia was confronted with Shanzkovski's two sisters. They also refused afterwards to swear that the woman they had just met was their sister.[1]

* * *

As can be imagined, the Shanzkovski business upset me very much; my nerves were in shreds and my whole state of health was once more set back. I slept very badly, and often had to have injections to calm me down. It was really incredible to try to make out I was a Polish peasant; I have never spoken Polish. One day, incidentally, the Duke of Leuchtenberg brought a Russian gentleman into my room, whose name I don't remember. First of all he spoke Polish to me for quite a while, so that I could not understand a word and just racked my brains as to what this could mean. All of a sudden, without changing his tone, he asked me questions in Russian; these I naturally understood, and answered them in German. Directly afterwards the Duke gave me the explanation for the Russian gentleman's strange behaviour, saying with a

[1] Translator's note—During 1958 a new witness came forward with a statement of having met Francisca Shanzkovski at Danzig in July 1920 (one of four girls intending to emigrate to England). Since Anastasia was then in Dalldorf, this finally disposes of the assertions that she and Francisca Shanzkovski are identical.

smile that he simply wanted to give the alleged 'Polish peasant Francisca' a test on her knowledge of Polish. The questioner had done it very cleverly, and I even had to laugh about it.

From this period I remember something else connected with my languages. Both at Lugano and at Oberstdorf I had taken up English again. As a child I used to read a lot of English books, it was only French novels we were forbidden to read. Now I received the Memoirs, written in English, of my mother's friend Anna Vyrubova, and began to read them. Much as the book interested me, because it recalled the past, I found many memories very sad, specially Rasputin's death. I talked about it to the Duke, and he told me that this man, whom till then I had regarded as a saint, had done Russia great harm; at which I was utterly confused and despairing. Still, I did not entirely lose my faith in our Church, and it was indeed at Seeon, where there was a little Russian chapel in the house, that I again went to divine services more often again.

It was now Eastertide. The German Easter, which comes ten days before ours, was celebrated fairly quietly in the castle, since almost all of us here were Russians. Miss Wasserschleben took the opportunity to read the 'Easter walk' from *Faust* to me, and I must say that I was very impressed by Goethe, though I may not have understood everything. This is altogether the sad thing with me: I would so much like to improve myself, but keep stumbling on my ignorance of the most elementary things. When the war broke out, I was just thirteen, and then came the Revolution. Today I no longer have the necessary mental powers and can retain only a little of what I try to learn.

The real Easter for me, of course, was our Russian festival. I had observed Lent strictly, as we used to at home, with much fasting and services. Sometimes I found it hard to follow Vespers, and especially to remain standing till the end of it. But I refused to sit down when asked if I would like to; my parents never did that, they were very strict about our obeying the ritual.

At Easter, for the first time for ages, I went to Confession again and to Holy Communion. With all that had happened meanwhile, I was deeply moved by this, but for some time now I had felt the urge to make my peace with God, having lost it for so long. The best thing, of course, was the midnight service. Although the space at Seeon was limited, the procession with the lamps through the little chapel and the adjoining rooms was carried out quite in the Russian style, and our old hymns and anthems were sung. Then we returned to the chapel for the 'Christ is risen.' It was a great and uplifting moment.

After the service the Duke and Duchess invited me to the Easter Supper with them and their guests; they gave me the Easter kiss and presented me with little pieces of jewellery in the shape of Easter eggs, just as of old. I sat at a small table with them and their children and their closest friends who were part of the family circle; the Duchess had prepared a wonderful Easter meal. As in the old days I ate good food and drank vodka, and it was specially lovely when the children began singing Russian songs. That night I was once more happy and untroubled, only remembering my childhood and my family, forgetting all I had been through and all the strangers who were around me. But afterwards the sad thoughts returned, and I was again overcome by grief at the loss of my dear ones and my own powers, that loss which kept forcing me to be inactive and live only half a life.

Soon after Easter, the spring came to Seeon, and I enjoyed seeing everything becoming green and the flowers growing. Snow too was something I was always very fond of, at home we used to ride on sledges a lot and also tobogganed down small mountains—at which Papa often joined us. But spring is my favourite season. Mama also liked spring best, and all the flowers there are in spring, specially violets. We had lots of flowers in our rooms, and when I haven't any now, I feel as if there were something missing in my life and get quite sad. For my birthday particularly, there were always heaps of flowers. I was very fond of their scent, and this is probably the reason why I like perfumes so much—it was one of my mother's great 'likes' as well. My sisters were fond of perfumes too, but not so much as I was. Even as a child it was almost an obsession with me: it went so far that I used to present my perfume to all the people I liked. I have forgotten its name now, but I remember what the bottle looked like. It was only when I came out of Dalldorf that I had lost my sense of smell, and also of taste. One *can* lose these senses, just as one can lose one's memory.

The thing which pleased me most at Seeon was the lake, on

which I sometimes rowed with the Duke's children and their friends. An expanse of water always reminds me of Finland. There were a lot of rushes on the banks of our Finnish lakes, we used to cut some of them off and plait rush-baskets. When I tried now, however, I could no longer remember how we did it. The park at home was far bigger than here, it was like a wood. We also looked for mushrooms there, I enjoyed that so much. Picking mushrooms was always my passion, and at Lent we used to eat salted Russian mushrooms instead of meat.

In the summer two elderly ladies who used to live in Russia came on a visit to Seeon: Miss Klemenz and Miss Baumgartner. The former used to come to the palace at Tsarskoe to accompany my mother on the piano. This was a reason for our making friends, and as Tatiana Melnik wasn't there any more, she now had to play me something every day. I have always been very fond of music, and have a specially good sense of rhythm. *Eugene Onegin* with its lovely ballet was my favourite opera. We used to play a lot of Tchaikovski at home, but I also liked hearing waltzes and marches and above all Russian songs.

As I used to play the piano myself and knew how to write down music as well, I thought I could surely do it again after a little practice. But my first attempts were a dismal failure. For one thing I could only play with the right hand, as my left-hand fingers had become quite stiff and my arm wouldn't bend at the elbow; and then things went wrong with my eyes, so that I could scarcely distinguish the different keys. The worst thing was that I had forgotten all the notes and had to learn to read music all over again. But then the patient Miss Klemenz began her 'lessons' with the children's song *Chishik*, which I used to be so fond of, and I could soon play it after her by ear. We also played other Russian songs, like *Po Ulize mostovoi* and *Ach vy Sseni moi Sseni*, all of which I had once known, and of course the *Volga Boatmen*, which made me weep as it does any Russian. There was only one tune I could not bear listening to: the Tsarist national anthem. Miss Klemenz once began to play it quietly but I asked her to stop; it was just too sad for me.

Another lady living at Seeon was Miss Lavington, the governess of the Duke's grandchild. Once she received a letter from her sister with two large picture pages from the *New York Herald*

*Tribune*, which contained a very good reproduction of our private rooms at Tsarskoe Selo, Peterhof and Livadia. Although these palaces and castles were guarded by the Bolsheviks, somebody had taken the photographs, which had then slipped through the Soviet censorship. I was shown them as a test, after they had first been cut out of the paper so as not to influence me. When I looked closer and recognised what pictures they were, I became extremely excited. Our dear old Livadia on the Crimea had been turned into a Soviet sanatorium, but even so I could recognise our rooms: my father's study, his bathroom with the miniature swimming pool, the bedrooms, the boudoir, the music room and our children's playroom.

When we afterwards compared the other photographs with the captions, it turned out that the paper had made some mistakes. One room was said to be part of the Winter Palace at St Petersburg, when it was really at Tsarskoe Selo. There was another room, that had once had two beds in it, which I recognised clearly as my brother's room; it also had the same wallpaper. On the desk in my father's study there was still a photograph in a frame, but nobody knew who the lady in the photograph was: in fact, it was my grandmother, the Empress Dowager Maria Feodorovna, who was now living in Copenhagen. On another picture, hanging on a wall, I saw my brother Alexi again in a sailor suit. The photograph was rather indistinct, but I clearly recognised the room in which it had always hung. Still another showed my brother's chute at Tsarskoe Selo. Anyone like Miss Lavington who did not know this room personally, would think there was a large wall-mirror to be seen there, which reflected a long flight of rooms; whereas in reality it was not a mirror but a door leading to our various nurseries. On looking at it closer, Miss Lavington had to admit that I was right. Miss Klemenz also remembered the room with the chute. At first I would not believe this, because to my knowledge she had only been to Mama's drawing-room. Monsieur Gilliard has asserted that the furniture in some of the rooms was different from my description, but he has been unable to prove that the errors I pointed out were in fact correct.

In the middle of September Miss Klemenz and Miss Baumgartner told me of the arrival of two gentlemen who had read about my fate in the papers and wished to see me. One was Mr Bornemann, a friend of General Hoffmann (who had lately died), and the other, whose name was at first not given me, was the former Captain Dassel of the 9th Kasan Dragoons, the regiment whose commander my sister Maria had been. As I heard afterwards, the winter before the Revolution he had been five months in the hospital at Tsarskoe Selo where Maria and I had worked; this was why the Duke of Leuchtenberg asked him to come to Seeon, to see whether he would recognise me. After all the depressing experiences I had had, I did not feel the least bit inclined to receive the two gentlemen. What had I to expect from them? I only wanted my peace. Even when Miss Baumgartner showed me some photos Dassel had given her from that time in the hospital, I could not make up my mind to it. I recognised the pictures of course; one of them showed Maria and me at the entrance to the hospital. But they made me too excited, I could hardly bear these memories.

I heard voices beneath my window. It was a fine day, the family were having their meals out in the garden. I looked down and felt I had seen Captain Dassel before, only he looked fatter and also fuller in the face. So I finally agreed to see the gentlemen in the afternoon. I even had my room decorated with flowers, so that it should not look too bleak; for the people who were coming *were* from home.

I had just drunk tea with my two ladies and was lying on the divan, when the Duke came in with the gentlemen. I first greeted Captain Dassel, who saluted, addressed me by my full title, reported his name, rank and regiment, and finally presented me with a bunch of roses and a small box of chocolates. Then I shook hands with Mr Bornemann. I must say I was extremely moved by this meeting with Dassel, so that tears came to my eyes; he too had tears in his eyes. First, I suppose, it was the joy of hearing an old Russian officer reporting present—it was like the great days, and I had not heard anything like it for so many years. But then I was again overcome with distress, and had to bite my handkerchief so that it would not be noticed—for after all my guest was someone from 'there,' from 'the old days.' We had spent happy times with the officers in the hospital, and I had always been gay, while now one of them stood before me in civilian clothes, and I lay here in my wretchedness, not having my own bed, my own room, or even anything I could offer him. It was too dreadful. The only way I could do him honour was to put his flowers in a place of honour—perhaps next to the icon and Mama's picture—for he must surely be poor too and yet had put himself to this expense.

I don't know if the Captain recognised me, nor could I be certain whether I recognised him. His figure was quite different, so were his eyes and his expression. But it was so long since I had last seen him. After all I had been through, I had quite forgotten about our old hospital; this memory had completely gone out of my mind. Another reason why I found it hard to recognise my visitor was because when excited I can hardly see anything; everything dances before my eyes, and all I see is black dots. So I did not talk to him much, only saying that I had not meant to hurt his feelings by not receiving him the day before. And because of my agitation I asked the gentlemen if they would not mind returning the following day when I should be calmer again. This visit lasted no more than ten minutes.

That evening in bed I could not sleep for excitement. I remembered something which might help us to recognise each other. I have already mentioned how we used to give the officers souvenir medallions when they were discharged from the hospital. The ones from Maria and me bore our monogram, 'M.A.' Perhaps he remembered this? The same evening I asked Miss Baumgartner to tell the Captain this; but the next day he said he had received no medallion, and had also been on leave at Christmas when presents were being distributed; his fellow officers had got swords and watches for Christmas. This was not correct, however—I never gave swords, only cigarette-boxes and watches. Afterwards he admitted having mentioned swords merely to test me. On this second day, when I was feeling better, he tried to find out by other small questions whether we had been together at the hospital. For instance, he declared that the billiard table where we sometimes played billiards with the officers stood on the upper floor, whereas in fact it was downstairs. I could answer all his questions correctly: that the hospital was not housed in the palace but in a building adjacent to the church, that we often walked there and that my brother Alexi never came along with us. After I had answered yet more questions, which he asked me in Russian, he was convinced of having recognised me as the Grand-Duchess Anastasia. For me that time remained very far away, there might have been a thick veil over it all.

While I was at Seeon, I received one more visit I was not prepared for. This time it was a really joyful surprise, and the reunion with this old friend was to have far-reaching consequences for me. It was Gleb Botkin, Tatiana Melnik's brother, who had come to Europe from America to discover in person what truth there might be in the sensational stories now being spread about me in the American papers also. As mentioned at the beginning, I had last seen Gleb at Tobolsk before we were taken to Ekaterinburg, and although I only saw him then at a distance, I still had clear memories of him, above all for those amusing animal drawings of his. On the day before that dreadful journey he greeted me from the window of the Kornilov House opposite us, and I returned the greeting with a wave. That was now nine years ago.

Yet when the Duke told me of Gleb's visit, I was at first so surprised that I did not want to receive him. What had become of me, I asked myself, what did I look like, what possessions had I today? Would this meeting not prove a disappointment for us both? Gleb Botkin had found an occupation in America as journalist and artist. Of course he would write about me—but how would he do it? I could not then know that it was just the Shanzkovski saga which had made him go after the truth.

Gleb had been in the castle several days when we happened to meet in the hall. I was obliged to greet him, and gave him my hand, which he immediately kissed, recognising me on the spot, as I had recognised him. I felt at once that he had come as a friend not an enemy, and this gave me the courage to invite him to visit me on the following day. All my fears that he might write something unfavourable about me were dispersed, nor did I ever mention them to him.

The next day he came to my room with one of the Duke's daughters, Baroness Meller. Like her husband, who had occasionally seen me before the Revolution, she belonged to the part of the family which was well disposed towards me. I did not feel particularly well that day, because I am always agitated before visits, and I had to receive my guests from the divan. But when I saw from Gleb's face that he recognised me today just as much as yesterday, the spell was at once broken. Everything was as if we had never been parted from one another.

I was sure that Gleb would ask me about a thousand things which had happened in the last ten years, as would have been only natural, but he was considerate enough not to ask me any questions at all. Once when the conversation happened to turn to the palace at Tsarskoe, I put up my hand in a defensive gesture, because it made me feel sad; at which he immediately changed the subject and began to tell a funny story, so that I could not help laughing just as I used to do. That was like Gleb, and that was why I was so fond of him. Later on, though, we talked of the past as well.

Of course I also wanted to see something of his caricatures. Whenever he wanted to cheer us up at Tobolsk, he sent us girls his drawings in all secrecy through his father or Tatiana; and we sent them back to him the same way. As he was very gifted and had gone on with his art, I very much hoped he had brought some of his work to Seeon, and sent this message to him through Baroness Meller. When he next came to see me, he brought a whole mass of drawings, mostly from his time in Japan and America. On looking at them, I saw that he still drew in the same style as before, mainly animals, which he depicted as human beings in all conceivable comic situations. Among the numerous caricatures, however, I at once recognised the ones he had done in Siberia, and put them on one side. If he had still had the slightest doubts of my being the Emperor's daughter, the mere fact that I picked out the drawings from the Tobolsk period, which were scattered through the whole collection, would have been enough, he said, to prove it to him.

Gleb stayed at Seeon about a week after our first meeting. We talked of many other things, and I was specially interested to hear something from him about America, where he now lived. I wanted to know how big the country was, what sort of religion they had there, whether the people were happy under their democracy; and he told me about all these things. My interest in America had evidently given him an idea, for the last day we were together he asked me if I would like to live there. I was amazed; it had never occurred to me. I told him I should indeed like to go to America, because it was a long way from Russia and I should no longer feel as hunted as I did here. But then I had no money, and the Hessian police wanted to take away my passport so that I get another one with the name of Francisca Shanzkovski and could then be arrested as a swindler. Anyhow, my present passport contained a mistake. It had been obtained for me from the Berlin Foreign Office at the recommendation of Zahle and General Hoffmann, when I was in the Mommsen Nursing Home, and gave the name Anastasia Tchaikovski; but it said I had been born at Tsarskoe Selo instead of at Peterhof.

So how was I to get to America? Gleb didn't know either at the moment, but asked me whether, in the interests of my security if for no other reason, he should try to arrange this. I told him I had no objections. We said good-bye that day; he went to Berlin to see his uncle Serge Botkin, and try to refute the Shanzkovski lies. I was to meet him again in America in the not-too-distant future.

* * *

Gleb Botkin himself recorded these impressions of seeing Anastasia again after nine years:

'I recognised Mrs Tchaikovski at once, without a shadow of doubt, as the Grand-Duchess Anastasia, youngest daughter of the late Tsar Nicholas and Empress Alexandra. This recognition is based on a close acquaintance of many years with the last Tsar's family. The Grand-Duchess, who used to be most talked about of the four girls, was always known as "the little girl" because of her short stature. With her irregular features she was not so pretty as her sisters; she had a rather long nose, a wide mouth, and a small straight chin, hardly curving in under the lower lip. But she had unusually fine eyes, which she had inherited from her father. . . . According to the accounts which we received about Anastasia in those days, and which I afterwards found confirmed in personal contact with her, she was a lively and high-spirited girl, usually gay and full of fun, although this sometimes turned into "cheek." She was absolutely honest, however, and never told lies to escape a "telling-off" for any naughtiness.

'The instant I set eyes on Mrs Tchaikovski now, I knew, as one knows of one's own existence, that I had before me the Grand-Duchess Anastasia—altered, certainly, in her features and figure, but still unmistakable. Physically, she looked frail and thin compared with the young, healthy, and I might almost say "strapping," Anastasia whom I had last seen nine years before at Tobolsk. The features seemed to me elongated, the nose stuck out more, no doubt because of the face's thinness. It was a face in which you could also read what she had been through, the development from a seventeen-year-old girl, relatively cheerful and carefree owing to her age and temperament despite all the troubles and fears of internment, to a woman sorely tried by suffering and illness. But it was still the face and the features of Anastasia, unmistakable, as I have said, for anyone who knew her well before, because of the eyes, which in colour, shape and animation had kept their same peculiar charm. Besides these, right from the first moment but naturally confirmed during the following days, were all the factors, like voice, intonation, particular movements, bearing, gait, etc., which make up a person's exterior and give her an individual quality distinguishing her especially for her friends, from everybody else. To recognise her, there was no question of my first having to discover Anastasia under her physical alterations or get used to her having aged; my first impressions confirmed for me without any doubt that here was someone I had known for twenty odd years, that Anastasia, in fact, had been saved.'

Among the first members of the Romanov family whom Gleb contacted in Berlin was Prince Felix Yusupov, son-in-law of the Grand-Duke Alexander and Grand-Duchess Xenia. He had at least made an unequivocal statement about the 'measles photograph' to Zahle and Mrs Rathlef, and declared himself neutral in the dispute over Anastasia's identity. At first, indeed, he told Botkin that owing to his name and reputation he was the only person above all suspicion of 'being influenced by later developments'; but he eventually admitted that he had only visited Botkin in the hope of drawing him into his mother-in-law's camp. And the same day, finding Botkin incorruptible, Yusupov wrote a letter for him to take to the Tsarina's elder sister, Lady Victoria Milford-Haven, in England, which in fact warned her to disbelieve everything he said:

'Dear Madam,

I am sending you this letter by Mr Gleb Botkin, son of Their late Majesties' personal physician. He is quite sure that the person claiming to be the Grand-Duchess Anastasia is speaking the truth and has various documents to prove it. I hold quite a different opinion, having just seen her at the Leuchtenbergs' castle near Munich where she is now living. I cannot understand how anyone can make such a mistake, since she is very common and has absolutely nothing to remind one of the Grand-Duchess. Nor does she understand a word of English, but answers questions only in German, and not even that unless she is feeling like it. She understands Russian but does not speak it. I feel such a situation should not be allowed to continue, and that something should be done about it. This is why I believe you should see Botkin, since he has all the evidence purporting to show that she is the Grand-Duchess and a lot of people believe it; whereas I myself am sure all that is untrue.'

Gleb had more luck with the Grand-Duke Andrew, who showed even more readiness than before to acknowledge Anastasia as his niece, although he warned Gleb in several letters that her identity must in any case be legally established, which would probably cost up to fifty thousand dollars for the law-suit, plus another four thousand for the further enquiries needed. He knew how many enemies Anastasia had in the family and realised that the case would have to be carried on over half Europe and America. Although many people had recognised 'the unknown woman' as the Tsar's daughter, the closest blood-relatives were missing as witnesses, while those who (in spite of the extreme exclusiveness of the Tsar's family circle) could testify for her with a claim to absolute reliability, had all been murdered. Nor could further necessary enquiries be made in Russia under the present regime; and enquiries in Rumania would prove very expensive owing to the changing conditions there. Finally Mrs Tchaikovski's own lapses of memory were very regrettable from a legal viewpoint, as the evidence so far available offered no convincing proof. So perhaps money could be found in America, Andrew suggested to Gleb Botkin—this was discounting the question of the Tsar's deposited fortune, which he (Andrew) did not believe existed.

Gleb returned to America, and soon afterwards heard from an old friend of his family, Mrs Margharita Derfelden, that a friend of hers, Princess Xenia of Russia, now a Mrs Leeds, would like to see him and listen to the strange story of the Grand-Duchess Anastasia. Princess Xenia (not to be confused with her aunt Xenia, the Tsar's sister), was a second cousin of Anastasia's; in later years she divorced her American husband, Mr Leeds, and married another American called Judd. Botkin had once met her, with her father the Grand-Duke George (the Tsar's uncle), at an exhibition of modern French painters. Like Anastasia, she was in her middle twenties, a smart and beautiful woman, who was also very rich thanks to her marriage to Leeds, a department store magnate. This wealth made her suspicious, and Botkin was first received with the remark: 'All Russian refugees are beggars.'

Ignoring this suspicion, he eventually succeeded in winning over Mrs Leeds to such an extent that she was ready to invite Anastasia to her estate at Oyster Bay, if she could first consult Prince Christopher of Greece (her maternal uncle and the Dowager Empress' nephew) whose arrival she was expecting shortly. Contact was thus restored with Copenhagen.

Botkin met the Prince at a meal in the Leeds' house, and was astonished to learn that he had not the slightest doubt as to Anastasia's genuineness; when asked about the Grand-Duchess Olga's present attitude, the Prince answered quite casually: 'Of course Olga knows better than anyone that she is Anastasia.' Xenia, like Botkin, was very pleased with this information, and asked the Prince whether he could give Anastasia a home in the unoccupied palace he owned in Italy, as she was not safe in Germany; Xenia herself would invite her cousin to stay with her for a time. Prince Christopher agreed to this idea at first, but had second thoughts the next day and withdrew his offer. Xenia rang up Botkin in some anxiety, for through her uncle's support she hoped to obtain an effective influence at Copenhagen. Although her position had now become more difficult, she was still resolved to invite Anastasia to America, and told Botkin she would herself accompany her to Copenhagen on her own, once Anastasia had convalesced a bit at Oyster Bay.

* * *

The year 1928 was to prove a very important year for me, and it almost looked as if after all the storms I should reach a quiet haven at last. Gleb Botkin had kept his word and arranged for me to go to America. My cousin Princess Xenia, whom I had last seen sixteen years earlier when we were both children, invited me to stay at Oyster Bay near New York, the estate of her husband, Mr Leeds. She had made arrangements for the crossing and sent to Seeon a Scottish nurse, Miss Agnes Gallacher, who was to accompany me on it; thanks to the combined efforts of Serge Botkin and the American consul in Munich, I had also obtained a United States visa valid for at least six months. The Duke of Leuchtenberg had managed to get me a new passport through the German authorities at Traunstein. As I still felt my safety was threatened from the German side, even if less than from the Soviet side, I was extremely pleased about this prospect; and although my host and hostess, the Duke and Duchess, were sad to see me go, they rejoiced to think that I might find happier times in America. All of us were wrong there, alas.

Behind my joy at the invitation from my cousin Xenia was the surely justifiable expectation that she would acknowledge my identity; she would scarcely have asked me to travel so far had I been Francisca Shanzkovski the Pole. Just about then I heard that my uncle the Grand-Duke Andrew wished to welcome me in Paris, and almost at the same time I received a letter from another relative, my cousin Gabriel, son of the Grand-Duke Constantine, in whose company I had so often been as a child in Pavlovsk and Petersburg, enquiring after my health with great warmth and addressing me as 'Du.' My happiness was naturally great: three members of my family suddenly wanting to see me again. I should have liked to shout for joy, yet had not even the strength left to feel grateful. It was all too much for me.

At the end of January, accompanied by the Duke and the Scottish nurse, I travelled to Paris, where I stayed for two days. A nice room in the Hotel du Palais had been booked for me, and decorated with flowers. It was there I was visited by my Uncle Andrew, who had come up from the Riviera specially to greet me. He came to the hotel directly after my arrival, bringing me more flowers and presents, and welcoming me very warmly by drawing me to his arms. We had recognised each other at once, I saw it in his face. This must have been realised also by his escort, who had tears in his eyes. But as always happens when so many impressions are crowding in on me, I simply could not speak, not even the next day when we were alone together. My uncle told me a mass of things, and asked after this and that; but in my wretched state of agitation I could only answer him by nodding my head, and scarcely uttered a word.

Nevertheless there was no tension between us; my uncle must have appreciated my feelings. He was a man of great sincerity and warm-heartedness, and after only these two days, which had been so intensely moving for us both, I found it really hard to part from him. As he told me, however, this was necessary on grounds of prudence and discretion; and as it turned out, his caution, alas, was only too well justified. All the same, I felt that I was parting here from a man who would now do anything to help me. That gave me courage for the journey into the new and unknown world.

The next day he and the Duke took me to Cherbourg, where a passage had been booked for me on the steamer *Berengaria*. After all the kindness I had been shown at Seeon, it was also hard to say good-bye to the Duke: how terribly distressing, directly after my arrival in America, to hear that he had suddenly died. And so, on this first day of February, 1928, I left for the first time the continent of Europe, which also contained my Russian homeland. What would my fate be in America?

* * *

After their meeting in Paris the Grand-Duke Andrew maintained that Anastasia's memories showed in every respect a clear picture of real facts. On the question which had evoked so much doubt, her resemblance to the girl his niece had been, he stated: 'Having seen her myself, I was struck most of all by the family likeness, which in a sense is almost more significant than the personal likeness. In any case my impressions were so overwhelming that the conclusion was inevitable: she is indeed the Grand-Duchess Anastasia.' Difficult as the process might be, he resolved to continue his investigations till the truth was proved, for if she *was* Anastasia, she could not be left in her present ignominious position. A confidential letter of his to Serge Botkin, written on 6th February, gives further expression to this attitude:

'... For two days I had the chance to meet and observe Mrs T. at close quarters, and can now say unequivocally that I have no doubt she is the Grand-Duchess Anastasia. Not to recognise her is completely impossible. Of course there are signs of the passing of years and of all her experience, but even they are far fewer than I had expected. At some moments one can see a despondency, the face shows the deep sadness and anxiety of someone who is constantly ill. But when her face lights up with a smile, Anastasia is so vividly recognisable that no further doubt can remain.

'Unfortunately my visit affected her so very powerfully that she could not speak, either to me or even to other people. ...

'To sum up my observations, I have no doubt left about acknowledging her. I have already written this to the Grand-Duchess Olga Alexandrovna, and am now awaiting her reply. Till I receive it, I shall make no statement to the papers. If it should prove necessary to give out in the press that she has gone to America, an article can be written without saying to whom she has gone there.

'I was as sad as you at her departure and especially at the circumstances in which we saw each other again. But prudence and discretion require that decisive measures be taken, which will in the end be for her own good. They will make her well again, she can convalesce in the most suitable environment, and that is a precondition for her being recognised. Meanwhile we should be able to complete our investigations.

'In case this letter is not quite clear, I should tell you of my deep conviction that certain people are set on destroying her . . . and their best chance to do so would be after she has been acknowledged. While she is still suspected of being someone else, she is not dangerous; but when acknowledged, who knows? I myself should hardly be in a position to express myself so openly if she were still in Germany—and other competent judges shared my fears. In any case I am profoundly thankful that she has now left Germany, where such grave danger was threatening her. . . .

'I should be very glad if you could follow the local papers to see how they react to her departure, and could send me cuttings. Probably G. will come out with something. Everything depends on Copenhagen and how they behave there in face of my categorical testimony. Anyhow I shall do everything to protect Mrs T., and am ready to maintain my statements on oath.

'The whole matter is now entering a new phase, and I very much hope you will assist me as much in the future as you have given her your help all the time. I feel we are reaching the last act of what has been one of the world's most pathetic tragedies. Now that I have seen "the patient" and know who she is, I have not the right to lay down my arms, but am in duty bound to do everything to help the triumph of right. I have absolute faith in the success of this difficult mission.'

The Duke of Leuchtenberg had written to Captain Dassel (on 7th February): 'Your letter of 31st January reached me here in Paris, where I had accompanied A. N. She sailed safely, and I am expecting a wire any time now to say she has arrived according to plan. Andrei Vladim. visited her here, and feels no further doubt as to her identity. He has written in vigorous terms to the two aunts. Will that help?—I fear not. But it was most moving to see the man's excitement, he was almost beside himself the whole day. She was extremely excited too, and said nothing, but this time did not take offence. Well, it has taken a load off my chest to know that she is safe, and I only hope that nothing goes wrong at the last moment—I mean any formal difficulties on the part of the United States, which has after all agreed to admit her. . . .'

* * *

My arrival in America was obviously ill-starred. The *Berengaria* reached New York on 7th February, but there was so thick a fog that we had to lie at anchor for twenty-four hours and could not enter the harbour till the 9th. On the 8th, despite the fog, a small vessel came out with the immigration officers to deal with the formalities. Gleb Botkin was on it also, and I was very glad to see someone I knew in this strange world. But he was not alone, a whole host of reporters and film people had also come to meet me and stood outside my cabin door.

Gleb was accompanied by a Mr Foley, Rachmaninov's agent; for the great Russian musician, who was living in America, had offered me his assistance. I really needed that now, as the reporters became more and more noisy and obtrusive, and had no appreciation for the fact that I disliked being dragged into the limelight like this; some of them even thought my refusal to show myself must mean I had something to hide and was an impostor. While Gleb and I prepared an interview for them in my cabin, Mr Foley and Miss Gallacher had to hold the savage mob in check till I said a few words to them and they could take their photographs. Eventually I was saved by the immigration officers who stamped my passport; now the reporters left me again, seeing that everything was in order with me. Only Gleb and Mr Foley stayed the night on board. Mr Foley was afterwards to figure in my life in a most equivocal way.

The next disappointment was that my cousin Xenia, who after all had invited me to stay with her, had not come to meet me, but had asked Gleb to do so, as she had gone to the West Indies with her husband, who apparently could not take a holiday any other time. So having expected to go to her house at Oyster Bay, I got a message that instead I should be staying in New York until her return with a Miss Annie Jennings. I was shattered by the prospect of going to a completely strange person I had never heard of, and should have liked to return to Europe by the next boat. What could this mean? Gleb did not conceal that he was also very surprised at Xenia's behaviour and connected it with his articles in the papers, which my cousin might not have liked. He had reported in the *New York Herald Tribune* everything that had happened to me in Germany, and in particular had refuted the Shanzkovski fable. As he had previously promised Xenia he would not do this, she had reproached him. I too should have preferred absolute discretion, but he said he had only meant to help me.

Disembarking from the *Berengaria* was like running away from pursuers, and the reporters pressed me so hard that I almost fell into the water. With great difficulty we finally succeeded in reaching a car which was waiting for us on the jetty, and a friend of Gleb's, Mrs Hetty Richard, drove it to Miss Jennings' house on Park Avenue. There Miss Gallacher and I had had two rooms reserved for us on one of the upper floors, which were furnished in rather poor taste. I told Gleb I should not be at all happy here and found it horrible. But soon afterwards a friend of Xenia's arrived, a Mrs Derfelden, and bade me welcome with tears of emotion. And then Miss Jennings came too, a very ugly old lady, who greeted me in a manner that was conventionally cordial. For all the flowers she had put into my room, I felt like a prisoner. They were tied in huge bunches, but without love. Everything here felt loveless to me, and I sensed that this was someone I had nothing in common with. When Gleb had gone, I felt quite deserted.

Although I felt so uncomfortable in Miss Jennings' house, I found it still more dreadful to go into the town with its seething traffic. I preferred to stay in my room, contenting myself with the company of Miss Gallacher, who was a friendly woman. I had expected that Gleb would come and see me fairly often, but he made himself rather scarce, and explained that he was terribly busy with the newspapers. Of course they had all reported my arrival in America and given their views, some favourable and others hostile; but I did not want to hear about all that. Xenia too apparently wished to avoid the sensational publicity, and Gleb told me that for the moment I should be better off here, where nobody knew me, than staying at her house, which was continually besieged by reporters; this was probably why she herself had not yet returned. I then asked him how she had come to be friendly with Miss Jennings of all people, and learnt that Mr Leeds' house at Hempstead in Oyster Bay was next door to a farm belonging to Miss Jennings' brother at Cold Spring Harbour; also, this brother's son had married the daughter of Xenia's friend, Mrs Derfelden.

When I had recovered from the excitement of my arrival, Gleb came to take me to the cinema. Now I saw part of this huge town, which was so strange to me and will probably always remain strange. What a difference between St Petersburg and New York or even the Kurfürstendamm and Broadway! I was quite dazed and felt glad when I got home again. Then Gleb suggested one day that I ought to receive Mr Rachmaninov, who would like to see me. Rachmaninov had already rung up Miss Jennings without her saying anything about it to me. But I did not wish to see him or anyone else. Gleb said he was famous and a rich man, and had offered his help even before Xenia came into it; also, he had sent Mr Foley to meet me on the *Berengaria*. I was annoyed that Gleb should insist so much on this visit, but finally agreed. When Rachmaninov came, however, I happened to be not very well and was in bed. When I saw that Miss Jennings had come with him, I simply could not talk to him; he only stayed a few minutes. He was certainly disappointed, and Gleb was even more so.

Just about then Xenia at last returned from the West Indies. Luckily Gleb had arranged that Miss Jennings should not be present at this meeting, though I was glad he was there himself, for I was very agitated; so was Xenia, as I noticed afterwards. I had last met her as a child, so there could be no question of direct recognition as with Gleb or Tatiana; we could only be brought together by common memories.

Xenia came into my room with a shy smile, perhaps a certain embarrassment. Yet I must confess that I looked at her face for only a moment, because my whole attention was occupied by something else: she had brought back a pair of tame parrots for me from the West Indies, and she let them fly round the room. These cheerful and colourful birds felt at home with me at once, fluttering hither and thither, settling down again, beginning to chatter or stare at us. As I am so fond of animals, it was really a charming thought of Xenia's, so that our conversation took on a friendly note straight away; although I somehow sensed that she was not quite sincere. Before she left, she told me she still could not take me with her to Hempstead immediately, but would come and fetch me quite soon; meanwhile she would often visit me. Why was this, I wondered. We kissed and embraced on saying good-bye.

Gleb stayed a bit longer and asked if I had recognised Xenia. I shook my head—how could I have done this after so long? She was no longer a child but a mature woman. Then he asked me if I liked her. I told him I had nothing against her, but did not care for her eyes. He said he thought she had such fine black eyes, but it wasn't that—I had never been able to read dark eyes. Light eyes are far more transparent, and people with dark eyes can hide things better. Gleb listened with interest, though he probably did not agree. The next time he came to see me, he told me what Xenia had said about me. He hadn't seen her again, but had heard from Mrs Derfelden that Xenia was firmly convinced I *was* Anastasia, although she had been rather sceptical at first. Was that why she didn't bring me to Hempstead straight away?

A day or two after she had been with me, I was thrown into dreadful agitation. Mr Leeds had been informed that an attempt on my life was planned. He told me of this himself on the telephone, and of course I was terrified. Miss Jennings was equally disturbed by the news, and asked Gleb Botkin to come over to us that same night; she phoned the police, who had our block of houses watched, and a private detective sent two of his men to search the house for bombs, but they did not find anything. They carried sub-machine-guns and looked like criminals themselves. One of them stayed the night in the hall, while the other watched the house from outside; for this they demanded a hundred dollars advance, which Miss Jennings paid them. On seeing these armed fellows, I was reminded of Ekaterinburg, hard as I fought against the thought. Since I did not feel like going to bed, we sat together in the hall, and I must say Miss Jennings won my respect, however little contact I had otherwise made with her. She was the first to calm down, and began telling stories which made both of us laugh; when half the night was past, we went to bed and Gleb returned home. We never knew whether anyone really meant to make the attempt, but it was a proper gangster night I experienced in that strange house.

In early spring Xenia at last came to New York to fetch me, and took me to her country house at Oyster Bay. I was glad to get out of the big city, and soon felt very comfortable in my new surroundings. Mr Leeds was away when I arrived, and was only expected back in a few weeks; but Xenia's sister Nina and Mrs Derfelden were staying with her. I liked the house at Hempstead, it was very tastefully furnished, and the wealth was not so ostentatious as it had been at Miss Jennings'. I found the safety and informality specially beneficial; I could do or not do just what I liked, could stay alone in my room, and also take my meals there, without needing to talk to the other guests. Xenia now treated me really like a cousin and we got on extremely well. She talked of planning to go to Copenhagen with me to visit my grandmother, and after the unsuccessful meeting with Aunt Irene this was my dearest wish.

She had told Gleb Botkin that no one who had once seen me could have the slightest doubt about my identity. This soothed me greatly; everything seemed to be quite all right. Of course Xenia often came up to see me, whereupon we talked about Tsarskoe and the family like the relations we were. We had so very much to talk about, and laughed together like sisters. Once there was an incident which both agitated and amused us. I had forgotten to close my parrots' cage at night, and the first thing they did next morning was to escape and fly out through the open window. I woke the whole house, it was just getting-up time. Xenia was in her bath, and the servants were only half dressed. Everyone rushed into the garden, more or less clothed, in order to catch the fly-aways. It was a scene that couldn't have been filmed more happily in Hollywood.

Then came sad hours too, when I remembered my situation and my dependence, and felt as if I were in a golden cage. Xenia, the only person with whom I had any family bonds, was often away. Once during these periods Mrs Derfelden took me to spend a few weeks at Miss Jennings' country house at Bridgeport, Connecticut, but I did not like it much there. It was depressing that this made me lose contact with Gleb Botkin, and I now had no one to whom I could speak freely in this strange country and environment. Should I ever feel at home here? When I returned to Oyster Bay and the summer began, I was to find out that there was a particular purpose behind my isolation from the world, though at first I had only a presentiment of what it was.

* * *

There is such positive evidence of the stages in Xenia's acknowledgment of Anastasia that it makes even more tragic the subsequent break between the two cousins.

On 28th February, 1928, Mr Leeds said in an interview with the New York *Daily Mirror:* 'It will probably never be proved whether the young lady at present staying with Mrs Leeds is or is not the Grand-Duchess. At any rate she herself will make no efforts to prove her identity to the Russian circles close to the Romanovs who doubt her genuineness. Her present chaperone, the former Princess Xenia of Russia, believes in her identity, and that is enough.'

In April Xenia wrote to her relatives in Europe that she simply could not escape the conclusion that it *was* Anastasia; they talked all the time in English, she said, and every day something interesting would come up, although they had not seen each other since they were both ten years old.

At the end of May she declared in *World:* 'As a child I often played with Anastasia, who was the same age as I. Mrs Tchaikovski has astonished me by recalling where and what we played. She also reminded me of other events. I have not the slightest doubt as to her identity and am ready to stake all my money to prove it.'

Ten years later (in July 1938) Gleb Botkin stated: 'The Grand-Duchess stayed in the house of her cousin, Princess Xenia, about four months—up till 8th August, 1928. The Princess received her from the start as her cousin Anastasia and assured me repeatedly that there could not be the least doubt about her cousin's identity. From the day of the Grand-Duchess' arrival in America up till the beginning of 1929 I saw her frequently, and for a period of six months almost every day. In all conversations with me she showed a knowledge of people and things such as only she could have. She talked to me about all the phases in her life, even about the tragedy of Ekaterinburg and her flight to Rumania. It often happened that she remembered details from the time before Ekaterinburg which I had forgotten, but which returned to my mind when she mentioned them and always proved accurate. I should mention especially her extraordinary familiarity with the unofficial history not only of the Russian imperial house but of all Europe's princely houses. Her statements sometimes showed a knowledge not readily available even to historians and inexplicable unless she belonged to one of the great princely families and had a close acquaintance with court archives accessible only to the immediate imperial family. In America the Grand-Duchess has always spoken English, a language familiar to her from childhood.'

On the other hand, Anastasia's enemies among the Romanov family issued a joint statement against her soon after her arrival in

New York, and had it syndicated through the *Associated Press;* the Grand-Duchess Olga apparently agreed to sign it only at the last moment, having previously refused to do so. It was so worded that the public was bound to think the whole of the Tsar's family had now withdrawn from Anastasia, an impression which was in fact completely false. For according to the Grand-Duke Andrew, the *Associated Press* statement was signed by only twelve of the forty-four members of the family living at the time. Significantly enough, they were the twelve who if all the Tsar's daughters were dead, including Anastasia, might have claims to his fortune in England: the Tsar's sisters Olga and Xenia, their husbands Colonel Kulikovsky and the Grand-Duke Alexander, Alexander and Xenia's six sons, their daughter Irene and her husband Prince Felix Yusupov.

In December 1928 Anastasia was to defend herself with a restatement of the position concerning the fortune in England, of which she alone had originally had knowledge:

'I the Grand-Duchess Anastasia Nikolaievna, youngest daughter and only surviving child of the late Emperor Nicholas II and Empress Alexandra of Russia, declare herewith that after our family had left St Petersburg and been banished to Ekaterinburg in Siberia, and shortly before my father and the rest of my family were killed, he informed my three sisters and myself that before the outbreak of the world war he had deposited five million roubles each for the four of us with the Bank of England.

'In 1925, when I was in Berlin, Herluf Zahle, the Danish Ambassador, whom I had told about the depositing of this money, made official enquiries and soon afterwards let me know that according to the reply he had received there *was* money which had been deposited with the Bank of England for my sisters and myself, but the Bank refused to state the amount.'[1]

* * *

Since my return to Oyster Bay I had not seen Gleb Botkin again. Mrs Derfelden too had returned to New York, where she had a flat. I didn't see much of Xenia, and heard no more about the journey to Copenhagen which she, after all, had proposed to me. I felt deserted, almost like a prisoner, for I did not receive any post either. That was strange. I remembered that Xenia had recently spoken of Gleb in not exactly friendly terms and repeated her criticisms of him for writing about me in the papers. Mrs

[1] See translator's note on page 262

Derfelden had also hinted at this attitude of Xenia's. Much as I fought shy of having my 'case' discussed in public, I did not know what to think and whether that was the real reason for their quarrel. Xenia might be deliberately keeping Gleb away from me, but he might just as well be prevented by other reasons from coming to see me.

I tried to find clues to this mystery from my last conversations with him, and decided that there must be some connection between the question of my identity being acknowledged and that of my father's inheritance. Gleb had told me on one of his first visits that this had been the subject of several reports in the American papers. One spoke of my having been acknowledged in Paris by my uncle, the Grand-Duke Andrew, while in another I was exposed as an imposter by some of my relatives. A third discussed a cable from the Grand-Duke Alexander, the husband of my Aunt Xenia in London, to the effect that my whole case was something fabricated by Gleb Botkin, whose exclusive interest was to obtain control of my father's prospective inheritance in England for his wife. Understandably, Gleb was very much hurt and bewildered at this, since it was just my aunts Xenia and Olga who till then had stubbornly denied the existence of such a fortune. Moreover, Aunt Xenia had repeatedly declared that she could only get at this money through a law-suit, which was beneath the dignity of a Grand-Duchess.

The inheritance came up again during a later meeting with Botkin, and I told him of my father's declarations at Ekaterinburg and also what I had said about it to Aunt Olga when she visited me in Berlin. My aunts' change of mind, or that of their husbands, must have dated from this information of mine, because they had since found out that my statements were true. Mr Zahle, who at that time was managing my financial affairs, had also made enquiries to the Bank of England and received appropriate confirmation. Now I recalled his telling me then that if I made no claims to the money, it would be paid out to my two aunts (my father's sisters) ten years after the death of my sisters and my own assumed death; since according to the legal provisions applying in the West, if a man's inheritance is not claimed by his immediate heirs within ten years of his death, it then goes to his nearest surviving relatives. I was not concerned with the money, no money could compensate me for the death of my father and my family; but I *was* concerned that my aunts, who had betrayed me, should not get their hands on it. For once they had it, that would be taken as a proof that I was no longer alive, which would settle all my hopes of getting my identity acknowledged in these quarters. Was this why Xenia kept putting off our journey to Copenhagen? Eventually I said as much to Gleb Botkin, and made him promise he would do everything he could to stop my aunts coming into the inheritance.

Meanwhile June had come, so it was not much longer till 17th July, the tenth anniversary of my father's death. From week to week, from day to day, I waited for Gleb's return to find out what he had been doing; but he did not come. Nor did Mrs Derfelden; and Xenia, so far as she showed herself at all, seemed changed. Could she really have decided to go over to my aunts' side, although she had acknowledged me and still did so? My anxiety was very great, but the 17th July came and went without my seeing Gleb or hearing from him. One day I asked Xenia about him, at which she merely shrugged her shoulders and said I should not believe in his friendship, for he was now siding against me. After all that bound me to Gleb, I could not grasp this, I simply refused to believe it. Xenia, of whom I had recently seen little, was specially friendly to me that day. She had come to my room and stayed there a long time. She kissed me, and said I should not worry, she would do everything to get my identity acknowledged and never let my aunts come into the money. After that I did not see her again for a fortnight, and I began to suspect that her particular cordiality might not have been altogether sincere.

On 1st August, when Gleb came to see me in the end, I at first received him rather coolly, being not sure where he stood after what Xenia had said. But I soon realised that it had been unjust of me to doubt him. The first thing I asked him, of course, was what had happened to my father's money in the Bank of England. He said he had stopped my aunts getting it, and that through his intervention the money had been blocked on 13th July. At first I would not believe him, being unable to understand his not having told me this before. He asked if I had not received his letters. Afterwards it transpired that they had been kept from me and that Gleb himself had not been admitted when he tried to see me. Indignant as I was at Xenia's behaviour, I was very happy to know that he had remained loyal to me. He had not seen her either till the previous week, but luckily had been told of her attitude by Mrs Derfelden, and had acted independently on hearing that although Xenia still acknowledged me, she had decided to help my aunts to get the money. This was also why she did not want to go to Copenhagen with me.

Gleb had been to see a lawyer called Edward Fallows, son of a bishop in the Reformed Church, who not only had considerable influence in America owing to his connections with the Roosevelt family but also had valuable contacts in England. He had already shown an interest in me, so Gleb consulted him on what to do to stop my aunts getting the money, and told him how he (Gleb) had been refused admittance at Hempstead. Fallows at once got in touch with another lawyer, a Mr Gilbert F. Kennedy, who had been looking after American interests in England, and had him block my father's fortune in London. Gleb gave the Bank of England a declaration to the effect that I was the true heiress and was still alive; so the money was not paid out to my aunts.

He at once wrote informing me of this and also wrote to Xenia that he had felt obliged to take this step because of her silence; but she returned the letter unopened and refused to see him. She merely told Mrs Derfelden in a high fury that if I were formally acknowledged it would seriously affect the reputation of my Aunt Xenia in London and other members of our family; also that I did not need the money, anyhow, since she was herself providing for my upkeep. So evidently her idea was that I should live the rest of my life branded as a swindler simply because my formal acknowledgment would not help my aunt's reputation; and for this reason I was not to justify my rights either to my name or to my inheritance. Of course I was extremely angry when I heard this, and finally Mr Leeds let the cat out of the bag by declaring in the press that although convinced I was the Grand-Duchess Anastasia, he and his wife would neither try to prove it nor to help me obtain my fortune.

Immediately Gleb read this in the paper, he at once published a counter-declaration, which openly accused my aunts of wishing to usurp my inheritance and denied Mr Leeds' right to renounce *my* rights for me; such a step was obviously part of the conspiracy to deprive me of those rights. Gleb's statement led to Xenia and her husband at last asking him to come and see them.

* * *

Gleb Botkin had two interviews with Xenia, in the second of which she told him she could no longer harbour Anastasia under her roof, since the situation between them had become intolerable. As Gleb was the only person Anastasia trusted, he should accept responsibility for her; and Xenia repeated an offer she had already made, only this time it was in the form of an ultimatum: 'Take Anastasia to some remote spot in Europe, and give up the struggle to get her identity acknowledged. If you do that, we will support her all her life and are ready to pay all her expenses. Otherwise you must take her away from here within forty-eight hours.'

When Gleb reported this to Anastasia, she had no need to reflect, and could only ask him to take her away within the time demanded.

* * *

On 8th August I left the house at Oyster Bay, though I had never thought of leaving it like this. Once more I faced a very uncertain future, in a strange country, without any resources of my own. I had consulted Gleb on where I should now go, and he offered to put me up in his flat, although he and his family were rather cramped for space. However, we abandoned that idea as not being safe for me. Another possibility was to get in touch with Rachmaninov or Miss Jennings, who Gleb thought would be pleased to give me a home; but they both happened to be in Europe just then, nor did I like the plan much anyhow. Finally he made an arrangement with his journalist friend John Colter, who was married to an actress and had a modest studio in Lexington Avenue, New York. It was there I was to stay for the moment.

Gleb came to fetch me with Mr Fallows in the latter's car. He had seen Xenia again before, and she suggested having another talk with me; perhaps I had changed my mind and would prefer to leave the house under the conditions she had offered. Of course I refused, and when she heard this Xenia was raging mad. Perhaps she still had some liking for me, or was merely very disappointed not to have got anywhere with me. We never saw each other again, though afterwards she did enquire several times after my health. Then I also talked to Mr Fallows about the legal chances of my getting acknowledged and the registration of my financial claims; as he made a good impression on me, I appointed him my lawyer and signed a power of attorney for a contract I shall speak about shortly. On Gleb's advice Mr Fallows first discussed the whole matter with Mr Leeds and his lawyer; Mr Leeds had always remained neutral in the whole quarrel with me. I myself understood precious little of such things.

I stayed only two days with the Colters. Gleb had meanwhile introduced me to a wealthy industrialist called Richards, who invited me to be his guest for some weeks at the Garden City Hotel in Hempstead, Long Island. His wife had been one of those who came to meet me in New York harbour when I arrived on the *Berengaria*. The Garden City Hotel was a fine building with a large garden, and was extremely near the Botkins' flat; I could feel well and safe there, providing I wasn't recognised. But Mr Richards was a very clever man. As I did not wish to be entered in the hotel register as Mrs Tchaikovski, he proposed to Gleb that he should introduce me as his sister, Mrs Anderson; while Mrs Richards gave me a friendly Frenchwoman, her former governess, as a companion. Little knowing what difficulties I should later have with the assumed name, I agreed to the change; and indeed I still face the world with it today. In the following years, as a matter of fact, I was saved much persecution and trouble by this inconspicuous name. Meanwhile Rachmaninov, who was still in Europe, had taken an interest in my lot and offered to pay for my living expenses until some other financial assistance should be forthcoming. I was specially pleased to hear that he had spoken up for me on a visit to my Aunt Xenia in London, and had refused to let her draw him into her camp, which she tried to do.

After this Miss Jennings approached me again with an offer to return to her. At first I declined, for I had never thought much of her, apart from that night when we feared an attempt on my life and she behaved so well. But now she positively overwhelmed me with professions of kindness, calling me her daughter, for whom she would do anything, and proposing, should I not wish to live with her, that I go into a separate house, with one of my former servants from the Garden City Hotel to wait on me and protect me. There I should also have greater security.

I don't exactly know what finally decided me to accept her invitation. Since the quarrel with Xenia my nerves had been in a very bad state, especially after a second blow had befallen me—the death of my grandmother at Copenhagen in October 1928; because of Xenia's resistance I had never seen her again. It's true Grandmama never got on well with my mother, but still we were very attached to her as children, and now it had been my fondest hope that her authority would at least have some influence on the members of the family who were ill-disposed towards me. Who was left to me now of my nearest and dearest? Fate had again conspired against me, and I had become indifferent where I went. I did not want to see anyone, I just wanted to be left alone. Even with Gleb Botkin I was irritable and difficult. Although he had certainly acted with the best intentions, I really blamed him for my situation, since it was he after all who had brought me to America, where conditions had turned out so unfortunately for me; and arguments about these things led to an estrangement between us. When he advised me to accept Miss Jennings' offer, I felt he wanted to be rid of me. Anyhow, I returned to this lady. Had I known what new difficulties I was bringing on my head, I should doubtless have decided otherwise. I have not seen Gleb again since January 1929, although he went on working on my behalf and our friendship has lasted in correspondence till the present day. I stayed a year and a half with Miss Jennings—and terrible new experiences lay ahead of me.

The most important thing that happened to me at this time, and which was to claim my attention right up till the time I left America, was the launching of the so-called 'Grandanor Corporation' (an abbreviation from my name and title, the Grand-Duchess Anastasia Nikolaievna of Russia). The Company was founded on 7th February, 1929, and its aim was to start a fund through subscription of shares, with the aid of which my identity should be established and I should come into possession of my fortune in various countries, such as England, Germany and Finland. The proceeds from the shares were to enable me to cover my personal upkeep, to have investigations made to prove my identity, and finally to reimburse my solicitor, Mr Fallows, who was also president of the company, for his efforts on my behalf.

In return for the advances paid to me from the 'Grandanor,' I surrendered to the company Mr Fallows had called into being all the fortune to which I was entitled as my parents' heir; at the same time I made provisions in case of my death. I don't know why I thought of this; perhaps it was due to the recent excitements, which had affected me greatly, and perhaps too because I always felt threatened. I wanted first of all to provide for my son, who naturally kept on coming up in my mind, then for the Tchaikovskis, my rescuers in Rumania, also the Botkins, both Gleb and Tatiana, and their uncle Serge, everyone in fact who had been close to me and shown their loyalty to me. At first, therefore, everything seemed ordered for the best. But of course someone like myself, who has never had anything to do with money matters, could not see through a contract as complicated as the 'Grandanor's'; and it was only later, too late, that I realised I had put myself right in the company's hands by surrendering my fortune in advance. This afterwards led to quarrels with Mr Fallows, who doubtless followed up my affairs with great zeal, but did so in my opinion at far too high a price. He demanded twenty-five per cent on the first four hundred thousand dollars coming in, and ten per cent of all further money.

Mr Fallows went to Europe to institute the necessary investigations on the spot, and as my relations with Xenia and Gleb Botkin had been broken off, I was now thrown back completely on Miss Jennings, with whom I stayed at her New York house till June 1929, except for periodical visits to her estate in Connecticut; in July 1929 we moved to a new house she had bought. My accommodation there, however, was even worse than in her old home. I was given an attic room on the fourth floor, which was pretty sparsely and tastelessly furnished; from the very beginning I felt like a prisoner, and my premonitions were afterwards confirmed. At first, though, Miss Jennings took a lot of trouble to make life pleasant for me. We went shopping together, went to the theatre, and she introduced her friends to me; I believe she even hoped to marry me to a rich American.

Assuming at the time that she meant well by me, I told her my worries over the contract with the 'Grandanor.' She took advice on this, especially from a Mr Lloyd Smith, and informed me soon afterwards that after thorough study the contract could be regarded as fair and that in the given conditions Mr Fallows was acting in my interests. Soon after that, however, I heard that Lloyd Smith was putting in good order the tangled evidence connected with my case, had found new and most promising lines of investigation, and had also undertaken to deal with the authorities for me. Surprised as I was at such news, since I had entrusted this task only to Fallows and not to Miss Jennings or Lloyd Smith, I was soon to be given even greater cause for surprise. One day Lloyd Smith appeared in my room, asked to see the contract and claimed I had no rights whatever, they all belonged to Miss Jennings. At the same time he demanded an incredibly large advance for his work. This was all inexplicable to me, and I refused most decidedly to comply with his demands. From that time on Miss Jennings' behaviour changed.

At the end of May my position became more and more difficult. Miss Jennings was in Connecticut, where I had not wanted to follow her, because I no longer trusted her, and I was quite alone in the house; on her instructions I was not allowed to leave it. When I tried, I found the iron gate leading to the street was bolted. As I was not allowed free movement inside the house either, I remained confined to my room. I was served by an old Irishwoman, whose husband acted as caretaker; but she hardly ever appeared, so that my two parrots were my only companions. Understandably, I was very much disturbed, and sent a message to Miss Jennings through the Irishwoman that she should finally release me. Instead she tried to bring me to heel by starvation; I had to provide for my own meals, and since my ready money was giving out, my situation looked extremely distressing.

Once she let me telephone to John Colter, with whom I had stayed after leaving my cousin Xenia's house. But when he came to see me he was refused admittance. Afterwards he wrote to me that Lloyd Smith had told him I was well looked after here and everything was happening for my own good; that he had checked up himself on what was being done for me, and neither the administration of 'Grandanor' nor the distribution of money from it was in any way illegal; finally, that if I spread the story further that Miss Jennings and others were trying to deprive me of my money, I should soon be without real friends. It was all too obvious under whose influence John Colter had fallen.

Soon after this I was surprised to receive a letter from Xenia saying she had heard I was not happy with Miss Jennings, and although unfortunately she could not help me herself, she had heard of a delightful holiday resort where good friends of hers lived. She had asked these friends to keep a room ready for me; I should be better cared for there than here and could then go about my affairs in peace and complete freedom. Xenia sent this letter through a lady who was also to help me pack my things—she even gave me the good advice to leave straight away. Although my family feeling towards her was still strong enough for me to bear her no grudge, I was so startled that I could not make up my mind to accept her offer. Oh, if only I had done so!

It was not long before I received letters from Miss Jennings and Lloyd Smith, but I was so utterly furious about their behaviour that I returned the letters unopened. Lloyd Smith thereupon sent word through the Irishwoman that if I went on playing this game, he would no longer be able to consider me as a responsible person and would have me shut up in an asylum. Then Miss Jennings herself demanded that I leave her house without delay, saying that though she could not blame me for being suspicious after my experiences, she was unable to tolerate my unco-operative attitude towards her and her advisers, who had never been anything but helpful to me. So she proposed I go to a 'home' in the country where I should find all attention given to my care and comfort and should definitely be happy; she would take charge of all the expenses. The Home, she said, was in Westchester, in New York State.

I could only answer that I was very ready to leave her house as soon as possible, but would like her to return any of my things she had. Then suddenly I had a shock. Suppose Lloyd Smith's threat was being carried out and the 'Home' in Westchester was actually an asylum? Memories shot through my mind of the appalling time I had spent in Dalldorf, and I became extremely agitated. I called for the Irishwoman and asked her to let me telephone. The telephone was now in another room, but I got no connection, the Irishwoman said it had been cut off and two men would soon come to take me away. So it was already too late, as so often before in my life; and I was in a really horrible situation.

* * *

The Home in Westchester was indeed an asylum, and Anastasia was confined there despite sustained efforts on the part of Gleb Botkin, her one loyal friend in America, to prevent it happening. At the beginning of July Lloyd Smith and Miss Jennings were considering this as an alternative to getting Anastasia out of the way by sending her back to Germany. When Gleb was told about it by Colter, he immediately went to see Lloyd Smith, who asked him in the course of a stormy interview whether he did not consider Anastasia of unsound mind. Gleb answered that on the basis merely of her conversation she might perhaps be regarded as simple and that she also 'did silly things,' but that she was definitely not insane in the medical sense. Lloyd Smith insisted that she was, and they parted without reaching any agreement.

In a long letter to Fallows, Gleb declared himself deeply shocked by the asylum suggestion, commenting that Anastasia's mental state was much the same as it had been for the last two years, and certainly better than it had been five or six years before. 'You know,' he went on, 'that at that time many well-known European doctors and psychiatrists stated on oath that she was not insane and never had been. An American doctor, who examined her about two years ago at Oyster Bay, also found her completely normal. Yet her behaviour was no different then from what it is today. Miss Jennings was thoroughly informed of the Grand-Duchess' fits of temper and unfortunate habit of making absurd accusations in her fury. I myself received express assurances from Miss Jennings that she completely understood the state of the Grand-Duchess' nerves and mental condition, which only aroused all the more sympathy for her. . . .

'I also doubt whether Miss Jennings has any right to place the Grand-Duchess under public supervision. In the past she herself empowered me to inform the immigration authorities that she would support the Grand-Duchess for life and that the latter would never in any circumstances become a burden on public assistance. Of course I thought then that Miss Jennings was honest, responsible and rational . . . I know that her obligations towards the Grand-Duchess are more moral than legal, and one cannot do much about people who disregard such moral obligations. First of all Miss Jennings supports the Grand-Duchess, spending fantastic and unnecessary sums on her, accustoming her to luxury and making her almost laughable by exaggerated attentions; then, she not only plans to leave the Grand-Duchess stranded without a cent (which would be bad enough) but in her incomprehensible petty vindictiveness even tries to push her into a public asylum. . . .

'At the moment the first priority is to stop Miss Jennings succeeding in this aim. Next, a way must be found for taking legal action. In such situations a lot can be achieved through publicity also. Public opinion is on the whole fair and humane, particularly in America, and I feel there must definitely be a lot of people in the United States who are as indignant as I am at the way the unfortunate Grand-Duchess is being treated: they must be made to take fresh interest in the case. I shall therefore publicise as widely as possible the precariousness of her position and the dangers which threaten her.'

But at the end of July, before publicity could play any useful part, Walter Jennings, Miss Jennings' brother, acting on his sister's behalf, had applied to the New York public health authorities asking for Anastasia to be certified. According to Jennings Anastasia believed attempts were being made to poison her, refused any medical help, spent most of the time shut up in her bedroom where she talked only to her parrots, believed that her papers and her money were being stolen, abused Miss Jennings, rejected all suggestions that she should go to a nursing home, threatened to shoot a member of this nursing-home's staff, and finally claimed she had been kidnapped, was treated as a prisoner, was not allowed to leave the house, telephone or receive any visitors: on the basis of all this Walter Jennings and his sister suggested that she was a danger to herself and others.

Their opinion was then backed by two doctors, who found that she was over-excited, threatened to commit suicide, suffered from persecution mania, was hysterical, aggressive and suspicious; they concluded that 'Mrs Anderson being of unsound mind, it must be considered right and proper under prevailing regulations that she be placed under supervision and given treatment in a mental hospital.' The High Court of New York State thereupon pronounced that '. . . the allegedly insane person is truly insane. We therefore order that Mrs Anderson be taken to a Hospital in Westchester, New York, for treatment as an insane person.'

* * *

In the middle of the night the two men came of whom the Irishwoman had warned me, and with them a woman who had been in the house before. At first I refused to believe it and had already gone to bed, having first bolted all the doors. But these precautions availed me nothing, for the doors were broken in with an axe. I had dashed on my dressing-gown and fled to the bathroom with my parrots, but even this was no use, the door leading to it was also broken in. My parrots fluttered around in excitement. One of the two men was Lloyd Smith himself, the second man, as I found out afterwards, was the doctor from the asylum, and the woman was an attendant from there. They asked me to get dressed and come with them. I tried to resist, but all resistance seemed futile from the start. They took me between them and led me to a car waiting outside the house. Before this my things had been packed into a case and my parrots caught again. After an eerie night drive of several hours we eventually reached the Home.

Almost as soon as I arrived, I got into my first quarrel with the hospital doctor. He immediately took away my beloved medallion, my last souvenir of my mother. Then he wanted me to make a statement that I was staying in the hospital voluntarily. I told him I could not sign such a statement, since I had in fact been brought here by force, as he very well knew. After a few days he came to me again and declared I must apply to the immigration authorities to have my stay in America prolonged for a year. He put the form in front of me and said I should sign it with my proper name, Anastasia Tchaikovski. I refused angrily, and as all his attempts to persuade me were unavailing, he left me in a fury. Soon afterwards he sent an attendant to me with the threat that if I did not sign the application, he would take away my two parrots: these two little creatures were the only thing that had been left me. Then he returned again himself and threatened to kill the parrots. I jeered at him and shouted that he would not be capable of such cruelty. When he saw I was sticking to my refusal, he suddenly got hold of one of the parrots and wrung its neck.

I was beside myself, and now lost my own self-control. But the doctor had achieved his aim, for to save the second bird I had no alternative but to sign, thereby delivering myself completely into my enemies' hands. Had I refused, the second parrot would have perished, but perhaps I should have been released.

Now I faced the same terrible fate as I had already been through once before. This was the beginning of August 1930.

After the parrot incident I was shut up in a narrow, ill-lit cell, the door of which was left open day and night and continually watched, making it very hard to sleep even at night. So this was the friendly comfortable room in the 'home' Miss Jennings had boosted so highly. The country round was bleak, with rocks, stones, snakes, a bit of shrub, and that was all. Of course I heard neither from Miss Jennings nor Lloyd Smith, nor from Xenia, Fallows or Botkin. Only the doctor turned up every fortnight, finding every time some new piece of malice. I afterwards learnt that a lady from some women's organisation, who had been concerned over my lot and even formed a committee for my rescue, had made efforts to visit me. But the doctor told her it was a very complicated case and she should apply in the first place to Miss Jennings or Lloyd Smith, who held control over me; without permission from these two they could not 'show' me to her. Nor was it any good her mentioning the name of Mr Fallows, my lawyer. So it had come to this! What I experienced thereafter in the hospital was so appalling that even today I still feel incapable of entrusting my memories to paper. I was completely broken up by the ceaseless suffering both physical and mental. Only the thought that I should please my tormentors by dying gave me a strange strength to hold on to life.

I lived this humiliating existence in hospital for a whole year, till August 1931. Then a new attendant appeared one day, a Finn, who told me we were to leave at once; where we were leaving for I did not find out till later. A car waiting outside took me to New York harbour in a three-hour night drive, under escort of the doctor, a male attendant and a second female attendant besides the Finn. After a ghostly bustling about among people I did not know, I was taken on to the liner *Deutschland*, which was just about to sail, and on which a cabin had been reserved for me and my Finnish escort. With this woman, whose name I never learnt, I spent the whole of the voyage, being not allowed to wear anything but underclothes and never able to go on deck. She did not speak a word to me and kept me under a baleful stare all the time. It was not till shortly before we arrived at Cuxhaven that I was given the key of my case, so that I could put on a dress. There

I was fetched by an attendant from the Ilten Mental Hospital near Hanover, where Miss Jennings had arranged for me to be confined.

The three of us reached Ilten late in the evening. On the way there my Finnish escort had told the German attendant that I was a dangerous lunatic who had to be put in a closed block and kept under observation. What had I done to Miss Jennings that she should continue her vendetta even beyond the ocean? Was it the money she and her relatives minded about, was it revenge that she could not achieve what she wanted with me, or was Lloyd Smith the real evil genius? Afterwards I heard that he had committed suicide; so perhaps I was on his conscience.

I had been two and a half years in America, the same time as I was in Dalldorf Asylum. What would be my fate in Ilten?—this was my anxious question that evening. In fact I had a better reception there than I could have expected after the Finnish attendant's slanders. As I soon realised, it was a noted private home, under the direction of Councillor Wahrendorff, run by conscientious doctors on whom I can still look back today with great respect. What a difference from the American asylum! Dr Nieper, who took charge of my case, had me put into a closed room at first, because of course the Finn's report made him consider me a lunatic; and as after my experiences I was very sceptical and unresponsive myself, I could not blame him. After all, it was the third time I was coming into such an institution. But Dr Nieper realised at once that there was something wrong about my admission, and that the Finn was not a qualified nurse, as she had claimed to be when handing me over.

This last had happened under peculiar circumstances. In July, when I was still in Westchester, an American doctor, and shortly afterwards an American lawyer, had gone to Ilten to reserve a place for me. The lawyer asserted that I was a lunatic and my name was Anderson, but he could not say what my nationality was. An advance of a thousand dollars was then paid for my future upkeep; as I afterwards heard, it was from Miss Jennings and had been sent by Lloyd Smith as if coming from an address in Paris. At the end of August, however, when I was admitted to Ilten, the Finn had no transfer papers of any kind for me, not even a covering letter from Westchester, as would be normal; all she supplied was a passport supposed to be mine and giving the name

Anderson. Since she disappeared early the next morning, no one had the chance to interrogate her, as had been planned. I told the doctors at once that the passport must be false, that although in America I had been known as Anderson in order to avoid certain unwelcome attentions, I was really called Anastasia Tchaikovski and was the youngest daughter of Tsar Nicholas. Luckily I found in my luggage another, expired passport made out under this name by the Traunstein District Office, which I was able to show the doctors; and of course they were dumbfounded.

Dr Nieper then showed me the passport the Finn had given him. The picture was the smaller copy of a snapshot Miss Jennings had once had taken of me. The passport had no signature by me, only a cross, and otherwise a normal declaration from the American Treasury, dated 8th August, 1931, permitting me to leave the country. So it dated from a time when I was still being kept in Westchester. Curiously enough, the passport had been made out by the German consulate-general in New York, to which I had never been, let alone having applied there for a passport in the name of Anderson. It was quite obvious to me that Miss Jennings or Lloyd Smith had sent someone else to the consulate, who there obtained the passport illegally under my assumed name of Anderson; and by the description given me of the American 'lawyer,' it seems that this was no other than Lloyd Smith himself.

* * *

Anastasia is probably right about her passport under the name of Mrs Anderson being obtained illegally. The enquiries made in person by Dr Kiep, the German consul-general in New York, brought to light that the business had been carried out by Lloyd Smith and the Mr Foley, Rachmaninov's agent, who had met her on the *Berengaria.* What his motives were is not known, but like Lloyd Smith he was certainly acting for Miss Jennings or her brother. Dr Kiep also established that while Anastasia did not leave the institution in Westchester till the evening of 19th August, the day before this a woman apparently resembling her had appeared at the consulate and also at a public notary's office, and had made false declarations on oath. Lloyd Smith denied his part in the affair despite this convincing evidence, and Mr Foley professed not to know Anastasia.

* * *

I stayed only a few days in Ilten's closed block, where, however, I could be alone in my room. Apparently the one anxiety they had was that I might try to kill myself, so my luggage was searched; but the nurses were more interested in my wardrobe, the elegance of which astonished them and which did not look as if I were a would-be suicide or a lunatic. I possessed a lot of afternoon and evening dresses, as well as fur coats, some given me as presents by my cousin Xenia and others which I had bought afterwards in New York. Then I was examined by the doctors for my mental condition. Directly after the first tests I was told that there were not the slightest signs of a mental illness and that I was in no need of treatment; that they had no right to keep me in this hospital and I could leave it whenever I wished. But as I did not know for the moment where I should try to go, and as I also did not feel safe, I asked if I might stay at Ilten, whereupon I was put in the ordinary nursing home. Here I got two very nicely furnished rooms, and was from then on treated simply as a guest.

Understandably, I at first avoided all contact with other patients. After all my unhappy experiences with people in the last years, I had to be particularly careful. I had also heard from a reliable source that Count Hardenberg, the marshal of my uncle's household at Darmstadt, had threatened to have me arrested if I ever dared return to Germany; and now I had come he said he would have me seized the moment I left the hospital. Hardenberg had his spies in America, of course, but he had also learnt about my move to Germany through the American press, in which my enemies—obviously to divert suspicions from their own scandalous behaviour—spread the story that I had secretly escaped from there and returned to my German friends. So I preferred to stay in my room and not even go for walks in the park, which I felt was too dangerous; I did not feel safe except in my room.

As time went on, I got on familiar terms with the doctors and nurses. Besides Councillor Wahrendorff, whose daughter was very friendly and taught me modelling, Dr Willige took a special interest in me. Dr Nieper and his wife, who for months came to see me almost every day, also cared for me with extraordinary conscientiousness and kindness. When I felt safer, I went for walks in the grounds, the park and the village, made excursions all over the district and visited nearby Hanover. Otherwise I occupied myself a good deal with reading and writing; I also learnt to type. English and German books and papers were my chief reading matter. If I had enough of them, I did embroidery, drew, played patience, or looked after the flowers and birds which had been put in my room and of which I was exceedingly fond.

Finally I also had to put my letters and papers in order; with Dr Nieper's help I began once more to work on proofs of my identity. He spent a great deal of trouble on my behalf, and tried to carry out my none too simple wishes. It was fortunate that through him I made pleasant social contacts in the house of Dr and Mrs Paul Madsack. Dr Madsack and his brothers were owners of the *Hannoverscher Anzeiger*, and this noted journal was the first German paper to describe the story of my life in all accuracy, which was particularly important just then, because other papers, susceptible to Hardenberg's influence, had been writing about me in an odious fashion.

Gertrude Madsack 'adopted' me with special warmheartedness. In January 1932, when I left Ilten and my claims had still not been settled, she made it possible for me to stay in a small flat in Hanover, where she paid all expenses for me. She helped me afterwards as well wherever I was, and even if I failed to get on with many other people, I continually returned to her with a great sense of gratitude; she always kept an open house for me, and I could talk over everything with her freely.

It was she who was present at my confrontation with the two sisters of the legendary 'Francisca Shanzkovski,' which took place at Hanover Police Headquarters in 1938. This confrontation, of course, was bound to be as negative in result as the one at Seeon with Felix Shanzkovski; in fact, it was simply grotesque. The police officers made me walk up and down the corridor, and really took great trouble to see the Shanzkovskis had every help towards recognising me; but they refused to state on oath that I was their sister. The only surprising thing is that the confrontation did not take place eleven years before; my enemies in Darmstadt were certainly very persistent in making this new attempt now. Right up till his death, indeed, Hardenberg carried on his vendetta against me in a manner bordering on obsession.

There was great excitement at Ilten when I was visited one day by the Empress Hermione, the Emperor William's second wife.

This meeting passed off very amiably. We were together the whole day, we went for long walks and had meals in the village inn. Hermione was interested in my case, but of course she could not help me much as she had not known me before. Apart from Aunt Irene and Aunt Olga, who had now turned away from me, the only one of my near relatives I had seen was my Uncle Andrew, who recognised me in Paris. The other relatives who visited me in the course of time could form no judgment from earlier days and came more from curiosity—among them Hermione.

An exception, however, was Prince Frederick Ernest of Saxe-Altenburg, who has been a faithful friend from the time at Ilten right to the present day. He has worked tirelessly to get me acknowledged and also stood by me at great personal cost in the hard days after Germany's collapse. His father's sister, Aunt Mavra, had been married to the Grand-Duke Constantine, and as I have already mentioned, we used often to be with their children at Pavlovsk, since Mama was particularly fond of Aunt Mavra. After the murder of her three sons in the Revolution, she lived at Altenburg with her daughter, my cousin Vera, whom I was one day to meet there. So from childhood Prince Frederick was extremely familiar with our family relationships, besides which our grandmothers were cousins and had met in Denmark in the old days. A far stronger bond between us, however, was the fact that my cousin Sigismund, son of my Aunt Irene (Princess of Prussia), is also Prince Frederick's brother-in-law. Since 1926 both of these relatives have worked very loyally to rescue me from my sad situation and to support me in my struggle to establish my identity.

When the Ilten doctors told me Prince Frederick had come, I was ready to receive him, of course, but wondered if my visitor really was the prince. After my experience with strangers I was always suspicious lest a spy from one of my enemies should sneak in; so I asked the doctors whether anyone knew him. Happily this was easy to answer, since Dr Willige's wife used to know the prince well. She invited him to tea, and had soon identified him, after which we met in the presence of Dr and Mrs Nieper. A little later we were left on our own.

During the conversation Prince Frederick spoke to me of Prince

Sigismund, who had meanwhile bought a farm in Costa Rica. After the unfortunate meeting with his mother, Aunt Irene, I was naturally delighted to know that he took an interest in me. As I heard later, he had recognised me at the time when I was in Berlin, from pictures Uncle Ernie had sent to Hemmelmark—specially from my very characteristic smile; but he had not been able to talk his mother out of her hostile attitude. Since Prince Sigismund had never been satisfied at the mystery over me being left unsolved, he wrote to Prince Frederick with some very precise questions which should be put to me, relating to our last meeting before the First World War, where and when it took place, and about various things which had happened then. Only someone in the family could have known all this, and I gave accurate answers to all the questions.

This year, 1957, when Prince Sigismund came over from South America to visit me at my hut in the Black Forest, we talked of that meeting for a long time and in great detail. It was in 1912, at the castle of Spala (in Russian Poland), where Papa hunted and Aunt Irene was on a visit with Sigismund—though he could only come during the school holidays, and so did not stay as long as his mother. He asked me if I still remembered the fat Prince Orlov. I knew at once who this was, and thought I had heard of his having died a few years afterwards. We spoke too of the beautiful woods, the mushrooms we had picked there, and all the pranks I had played. I was eleven then and had always been a little imp and a clown. Prince Sigismund also remembered my brother, who had been very ill at the time; and I said it might have been better if Alexi had died then, which would have saved him a lot of suffering. Sigismund knew Alexi's personal servant, Derevenko the Marine, who had been one of the worst fanatics at the outbreak of the Revolution, as, alas, were so many from the crew of the *Standart*. Only Nagorny and Dr Botkin remained true to us, and they both had to pay for it with their lives.

We also talked of one of Papa's adjutants, who had accompanied him on a trip to Germany and afterwards left him; this brought us to my family's visit in 1910 to Friedberg Castle, Hesse, which belonged to my uncle at the time and where we stayed with all our relatives. Prince Sigismund said he had seen Papa on one other occasion before the war; I knew he meant my father's visit to Berlin for the wedding of Prince Victoria Louisa, the

German Emperor's daughter. From the very beginning I had no real contact with Uncle Ernie. Just as I had written a letter to Aunt Irene during my escape—which ostensibly never reached her—I had also sent news to Uncle Ernie at Darmstadt through a German prisoner-of-war being repatriated; I don't know whether it reached him either. My cousin was most interested in that meeting with his mother at Dr Grünberg's house in Funkenmühle, which I described to him very fully. He found it extremely tragic, and said my life would certainly have been different if she had accepted me then. After our various conversations he was firmly convinced he was indeed seeing his cousin, and he confirmed this in a detailed declaration on oath.

After I had been some while at Ilten, my New York lawyer, Mr Fallows, unexpectedly turned up. He said he had been quite unable to get in touch with me till then, being deliberately kept away from me. It was only while in England that he had read in the papers about my being back in Germany. Although Fallows went on working for me quite a time longer, we could never reach a proper understanding; I was very bitter about his behaviour and eventually handed my affairs over to German lawyers. Apart from the contract with the 'Grandanor,' for which I still blamed Fallows, he was too unversed in some of the important factors in my case. Through Montagu Norman, the director of the Bank of England, he had a good introduction to the London banking world, but because of his complete unfamiliarity with conditions in the old Russia, he failed to enlist the advice of important personages who were then still alive, or to take advantage of others who would have been ready to testify on my behalf: valuable help was thereby lost irretrievably. I have been criticised for ingratitude to Fallows, but I am afraid that with the best will in the world I could not have acted differently towards him. Still, I must admit it was through his efforts that the Bank of England has not yet disposed of my fortune there, nor will do so until my claims as the rightful heir are settled.

* * *

Besides England, the Tsar's disputed fortune extended among other countries to Finland. Early in 1928 Xenia had sued that country for the recovery of valuable estates in Eastern Finland which she claimed as the sole heir of her brother, Tsar Nicholas. One of several reasons why her claims were rejected was that she failed to prove that the Tsar and his family were dead and that she was the sole heir. But the defence counsel also referred to official documents purporting to prove that in 1900 the Tsar had formally transferred the property to the Russian State to be used for the Empress Maria's large benevolent institutions, and claimed that the Soviet Government had therefore been entitled to cede it to Finland (by the Treaty of Dorpat) with full right of possession.

There were also assets in Germany. In December 1905, at the time of the first revolutionary plots in Russia, the Tsar opened accounts for all five children at the Berlin Bank of Mendelssohn & Co. (Mendelssohn was then Danish consul), under the letters A.B.C.D.E., paying several million roubles into them; and the following year he opened a further account at the same bank, with a cheque of a million and a half pounds, to take the interest on the five original accounts. The inflation in Germany greatly reduced their value, which at the beginning of the 'thirties was approximately a million Reichmarks.

In 1933 the Berlin Civil Court granted a document of inheritance (relating to the Tsar's property in Germany only) to Countess Natalie Brassova, morganatic widow of the Tsar's brother Michael (murdered at Perm in 1918), as the heir of her deceased son, Prince George. In her application for this document the following were named as the heirs of the Tsar's four daughters:

1. The Dowager-Empress Maria Feodorovna.
2. The Grand-Duchess Xenia (the Tsar's sister).
3. Countess Natalie Brassova.
4. The Grand-Duchess Olga (the Tsar's sister).
5. Princess Victoria Mountbatten, Marchioness of Milford Haven (the Tsarina's elder sister).
6. Princess Irene of Prussia (the Tsarina's younger sister).
7. The Grand-Duke Ernest Louis of Hesse (the Tsarina's brother).

The Dowager-Empress was dead, but only five of the remaining six came into their share of the inheritance; either Princess Irene or the Grand-Duchess Olga presumably had scruples about applying for it and thus assuming Anastasia's death.

Anastasia herself was naturally furious at the granting of the document, in which for the first time she was officially declared to have been killed and was supposed to be putting in claims as an impostor. In 1938 her lawyers applied for the document's cancellation; and the law-suit which started at Hamburg in December 1957 is a continuation of these proceedings, though of course it is also concerned incidentally with the assets in England.

Doubts as to the existence of these have continually been expressed, and in January 1928 the *New York Evening Post* professed to have heard from 'authoritative circles, familiar with the most intimate details of the Tsar's financial position,' that the fortune, which had amounted to forty million pounds, then nearly two hundred million dollars, had been withdrawn by the Tsar at the outbreak of the First World War; that this fortune dated from the reign of Alexander II, was private and not state property, and was probably meant for the Tsar's personal safeguard in case of a revolution; but (the paper went on) when war broke out, Nicholas II considered it unpatriotic to leave so large a sum outside Russia; so the money was then used towards the development of the imperial air-force (according to other accounts, for the purchase of arms or equipment for hospitals).

This story was subscribed to with great vehemence by the Grand-Duke Alexander, husband of Xenia, who wrote in his Memoirs (published in 1931): 'Financial experts and awestruck laymen have always claimed that the late Tsar was one of the ten richest men in the world. Even today, thirteen years after his tragic end, the gentlemen of the press tell us periodically that the Bank of England is still in possession of the "vast fortune of the Romanovs." Not long ago a poor irresponsible girl came to New York, was presented as the Grand-Duchess Anastasia, Nicholas II's youngest daughter, and expressed the intention of claiming "her share in her father's millions." But . . . since the summer of 1915 the Tsar had not a penny to his name either in the Bank of England or in any other bank outside Russia . . . had his reign lasted longer, by the end of the World War he would have been a relatively poor man.'

Since then, however, such statements have been contradicted, and the existence of a large overseas fortune confirmed, by several more reliable sources, including Mrs Lili Dehn, a very close friend of the Tsar and Tsarina, who often mention her with affection in their published diaries. Anny Vyrubova's Memoirs also describe how closely they confided in Mrs Dehn during the tragic days following the Tsar's abdication—soon after which Kerensky had her arrested and sent away from Tsarskoe Selo, to deprive the Tsar and family of her loyal support. In September 1955, at the German Embassy in Caracas (Venezuela), Mrs Dehn stated the following: 'In March 1917, when I was at Tsarskoe Selo with the imperial family—the situation being very grave because of the Revolution—Her Majesty the Tsarina said this to me: "At least we shan't have to beg, for we have a fortune in the Bank of England." I don't remember exactly how much it was, but I know she spoke of millions and in gold.'

The position regarding the twenty million roubles deposited with the Bank of England (of which the Tsar told his wife and four daughters shortly before he died) is still uncertain. In 1928 and 1929, when Mr Kennedy was making his enquiries, he approached Barclays', Lloyds' and other English banks, who replied to the effect that they did not think they held any such funds. The Bank of England refused to give any information, saying it was a bank secret—which gave the impression that there *was* a deposit.

*Translator's note:* In 1958 the Bank of England answered my direct enquiry with a denial that they had ever held funds deposited by the Tsar in any name. Reference to Anastasia's lawyers revealed that during the 1920's she altered her original statement: the money had been deposited *with an English bank*. The mistake of language is very understandable, and Anastasia with her faulty memory has probably been convinced in later years that it was the Bank of England. Presumably her lawyers will now be making new efforts to track the deposit down to one of the private English banks.

* * *

Soon after leaving Ilten, I parted from Mr Fallows, and in his place entrusted Mr Friedrich Völler, a lawyer in Bad Salzungen, to look after my inheritance interests and investigate my rights and responsibilities towards the 'Grandanor.' After Völler's death I returned to Fallows, but in 1938, as he was making no progress with my German claims—he did not speak a word of German—the American embassy recommended to him the Berlin lawyer, Mr Paul Leverkuehn. Mr Leverkuehn, originally from Lübeck, asked an old friend of his, Mr Vermehren of Hamburg, to work on my case with him. These two lawyers clearly did not agree to represent me without having first studied very carefully the documentary evidence for my identity given them by Fallows. They would scarcely have made my case their own had they been afraid they were dealing with an impostor or a lunatic. Because of my sad situation, in fact, they were generous enough to carry on their extensive work on my behalf for many years without fee, their only wish being to see right prevail where they felt injustice was being done.

For in 1933 the Berlin Magistrates' Court had granted a document of inheritance to my relatives for my father's German fortune. This was a disgrace, and in 1938 my lawyers applied to the Court to get it revoked. The proceedings which followed were influenced from the outset by questions of politics and war, possibly including the special relations between Nazi Germany and Soviet Russia; in 1941 the decision was given against me. During the bombing raids my two lawyers' offices in Hamburg and Berlin were totally destroyed, involving the loss of irreplaceable documents; but fortunately the court files remained intact. Before the necessary copies could be taken from these, however, most of the original documents my lawyers had submitted in proof of my identity disappeared in a manner which has never been explained; this led to extraordinary delays and difficulties in the resumption of proceedings after the war.

I hope to God the legal proceedings soon reach an end, for I find it a dreadful strain trying to follow what is happening, and even then understand only part of what is going on. I was so much hoping the court would agree to my lawyers' request that my witnesses living abroad should be heard—such people as Uncle Andrew in Paris, Gleb Botkin in America and his sister in Paris, my cousin Sigismund of Prussia in Costa Rica, and my mother's good friend Lili Dehn in Caracas, all of whom knew me from childhood. I can only pray that the worry of this endless dispute will be ended by my relatives seeing reason. My Hessian relatives started fighting me much earlier with weapons from 'anthropometry,' and I had various photographs taken of me. But all their 'measurements' and 'expert opinions' are irrelevant against my own knowledge of my descent. I hope these 'anthropometric findings' in the files will one day be checked by some competent and unbiassed person, whose judgment is based on quite unexceptionable photographic evidence.

Apart from all the agitations caused me time and again by the dispute over my acknowledgment, my life in the next few years flowed in quieter channels. I found friends in the most varied parts of Germany, who assured me a reasonable existence. Among these kind friends of mine in the 'thirties I think specially of Mrs

Stahlberg in Berlin and her mother, Baroness Kleist-Retzow, in Pomerania; Countess Astrid Bethusy-Huc, daughter of General Moltke (former chief of the general staff), who for many years invited me to her estate at Bankau in Upper Silesia and also to Starnberg and Berlin; and Mr and Mrs Gerlach at Rohrbeck in the Uckermark. As the Emperor William's adjutant, General Moltke had once met my father personally, and his daughter still wore a beautiful diamond ring he had had made for her from one of the stones in the order Papa had given him; his widow also took an extremely sympathetic interest in me right up till her death. The Gerlachs too had many connections with the old princely houses. Mr Gerlach had been with the Dragoons in Schwedt and handed his regiment's flowers to my mother at her engagement in Coburg; afterwards, at Queen Victoria's sixtieth jubilee in 1897, he had the privilege of handing to the Queen the roses of his regiment, whose patroness she was. They could surely judge whether I came from a princely house or not. I always felt very much at home with them, and for quite long periods I was sometimes the guest also of Prince William of Hesse-Phillipsthal at Herleshausen Castle on the Werra near Eisenach—he was killed in the Second World War. I was specially fond of the landscape of Hesse and Thüringen, but above all derived satisfaction from the fact that the Prince and Princess never swerved from their conviction that I was Anastasia of Russia, although the Prince's mother was the sister-in-law of my Uncle Ernie at Darmstadt.

Having resolved to describe my life with absolute frankness, I must confess that I often quarrelled with my friends, even the best of them, despite the hospitality and kindness they showed me. After all I had been through, I had not only become very suspicious with most people; my nerves were simply worn out, so that I grew touchy and irritable, and spoilt many chances through my moods and obstinacy. If I admit this freely, I do so because I am really aware of these shortcomings; but sooner or later I have usually made it up with my friends, as I did with Harriet Rathlef in 1932 and with Gleb Botkin. I was deeply sad when the former died very suddenly. I correspond quite often with Gleb, and I recently had a visit from his sister Tatiana. For a long time, though —often through my own fault—I led quite a gipsy life.

I have particularly pleasant memories of Siebeneichen Castle near Meissen, which belonged to Baroness Monica Miltitz. I was taken there by Prince Frederick, who had also introduced me to Countess Bethusy and his Hessian relatives. I once stayed several months at Siebeneichen, because I again developed a glandular tuberculosis and needed the splendid nursing given me by Baroness Miltitz, 'the good fairy of Siebeneichen.' This place was right after my heart. The ivy-covered castle, surrounded by wonderful old trees, had a fine situation on a bend in the Elbe, set on a hill facing the fort of Meissen.

Once while I was there, Prince Frederick also took me to his home at Altenburg, where my cousin Vera, the Grand-Duke Constantine's daughter, was living—whom I mentioned earlier on. She was five years younger than I, and my real playmates were her elder brothers, so I could no longer recognise her by her appearance; but I asked Prince Frederick to arrange my first meeting with her without telling her who I was. She soon recognised me as her cousin Anastasia, and made efforts to get me acknowledged by my relatives, particularly my Aunt Irene. This was a special joy for me.

I have yet another memory connected with Prince Frederick. Towards the end of the last war, when it was very hard to get out of Hanover, which was being badly bombed, the Prince appeared like a knight errant and with great difficulty brought me to the estate in Thüringen of his cousin, Princess Louisa of Saxe-Meiningen, widow of Baron Wagenheim who had been killed in the war. For the moment, therefore, I was saved. But soon afterwards Germany collapsed, we came under Soviet occupation, and had to endure all the stresses one associates with that first post-war period. It was a bitter irony of fate that I had to fall under these of all Germany's enemies. Sometimes I was in deathly fear that I should be recognised as the Tsar's daughter and dragged off to Russia, especially on one occasion when one of the Red soldiers who had come into the castle was with me in a room to check on something. Had he guessed that the daughter of the Emperor of Russia was before him, he would surely have taken me with him as welcome booty. But Destiny, which has so often brought me to the extremes of what a human being can bear, and then saved me again, seems to have thought better of it once more—for the Red soldier left the castle without incident.

This was a warning to me, and I moved to a good old friend near the Wartburg, so as to be nearer the borders of the Russian Zone and then cross over to the West. Eventually, with the help of a courageous lady belonging to a relief organisation, I succeeded in crossing to the British Zone, where Prince Frederick was expecting me and from where he later took me to South Germany. To cross the Weser we had to use a boat in all secrecy. My faithful escort then took me to Bad Liebenzell in the Black Forest, in what was then the French occupation zone. I stayed there for a year and got the rest and good air which was so especially beneficial after my glandular tuberculosis; but then it was my dearest wish to have at last a home of my own, however small and primitive it might be. I did not want to be beholden any longer to strangers, kind as they had always been to me. So finally Prince Frederick—who was now himself a refugee, as a member of a princely family in Soviet-occupied Thüringen—managed with his last remaining resources to obtain an old army hut near Bad Liebenzell, which had been taken over by a farmer on Germany's collapse in 1945. We furnished it with the barest essentials, but later I got my dearest wish fulfilled, to possess my own garden.

There I have now been living for ten years, right in the woods, with my old companion, Mrs Heydebrand, who has cared for me with selfless devotion. I talk a little to the peasants and the children, look after my animals and above all my garden, which I have laid out like the gardens at Tsarskoe Selo and Tolbolsk where I once dug and sowed and reaped, when my parents, sisters and brother were still alive. The only thing that spoils my life is the crowd of inquisitive strangers who come and stand outside my house every day. Their attention was drawn to me by the play and the film, so now they disturb my peace and I hardly dare to venture outside the house.

I have still not completely lost touch with the people of my old environment; some from earlier times have returned, new people have come into my life, and there have every now and then been highlights in such meetings. I have several times been the guest of the Grand-Duke and Duchess of Saxe-Weimar at Weikersheim Castle near Mergentheim, where their Hohenlohe relatives took them in after their flight from their Thüringen home. It was a special joy for me to become godmother to the son of the Weimar house, for our families had long been closely connected. What pleasure I had in gazing on all the little personal mementoes of the Grand-Duchess Maria Pavlovna which by good fortune had been saved! She was Alexander I's sister, and it was to her Schiller dedicated his 'Homage of the Arts' on her arrival in Weimar.

From among my more distant relatives I became friendly with Princess Margarethe Urach, Countess of Württemberg, with whom I often stayed at Lichtenstein Castle; and she also visited *me* in the 'Three Kings' Hut,' as my dwelling at Unterlengenhardt was christened.

She it was, too, who arranged a new meeting with Princess Cecilie, who had seen me that time in Berlin, without our making real contact. At Lichtenstein Castle she had heard in detail, from Princess Margarethe and Prince Frederick, of all that happened to me during the thirty years since she had last seen me; and she thereupon decided to renew her personal impressions. She came to see me twice with Princess Margarethe, and we had long *tête-à-têtes* together. These meetings led to her recognising me unreservedly. With her knowledge of all my relatives on both my father's and my mother's side, she could certainly form the best judgment on whether or not I *am* Anastasia. When she was quite convinced of my identity, we reached a really warm understanding, and in her declaration on oath, which has already been quoted before here, she wrote as follows:

'. . . The political developments in Germany since the early 'thirties, and then the Second World War, made me lose sight of Mrs A. T. I did not know what had become of her till about three years ago, when I heard from Princess Margarethe Urach that Mrs A. T. was living in very distressing circumstances in the north of the Black Forest. On my own initiative I sought a first meeting with her through the Princess, because the latter and Prince Frederick of Saxe-Altenburg . . . had recalled the whole affair to me by expressing their conviction of her identity. What in the 'twenties I had felt no concern of mine, now seemed to me a moral obligation.

'I visited Mrs A. T. twice more after this, spending quite a long time with her on each of the three occasions. Today I am convinced she is the Tsar's youngest daughter: not only because, now she is an elderly woman, I can sometimes detect her mother's features in hers; but even more because the kinship is betrayed in her manner of behaviour and hospitality, in all the bonds of intimate knowledge and association which link people of the same origins together.'

After this she decided to bring her son, Prince Louis Ferdinand, and her daughter-in-law, Princess Cyra, to meet me. The meeting took place in Princess Margarethe's castle at Lichtenstein, and I can still recall that day very clearly. It was the middle of September 1952, I had arrived at the castle at five in the afternoon. Shortly afterwards Princess Cecilie came with her children, introducing me to them at once with the words: 'That's your cousin.'

I then stayed for a while talking to Prince Louis and his wife, Princess Cyra; and I also talked to her alone. As I have mentioned before, my family was not on the best of terms with the family of Cyra's father, the Grand-Duke Cyril; so it will be appreciated that I felt rather apprehensive. During our conversation I realised that Cyra was looking for the truth and was by no means prejudiced from the start by the negative attitude of her parents and brother Vladimir, but was trying to form her own impressions of me; even so, however, I could not feel the same close bonds as I did with her mother-in-law.

Yet what more could I want? The loving confidence of the German Crown Princess, who had known me and my parents in better days, was certainly a great consolation for much else in the last years. I no longer ask much about people's good or evil opinions. Only the memory of my parents, sisters and brother, has kept me from despairing of life. What am I still fighting for? My name, my honour—or money, as my enemies say? Having to carry on such a struggle must be a kind of penance, and perhaps it is this idea which has given me the strength to cling to life so resolutely. I am deeply grateful to Fate, which has compensated for all the ills of body and soul, which I must bear till my death as a legacy of the great tragedy, by continually giving me joys as well. They are all the greater for the unexpectedness with which they come to cheer my life; and I am glad I can still feel joy in spite of everything.

This summer of 1957 offered me three visits from people who

had come long distances for my sake out of loyalty and family devotion. It was over thirty years since I had seen my cousin Sigismund, son of my beloved Aunt Irene. For a long time he had known of my being the sole survivor of the night of murders at Ekaterinburg, and as I have already mentioned, in the early 'thirties he sent his brother-in-law Prince Frederick precise questions for me to answer; now he came to see me once more in this life. I have also spoken of the details of our meeting. We two old people did not recognise the children in ourselves, but found our youth again through many memories in common. We spoke the same language, and only Aunt Irene was missing to make our happiness complete.

The second visitor was Tatiana Melnik, daughter of our faithful Dr Eugen Botkin, who came from Paris to make a long-planned visit to me—she also thinking it might otherwise be too late. For she too is a sick woman, and who can say how much longer we shall be allowed? As at Oberstdorf and Seeon about thirty years ago, I was completely happy again and at one with her, although I could not feel quite the same joy in her presence as I did then owing to my health now being worse. But that made no difference to the warmth of our feeling for each other and our heartening friendship. I hope this has not been Tatiana's last visit to me.

The third visit was the one I least expected. I could never have guessed that Lili Dehn, one of my mother's two closest friends, who often stayed with my parents for weeks and shared their daily life, would come from Venezuela simply to convince herself that the youngest daughter of her friend and empress was still alive. Great as was my pleasure at this proof of her loyalty, I yet found it hard and painful to return with her to the happy years of our family life before the catastrophe. Few will appreciate the distress it causes, despite the joy of reunion and of taking up our friendship where it left off, to feel again through someone so intimate the deep bonds of the close family circle, which has been destroyed in so appalling a fashion.

Still, I find on looking back that the meeting with three faithful friends did me a lot of good, confirming me in the knowledge that I am not deserted. On the other hand, the thought that I may never again see any of these faces familiar from my childhood years is a painful one and doubles my feeling of loneliness. Yet I would like to live in this loneliness, for the quiet around me has become normal and familiar to me, and I hate inquisitive strangers coming to disturb my peace.

* * *

## Translator's Note, June 1958

Anastasia's story is not yet ended. After immensely long hearings and several adjournments, the Hamburg court may one day at last give their verdict that she *is* Anastasia, thus fulfilling the one remaining great desire of her life; or else even those hopes may be cheated both by the loss of evidence due to the last war and the lapse of time, and by the power of her surviving enemies. Meanwhile the seventeen-year-old girl, who was born and brought up in a palace, is a sick elderly woman occupying a primitive hut in the Black Forest, existing alone 'in the shadows,' and content with the loneliness if only she can be given back her name: without which, as she herself has said at the beginning of this book, no human being can really live.

There are several reasons why her fate as a human being may be disregarded—despite, or because of, all the publicity she has received in the last few years from plays, films and countless articles in magazines and newspapers. The play and the American film were largely fictional, and they have somehow turned her into a legend, the legend of an unsolved mystery; this is dangerous, because it means that few will expect or demand a solution. Many people in England, for instance, seem surprised to learn that Anastasia is a real person and still alive, let alone that she is still longing for general recognition. For another thing, the world she lived in, with its exclusive courts and relationships, has gone for ever; and the whole atmosphere of her own nostalgic memories is remote for us in these egalitarian days. We still cherish and publicise our royalty, it is true, but the remnants of Europe's pre-1914 royal families make little appeal, and intrigues among their members have largely been replaced by intrigues among ruling politicians.

Thirdly, the last war left in its wake millions of refugees and 'displaced persons'—that sad and terribly apt phrase—many of whom have suffered as much from bereavements, uprooting, poverty and sickness, as this innocent victim of a war and revolution which are now 'old unhappy far-off things and battles long ago.' Memory of Anastasia as an individual can easily be swamped by the thought of all those other millions; but it can still be said that she has suffered longer than they, and that while many of them are stateless, homeless and lonely, hardly any have been denied their own identity, as Anastasia has, by unscrupulous and self-seeking members of their own family. It is one of the penalties of being born in high places that there will usually be plenty of people to watch your downfall with a satisfaction born of earlier envy. But no impostor could have kept up the deception for forty years without once giving herself away, and through all the vicissitudes of the last forty years Anastasia has remained true to herself, her courage triumphing alike over circumstances and 'malice domestic.' As the supreme instance of a displaced person from an earlier generation, she still merits our sympathy—and our hopes that at least in this one case justice will finally prevail.

# BIBLIOGRAPHY

A great many books have been written about Anastasia by friends and enemies. She knows about such books and has read them, though it can be imagined with what feeling she reads the accounts they are bound to give of her family's terrible fate.

All these books, both for and against, have been carefully studied in the documentation of her autobiography; and so that it should achieve the greatest possible accuracy, care has been taken to consult all available 'witnesses' who have given reliable and significant testimony concerning anything in her life. This was in accordance with her own wish, and has been particularly important for periods where she was seriously ill and suffered from partial amnesia; it has thus helped to bridge the gaps in her memory which are a natural result of the physical and psychological stresses she has been through.

Harriet von Rathlef-Keilmann's book, extensively quoted from here, *Anastasia, ein Frauenschicksal als Spiegel der Weltkatastrophe*, was published in Leipzig and Zürich in 1928, and an English translation was brought out by Putnam's with the title *Anastasia—The Survivor from Ekaterinburg?;* the book has long been out of print. So has a pamphlet by Felix Dassel called *Anastasia lebt!;* in fact the whole edition was mysteriously bought up soon after its appearance and disappeared from circulation. Gleb Botkin's book, *The Woman who Rose Again*, first came out in 1938 in New York (Fleming H. Revell & Co.) and London. The book by Pierre Gilliard and Constantin Savich, *La Fausse Anastasie*, was published in 1929 by Payot in Paris.

There are, of course, countless works on the end of the Romanovs, including Anna Vyrubova's *Memoirs;* the small book by the Bolshevik leader Bykov, *The Last Days of the Romanovs* (1926); and Sir George Buchanan's Memoirs, *My Mission to Russia* (Cassell, 1923). The extracts quoted from the Tsar's diary were published in German (Ullstein, Berlin, 1923) and the Tsarina's letters to her husband in French (Payot, Paris, 1924). Lili (von) Dehn has reproduced many conversations with the Tsarina in her book, *The Real Tsaritsa* (Little, Brown & Co., Boston, 1922), also long out of print. Mrs Dehn was an eye-witness in intimate touch with the Tsar's family till the days of the Revolution. This cannot be said of the authors of many other works about the imperial house, who either relied on the accounts of others or else were in such subordinate positions that they could not gain any real view of the imperial family's daily life. Mrs Dehn's unqualified testimony in favour of the Tsar's still surviving youngest daughter is therefore all the more valuable.

In 1953 Marcelle Maurette wrote the play *Anastasia*, which was performed first in London, then in other European countries and in the United States, with the Swede Viveca Lindfors in the title role; it was immensely successful, and in 1956 was filmed by 20th Century Fox with Ingrid Bergman as Anastasia. As mentioned above, play and film are largely fictional, and Anastasia's meeting with her grandmother, the Empress Dowager, which forms the climax of both, never took place. On the other hand, the German film which appeared the same year with Lili Palmer in the title role (English title *Is Anna Anderson Anastasia?*) tried to keep as near the truth as possible, though certain cuts, omissions and inessential changes were unavoidable in the interests of conciseness. Lili Palmer gave a magnificent performance, feeling her way into the personality of the Grand-Duchess Anastasia with outstanding conviction.

ALEXANDER III *m* MARIA FEODOROVNA
1845–1894 Princess of Denmark
(*reigned* 1883–1894)

(*her youngest brother*)
VALDEMAR, Prince of Denmark

NICHOLAS II *m* ALEXANDRA
1870–1918 Princess of Hesse
(*reigned* 1894–1918)

OLGA
TATIANA
MARIA
ANASTASIA
ALEXI

MICHAEL *m* NATALIE
Countess Brassova

GEORGE
Prince Brassov

XENIA *m* ALEXANDER
Grand Duchess of Russia MICHAILOVICH

six sons and
one daughter *m* Prince Felix Yusupov

OLGA *m*
COLONEL
KULIKOVSKY

(*her brothers and sisters*)

ERNEST LOUIS
Grand Duke of Hesse
1868–1938

VICTORIA *m* PRINCE LOUIS MOUNTBATTEN
Dowager Marchioness
of Milford Haven

IRENE *m* PRINCE HENRY OF PRUSSIA

PRINCE SIGISMUND

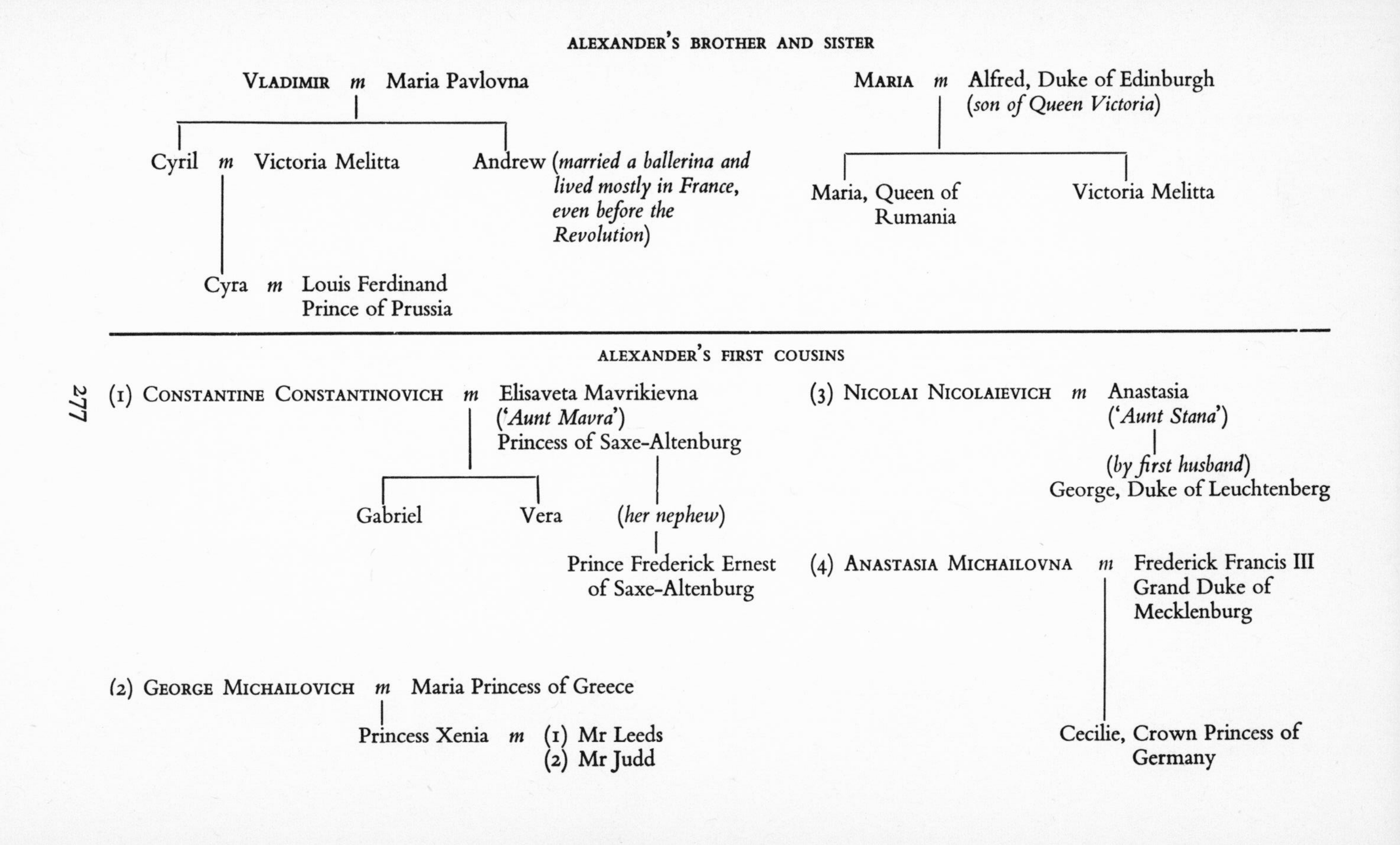
ALEXANDER'S BROTHER AND SISTER
VLADIMIR m Maria Pavlovna
Cyril m Victoria Melitta
Andrew (married a ballerina and lived mostly in France, even before the Revolution)
Cyra m Louis Ferdinand Prince of Prussia
MARIA m Alfred, Duke of Edinburgh (son of Queen Victoria)
Maria, Queen of Rumania
Victoria Melitta
ALEXANDER'S FIRST COUSINS
(1) CONSTANTINE CONSTANTINOVICH m Elisaveta Mavrikievna ('Aunt Mavra') Princess of Saxe-Altenburg
Gabriel
Vera
(her nephew)
Prince Frederick Ernest of Saxe-Altenburg
(2) GEORGE MICHAILOVICH m Maria Princess of Greece
Princess Xenia m (1) Mr Leeds (2) Mr Judd
(3) NICOLAI NICOLAIEVICH m Anastasia ('Aunt Stana')
(by first husband)
George, Duke of Leuchtenberg
(4) ANASTASIA MICHAILOVNA m Frederick Francis III Grand Duke of Mecklenburg
Cecilie, Crown Princess of Germany

# INDEX